# Backcountry Trails of Florida

*Wild Florida*

UNIVERSITY PRESS OF FLORIDA

Florida A&M University, Tallahassee

Florida Atlantic University, Boca Raton

Florida Gulf Coast University, Ft. Myers

Florida International University, Miami

Florida State University, Tallahassee

New College of Florida, Sarasota

University of Central Florida, Orlando

University of Florida, Gainesville

University of North Florida, Jacksonville

University of South Florida, Tampa

University of West Florida, Pensacola

# Backcountry Trails *of* Florida

## A Guide to Hiking Florida's Water Management Districts

Terri Mashour

University Press of Florida

Gainesville / Tallahassee / Tampa / Boca Raton

Pensacola / Orlando / Miami / Jacksonville / Ft. Myers / Sarasota

This book may be available in an electronic edition.

22  21  20  19  18  17    6  5  4  3  2  1

Library of Congress Control Number: 2017938941

ISBN 978-0-8130-5454-4

The University Press of Florida is the scholarly publishing agency for the
State University System of Florida, comprising Florida A&M University,
Florida Atlantic University, Florida Gulf Coast University, Florida
International University, Florida State University, New College of Florida,
University of Central Florida, University of Florida, University of North
Florida, University of South Florida, and University of West Florida.

University Press of Florida
15 Northwest 15th Street
Gainesville, FL 32611-2079
http://upress.ufl.edu

I'd like to dedicate this book to my daughter, Picchu, for creating the need to write it when she was six months old and for encouraging me to finish it when she was four years and six months old. To my husband, Hugh, for his edits, support, and humor. To my son, Hamilton, who made me a better person for making me figure out how to hold him while he slept while still typing this book. To my mom who helped babysit many hours so I could work. And finally to my cowboy friend and second dad, Danny Mills.

# Contents

# Foreword

As one of the most populous states and with hundreds of thousands of new residents moving into Florida every year, it seems impossible that truly wild places can remain anywhere in such a densely inhabited region.

Yet in spite of the tremendous influx of people wanting to enjoy the Sunshine State's warm climate and active outdoors lifestyle, significant sections of original, natural Florida do still endure.

The amount of Florida land set aside for preservation surprises many people, especially first-time visitors and newly arrived residents. As this is written, the Florida landscape is protected by three national forests, three national parks, one national preserve, two national seashores, thirty national wildlife refuges, thirty-seven state forests and one hundred seventy-four state parks. In addition, individual Florida counties have designated their own protected public lands

Yes, there is quite a lot of Florida that hasn't been paved over or badly disturbed by development; and it never will be.

The University Press of Florida celebrates the essential natural qualities of Florida, its environment, its creatures, and its people through the broad-ranging series Wild Florida.

In *Backcountry Trails of Florida: A Guide to Hiking Florida's Water Management Districts*, Terri Mashour takes us into one of Florida's least-known and untamed natural areas. All the walks take place in Florida's five water management districts that encompass almost two million acres. Since these state agencies are charged with preserving and managing the state's water resources, many trails traverse not only flatwoods but also swamps, river frontage, cypress stands and marshes. Some also meander past sinkholes and springs.

To guide her readers through these remote backcountry regions, Mashour calls upon her experience not only as a hiker but also as a former land management specialist with the St. Johns River Water Management District. It is the perfect background for compiling a detailed and comprehensive guide to some of Florida's least-known hiking regions where it is possible to discover real wilderness.

As Mashour points out, the main purpose of Florida's water management districts is to provide protection, not recreation. As such, the trails in some places are anything but strolls in the park, particularly in areas like the Northwest Florida Water Management District which has limited access roads. The trails located there tend to be long and linear, following the rivers, but with limited maintenance, few facilities, and a scarcity of direction signs and trail blazes so common elsewhere. Still, it should be easy to find your way on these true backcountry hikes thanks to the guide's GPS coordinates and the URL addresses for trail map downloads.

Fortunately, many district hikes have fairly easy access. The Suwannee River Management District, for instance, includes several sections of the well-marked Florida National Scenic Trail that lead to such well-known (and crowded) spots as the Big Shoals class III rapids or the less-traveled but equally scenic banks of the Aucilla River.

The majority of the hikes are found from North Florida to the Everglades. You are sure to find numerous hikes with strong appeal regardless of your interest. And the way will be made easier with Mashour's detailed hike descriptions, which include the amount of shade and wildlife you could see on each.

Particularly worthwhile are uses and restrictions detailed for each trail. Water management paths are often multiuse trails open to those on bikes and possibly horseback as well as people on foot. It's good to know what to expect ahead of time in order to match your hiking expectations with the reality of the trail.

With a guide like *Backcountry Trails of Florida: A Guide to Hiking Florida's Water Management Districts*, it is always tempting to go straight to the hike descriptions and bypass front matter like the introduction. That is a serious mistake here. In a sense, the introduction contains the heart and soul of the book as Mashour explains the history and role of the Northwest Florida, Suwannee River, St. Johns River, Southwest Florida, and South Florida Water Management Districts.

She describes when and why the agencies were created, how well they are completing their mission, their accomplishments, and the political pressures that may hinder them. Considering that Florida's vital and limited fresh water supplies face unrelenting pressure from residents, various industries, and 100 million tourists who visit annually, this is important information to know.

With *Backcountry Trails of Florida: A Guide to Hiking Florida's Water Management Districts*, Terri Mashour delivers a complete and timely package

M. Timothy O'Keefe
Series Editor

# Preface

Life is much like a hike. We plan, set out, explore, sometimes struggle, sometimes get lost, and sometimes discover serendipity. In the end we look back at our experience with satisfaction. The trail that led me to the writing of this book has been a voyage through many different terrains, and the journey itself has been the reward.

As a native of Jacksonville, Florida, I grew up exploring the rich Florida landscape from the woods to the sea. As I grew older I sought hiking opportunities all over the nation and the world. I ventured into the Alaskan big wilderness and vast temperate rainforests. I climbed rugged volcano trails in rural Guatemala where the heat of flowing lava seared my skin. While pregnant with my first child, I trekked the four-day Inca Trail, arriving at Machu Picchu as the sun rose over the Peruvian Andes. Slightly closer to home, my feet have pounded the arid sandstone of Arches National Park in Utah and scrambled across the folded bedrock topography of coastal Maine. On the trail, my lungs have gasped at the dry thin air of Colorado, and filled with the sweltering mugginess of the South Carolina low country. With every trip and every new terrain, I was inspired to continue seeking more opportunities. As the motto for a national outdoor apparel company goes, "Never stop exploring." But, unfortunately, I'm not a globe-trotting millionaire with unlimited resources! And so, as I settled down in Florida to pursue my career and raise a family, imagine how lucky I felt to discover my own world-class personal wilderness right here in the woods and swamps of my home state.

After finishing my graduate degree in forestry, I found my calling as a land management specialist with the St. Johns River Water Management District. In this position, I was blessed to be able to lace up my boots to go out in the Florida woods every day. My experiences in this position were the catalyst for this book. The job duties were varied and challenging. I planned and executed prescribed burns to manage our fire-dependent ecosystems. I responded to wildfires, joining multiple agencies to control the fire line and safeguard private homes and properties. I monitored logging contractors working on public lands, assisted with ecological restoration projects, put up fences, and painted boundary markers. I've climbed what I believe are the tallest, skinniest, and most swaying pine trees ever known in order to peek at the nests of endangered red-cockaded woodpeckers. I've explored properties to plan tours for the public and VIPs. I've written management plans for enormous tracts of conservation land, and I've walked and talked with "Old Florida" cattle ranchers in the green pastures of thousand-acre ranches along the St. Johns River. It was my job to be in the field every day doing these things, and I loved it.

Like any good hike, however, there have been times when this career has tested my perseverance. I have sweltered in the worst of Florida's heat and humidity while covered from head to toe in heavy fire gear. I've been stuck on the fire line, drenched in sweaty wet gear at night during the freezing months of January and February. I've seen grown men with drip torches scream as we walked face-first through the webs of banana spiders in June. I've waded through tannin-stained and snake-inhabited swamps to mark timber and determine sites for bridges. I have gotten four-wheel-drive trucks stuck on flooded roads during the rainy summer, and stuck them again on the same sugar sand roads in the dry winter. I passed the pack test for wildfire-fighting certification known as the Red Card, finishing three miles in less than 45 minutes carrying a 45-pound pack in 110-degree heat.

I have not only hiked Florida's trails; I have also been through the woods, off the trail, and in the wilderness where no one else is even allowed to go. By foot, horseback, ATV, fire engine, airboat, and heavy duty truck, I have experienced wild Florida. I lived the Florida woods, breathed the Florida woods, and flowed through the woods. I've made my way around palmetto patches and blackberry thorns, under banana spider webs, around strands of swamp, and through flooded paths. I've tip-toed up to wild deer, waded into cypress domes, and meandered through longleaf pine stands with swishing wiregrass and vibrant wildflowers. More than a lifestyle, hiking through the woods was my life at that time.

And sometimes, life's terrain changes suddenly. With the birth of my first child, Picchu (the Quechua word for mountain), my career took a left turn. Now my hikes are limited to shorter distances. Instead of tiptoeing up to deer, I chase my darting toddler down the trail. I bend over to help her through tough spots as she stumbles over roots and climbs up riverbanks, keeping her on the path and out of poison ivy patches. We stop every 50 feet, it seems, for diaper changes or Cheerios snacks. When it comes time to go home, I try to coax her back to the car, but she is never ready to leave. I carry her squirming in body plank–style as far as I can toward the car, until she inevitably breaks free and waddles back down the trail at top speed. The frustration is there sometimes, both at her stubbornness and at the sudden change in my life's terrain. But any frustration is overshadowed by a sense of joy, that she loves the woods as much as I do, even at age one.

So thank you for allowing me to get back out in the woods and bring you along! I hope to share some of the least-publicized backcountry hiking trails in Florida, but I also hope to share the beauty and importance of Florida's natural communities. The real, wild Florida will always be threatened by cuts to conservation budgets, unchecked development, and those who would exploit the beauty of nature without protecting it. I hope this guide enables and encourages you to get out in these backcountry areas of Florida's wilderness, to learn about forests, swamps, glades, wildlife, and ecosystems. To love Florida's nature, and be moved to protect it. And I hope that like any good hike, this book will inspire you to seek more trails, soon and always.

**St. Johns River**
Water Management District

**Northwest Florida**
Water Management District

**Suwannee River**
Water Management District

**Southwest Florida**
Water Management District

**South Florida**
Water Management District

# Introduction

Welcome to the Florida backcountry! This book is designed to present a comprehensive guide to the hiking trails of Florida's five water management districts—Northwest Florida, Suwannee River, St. Johns River, Southwest Florida, and South Florida—which together manage millions of acres of public land with thousands of miles of public trails.

The mission of the five districts is to preserve and manage the water resources of Florida, so trail hikers will find wide expanses of pristine swamp, floodplain marsh, river frontage, isolated basin swamps and cypress strands, depression marshes, seasonal wetlands, sinkholes, springs, spring runs, headwaters, flood control storage areas, stormwater treatment areas, and flatwoods that can stay wet much of the rainy season. Along with wetlands, these conservation areas protect the associated upland buffers with many habitat types and species of wildlife, including many endemic and unique to Florida, or the longleaf pine ecosystem that once ranged extensively in the southeastern United States.

This is original Florida in its untamed, natural state. Staffing is minimal, so there are no gatekeepers or ticket takers. Protecting water means limited development, less concrete, and few facilities. In essence, these properties are mostly primitive. The result is miles of hiking trails that remain undisturbed, off the grid, and off the beaten path, and allow for true Florida wilderness experiences. Whereas many resource managers measure recreation success by the number of people visiting their lands each year, studies have shown that hikers measure their satisfaction by seeing no other people in the woods (T. Stein, University of Florida, pers. comm. 2016). If that describes you, then these trails are where you want to be!

With these fragile wetland ecosystems and many threatened and endangered wildlife species under protective care, water management district hiking trails and other forms of recreation are resource based. This means that recreation opportunities are created only to the extent that the habitat can support them. Trails may be seasonal, with flooding in certain areas during the rainy season of July–November. Trails may be closed during wetland or upland restoration projects or prescribed burns. Trails may be routed and rerouted around sensitive areas or to bypass endangered species' nesting sites to protect wildlife and natural resources. This hiking book will guide you through what to expect while hiking the backcountry trails of Florida's water management districts, with information on the trail marking system, special trail highlights, rules and regulations, and habitats and wildlife species you might see on the properties. Be sure to check the websites provided prior to hiking for information about any trail or property closure or changes to trail maps.

You will see present-day Florida in its most primitive state but also in various states of wetland and upland restoration and with markers of past human habitation. You will see blooming flowers in wetlands, but they might be next to a levee trail installed by a previous owner, a farmer or rancher who once drained the wetlands to plant crops or graze cattle. You may see remnants of prescribed burns. You may see natural pine flatwoods on one side of a trail, a clear-cut harvest for restoration on the other. You may see miles of planted pine from when lands were owned by big timber companies—not a natural state, but better for the environment than if converted to development. Water management district wetland scientists and land managers work together to provide the best care for these conservation lands, and the recreation managers work with them to provide the best recreational experience, where possible.

For avid hikers, new and longtime Florida residents, and the 100 million-plus tourists visiting Florida each year, 65 percent of whom mention natural areas among their Florida destinations, I hope this book brings you new hiking adventures, that it guides you to experience something natural and wild, and that it might even help you introduce a young child, the next generation of conservationists, to the outdoors.

## Florida's Water Management Districts

Florida is water! Because Florida is flat for the most part, rainwater takes a long time to clear out. With a rainy season from June to the end of November, and with many areas covered in an impermeable soil layer, water stays put and the habitat stays wet. The rainy season is not just rain, but can also consist of hurricanes, tropical storms, and dependable everyday afternoon thunderstorms. We have an underground aquifer, owned by the people of the state of Florida, that provides our drinking water. We have sinkholes where water drains directly into the aquifer, so we must keep our water clean, because we will drink it again at some point. We have springs where water rises from the underground Floridan Aquifer through holes in the limestone layer. Many of the springs form spring runs, which are rivers of crystal-clear water where recreational users can see to the bottom and enjoy viewing flora and fauna such as sea grasses, turtles, manatees, fish, and more. The springs have a year-round temperature of 74 degrees, making for a refreshing place to splash and get wet during long, hot, humid Florida summers. We have rivers that flow to tide. We have large lakes, chains of lakes, the eternal river of grass in Florida's Everglades, and we have a peninsula surrounded on three sides by ocean.

With all this water, the natural inclination was for residents and governors to get rid of it. The goal was to drain, move, and control water from swamps and wetlands. Ranchers and farmers diked and leveed the lakes and rivers to keep them under control and planted crops in their fertile soils. Developers historically, and to this day, paved wetlands and built roads, homes, and businesses. Napoleon Bonaparte Broward—one of Florida's first governors and originally from Jacksonville—declared the Everglades a waste of space and attempted to drain the river of grass for development. The result was loss of thousands of acres of wetlands, loss of wildlife habitat, loss of wildlife, and loss of what we now know are ecosystem services like flood control, flood storage, and water filtration.

After World War II, farming was encouraged in Florida to help create jobs and provide food security. Lake Apopka was drained for prime fertile soils and planted in crops, allowing pesticides and fertilizers to run into the water. Canal C-54 was created to allow headwaters of the St. Johns River west of Vero Beach to be turned to tide so as to avoid flooding farms; the Kissimmee, the Ocklawaha, and other rivers were channelized to move water to tide quickly; cities like Jacksonville were built right up to the St. Johns River with no stormwater treatment and with grassed lawns spilling fertilizers into the river, all resulting in algal blooms and loss of wetlands. Bottled-water plants moved in and withdrew millions of gallons of water per day from the Floridan Aquifer. Agriculture operations maintained flowing artesian wells for watering uses, with unlimited water withdrawal from the aquifer, and residents watered green grassy lawns during the heat of the day at peak evaporation and with programmed sprinkler systems, running during and after rains. Mistreatment of Florida's water, water quality, and water supply multiplied with quick population growth in the 1980s and 2000s.

In time, with many hurricanes and other large storm events overpowering the man-made dikes and levees, with water quality on the decline, and with water quantity decreasing, Florida governments came to understand that Florida's water and wetlands, though not valuable for market production, could be valued based on nonmarket, ecosystem services. In other words, the public was willing to pay for wetland and water quality, for nice views of nature, and for enjoyment of fishing and other recreation on water. Leaders realized that wetlands have many benefits. They can be utilized to store floodwaters during tropical storms, hurricanes, and other 10-, 25-, and 100-year storm events. Curvy, sinuous, meandering rivers could slow down the flow of water during rainy season floods. Wetlands could filter and clean waters flowing off parking lots, roads, and roofs before flowing into the lakes and rivers and the Floridan Aquifer. Surveys showed the public willing to pay a certain dollar amount for cleanup and restoration of the lakes and waters they lived near or reminisced or felt strongly about.

In 1972, the Florida legislature decided it was time for change. They voted to create water management districts as agencies of the Florida state government. They would have taxing authority to fund restoration programs, land acquisition, public education, and staff for regulation and compliance. They would have permitting programs for regulating development within wetlands and to limit water withdrawal from the Floridan Aquifer. They would have boundaries defined not by political county or city boundaries, but by watershed boundary. Budget review would still be checked and balanced by the state's Department of Environmental Protection in the State of Florida governor's office, but they were set apart from the legislature for day-to-day operations.

The goal was to shield Florida's water from the political whims of various administrations.

Today, more than 40 years after the districts were created, hundreds of thousands of wetlands and upland buffers have been placed into conservation to protect Florida's waters. The Everglades are undergoing a multibillion-dollar restoration with federal support, the Kissimmee River has been restored to a slow, winding river, Lake Apopka floodplains are no longer in farming, and the lake's waters and wetlands are thriving with life. The Upper St. Johns River Basin now turns water to tide only in extreme circumstances.

## WATER MANAGEMENT DISTRICTS TODAY

Florida is the third fastest-growing state in the United States, with some counties ranked in the top 10 among fastest-growing counties in the nation. The five districts have handled the development to the best that regulations allow. There is much to celebrate in the creation of the districts and their mission to manage water and the related natural resources to ensure their continued availability, while maximizing benefits to the public.

Yet, even with the successes in land conservation, water regulation, and wetland restoration, each new state government and business lobby brings with it the threat of limiting and changing the protective measures and laws of the water management districts. Most recently, the 2011 state legislature reduced the tax rate for the districts, resulting in budgets millions of dollars lower than in previous years. Each district was required to release a certain number of state employees and contracts were terminated, contracted employees fired, and department staff thinned. Many restoration, research, and land management projects were forced to be canceled from lack of funding. Most of the executive directors were fired or retired early. One legal department director was fired for prosecuting a ranch landowner who was draining wetlands—in effect, fired for enforcing the very laws she had hand-penned 30 years earlier to protect wetlands. The conservation lands presented in this book for hiking were forced to undergo an evaluation to see which acres could be sold. The administration felt that public land was lowering tax rolls, that it was superfluous, that the money made from sales could be better spent elsewhere. The districts have conducted a thorough review of lands with the potential for surplus and are now waiting for the administration's next move.

This most recent hit at the water management districts, at Florida's water, is not new. Protecting Florida's resources will always be a fight; it will always be political. It will take bringing people into the woods so they can experience Florida's backcountry and also providing fun, educational experiences in nature for children and adults alike, to ensure the preservation of Florida's wilderness. I hope as you hike and enjoy these District lands and wildlife, that you will come to love them and be moved to preserve Florida, to vote for those working toward conservation.

## LAND CONSERVATION

Water management districts are the unsung heroes of public land conservation in Florida. With funding from taxing authority, five regional land acquisition departments, and great working relationships with federal, state, local, and nonprofits for funding partnerships, they have developed quick methods for completing the acquisition process. Whereas other state agencies may have a parcel of land in the acquisition process for years, the districts can close within six months, which may involve placing the site on the state lands priority list, contacting landowners, conducting a land-manager review of the property, negotiating a price, and closing the sale. Funding comes from many sources. Grants include Conservation and Recreation Land (CARL) funds designated by the Florida Legislature in 1979 and funded by an excise tax on mineral extraction and documentary stamp taxes from real estate transactions, and from Save Our Rivers (SOR) funds, a water management district land trust fund for the acquisition and restoration of water resources. This funding was designated for each of the five districts and used to purchase thousands of acres of land starting in 1981.

Preservation 2000 started in 1991 and used funds from the sale of bonds to fund SOR, CARL, and other land conservation programs. Florida Forever was created in 2000 as a successor to Preservation 2000 and has preserved more than 2 million acres of Florida land. Florida's land acquisition program has been one of the most successful and aggressive land conservation programs in the United States under the leadership of Charlie Houder at Suwannee River, my graduate school advisor, and Robert Christianson, my director at St. Johns River Water Management District and preservation genius who won an Audubon Award for Land Conservation in 2010. However, the positive attitude toward conservation of Florida's distinct and fragile habitats changed in 2012. Governor Rick Scott's administration did not budget funds for public land conservation through Florida Forever, and land conservation purchases dwindled. The districts have a long history of award-winning land conservation and management programs, and it is the hope that future legislatures will once again allocate funds for preserving Florida's ecosystems.

However, even with the hundreds of thousands of acres of land under the purview of the districts, land management departments are extremely limited in staffing. For example, the St. Johns River Water Management District manages 500,000 acres of land and 60 conservation easements with one recreation staff member. It has 17 land management field staff with additional invasive plant managers, for an average of 29,000 acres per person to manage. So water management districts have to get creative. Districts buy the land quickly, then enter into management agreements to add lands to state parks or state forests, or they work with national preserves to manage lands. The water management districts will usually keep a conservation easement on lands they purchase that are then managed by others to ensure management for the purposes for which they were acquired and funded. This is a creative and innovative way to continue to protect Florida lands without adding to the management time and costs of the districts. In this book, lands owned and managed only by the districts are presented and described in terms of their hiking opportunities, highlighting unique Florida backcountry wilderness.

## Natural Communities and Wildlife on District Land

The water management districts purchase land with coverage in wetlands and many types of natural communities. In most of the natural community types, hikers may encounter common Florida wildlife species such as white-tailed deer, feral hog, coyote, bobcat, raccoon, rabbit, armadillo, varieties of snakes, American alligator, bald eagle, wild turkey, Florida sandhill crane, other resident avian species, and more. Be on the lookout for wild turkeys with chicks, as the parent turkeys will be highly aggressive toward hikers in an effort to protect their young, as can be the case with many wildlife species.

Florida black bear are common in the panhandle near Eglin Air Force Base and Apalachicola, near Osceola National Forest and Ocala National Forest to the St. Johns River area, the Chassahowitzka area in the Big Bend, the Highlands/Glades region of south-central Florida, and the Big Cypress management unit of South Florida. They can, however, be found in any district conservation area. Hikers should beware of bears and make sounds while hiking.

Florida panther, which once roamed throughout the southeastern United States, are now breeding only in south Florida, with some roaming males found in central Florida. Panther might be found on any district property. Paw prints have been noticed as far north as Lake George Conservation Area in the St. Johns River Water Management District.

The remnants of the longleaf pine ecosystem of the southeastern United States can be found on district property. The now rare ecosystem hosts longleaf pine (*Pinus palustris*) in the forest canopy; at the forest floor it hosts palmetto/gallberry and wildflower mixtures in flatwoods, wiregrass and wildflower mixtures with high biodiversity in sandhills, or saw palmetto, oaks, and wildflowers in scrubby flatwoods areas. It also hosts 29 species of wildlife that live only in longleaf pine habitats, like the red-cockaded woodpecker.

Longleaf pine is a slow-growing evergreen tree that was heavily logged throughout the southeast for use as ship masts. Millions of acres were lost as fast-growing slash pine were planted in replacement of longleaf pine to enable quick harvest cycles, resulting in hundreds of thousands of acres converted from longleaf pine. Today the districts and state agencies are replacing slash pine with longleaf pine after those areas are cut to restore the habitat and wildlife of this long-lost ecosystem.

The following are descriptions of the plant communities, prescribed fire intervals, and districts where you can find them. Natural community descriptions are garnered from Florida Natural Areas Inventory, published in 2010 and listed in the bibliography.

## SANDHILL

Sandhill is characterized by widely spaced pine trees with a sparse midstory of deciduous oaks and a moderate to dense groundcover of grasses, herbs, and low shrubs.

**Fire return interval:** 1–3 years
**Wildlife viewing:** Gopher tortoise, gopher frog, snake species, white-tailed deer, Florida mouse, Sherman's fox squirrel
**Districts:** Found in all districts

## SCRUB

Scrub is a community composed of evergreen shrubs, with or without a canopy of pines and is found on dry, infertile, sandy ridges. The signature scrub species—three species of shrubby oaks, Florida rosemary (*Ceratiola ericoides*), and sand pine (*Pinus clausa*)—are common to scrubs throughout the state.

**Fire return interval:** 5–20 years
**Wildlife viewing**: Florida scrub jay, gopher tortoise, Florida mouse, sand skink, snake species
**Districts:** Found in all districts

## XERIC HAMMOCK

Xeric hammock is an evergreen forest on well-drained sandy soils. The short overstory is dominated by scrub oaks and can include pine. The understory is either leaf litter or remnant wiregrass and wildflower species, where sunlight still reaches the forest floor. This is remnant sandhill or scrub where fire has not occurred in seven years or more, so oaks have been able to grow to the canopy and create shade. The groundcover is then unable to grow and fire cannot run through the system, causing succession to a completely different ecosystem.

**Fire return interval:** 4 years; however, fire has been excluded from these ecosystems
**Wildlife viewing:** Gopher tortoise, red fox, wild turkey, rabbits, white-tailed deer
**Districts:** Found in all districts

## MESIC FLATWOODS

Mesic flatwoods form the most prevalent upland ecosystem on district properties. They are characterized by an open canopy of tall pines and a dense, low ground layer of short shrubs, grasses, and herbaceous flowering plants. Longleaf pine (*Pinus palustris*) is the main canopy tree in northern and central Florida, and South Florida slash pine (*P. elliottii* var. *densa*) forms the canopy south of Lake Okeechobee.

**Fire return interval:** 2–4 years
**Wildlife viewing:** Flatwoods salamander, red-cockaded woodpecker, Florida black bear
**Districts:** Found in all districts

## DEPRESSION MARSH

Depression marsh is characterized as a shallow, usually round depression in sand with grasses, herbs, and wildflowers, or small shrubs. Depression marshes are typically surrounded by natural communities that also burn, like flatwoods, dry prairie, or sandhill.

**Fire return interval:** Dependent on surrounding natural community; fires in those communities should be allowed to burn into depression marshes and extinguish naturally or burn through them
**Wildlife viewing:** Salamanders, gopher frog, eastern indigo snake, wading birds
**Districts:** Found in all districts

## GLADES MARSH

Glades marsh is a primarily herbaceous wetland, one that hosts only herbs and grasses such as sawgrass, in South Florida. It is found especially in the Everglades, occurring in broad shallow channels or depressions over a substrate of peat or marl that directly overlies limestone.

**Fire return interval:** 3–10 years
**Wildlife viewing:** Federally endangered snail kite, wading birds, American alligator
**Districts:** South Florida and Southwest Florida Water Management Districts

## FLOODPLAIN SWAMP

Floodplain swamp is a closed-canopy forest of hydrophytic (water-loving) trees such as cypress. It occurs on frequently or permanently flooded hydric soils adjacent to stream and river channels and in depressions and oxbows within floodplains. Trees are often buttressed, and the understory and groundcover are sparse.

> **Fire return interval:** Floodplain swamp is usually too wet to support fire
> **Wildlife viewing:** Alligator, snakes, wading birds, bats
> **Districts:** Found in all districts

## WET PRAIRIE

Wet prairie is an herbaceous community with no trees or shrubs. Wet prairie is found on continuously wet, but not inundated, soils on somewhat flat or gentle slopes dominated by wiregrass and water-tolerant grasses.

> **Fire return interval:** 2–4 years
> **Wildlife viewing:** White-tailed deer, grasshoppers, and wading birds
> **Districts:** Found in all districts

## SLOUGH

Sloughs are the deepest drainage ways within swamps and marsh systems. They are broad channels inundated with slow-moving or nearly stagnant water, except during extreme drought. The vegetation structure is variable, with some sloughs dominated by floating aquatics, others by large emergent herbaceous plants, and still others by a low or sparse canopy.

> **Fire return interval:** May never burn
> **Wildlife viewing:** Alligator and epiphytic plants like rare orchids
> **Districts:** South Florida Water Management District

## FLOODPLAIN SWAMP

Floodplain swamp is a closed-canopy forest of water-tolerant trees occurring on flooded soils along water bodies. Trees are often buttressed, and the understory and groundcover are thin. The canopy is sometimes a pure stand of bald cypress (*Taxodium distichum*).

> **Fire return interval:** Typically too wet to support fire
> **Wildlife viewing:** Alligator, bats, turtles, wading birds, Florida black bear
> **Districts:** All districts

## Recreation at Florida's Water Management Districts

Water management district recreation programs are defined as "dispersed recreation"; thus they do not have one recreation destination where a lot of people are located, such as a busy campground or swimming hole at a spring. The trails are dispersed throughout, with multiple user types on each trail. You may pass people or you may not, so be prepared to hike alone in Florida's backcountry, and also be prepared for an emergency.

Water management districts do not have the typical brown signs noting a conservation area at the next turn or a Florida birding trail in a few hundred yards. You will need to utilize the GPS points, directions, and possibly a 911 address to find the upcoming trailhead entrance, keeping your eyes open for the property signs. You can also note the blue or other colored boundary markings on trees to know you are passing water management district property and will soon come upon the sign for the property.

### RECREATION FACILITIES

Districts offer various recreational opportunities at each property depending on what the natural resources can support. District lands are purchased to protect wetland and water, so most properties are primitive, with few facilities. Typical uses are hiking, bicycling, horseback riding, geocaching, hunting, and paddling/fishing/boating where there is a lake or creek with a ramp.

Most properties have board-fenced, grassy parking areas. Some properties have primitive camping, portable toilets, picnic tables, shelters, fishing docks or fishing access, equestrian trails, parking areas, and boat or canoe ramps. Some are handicap-accessible, and some have access to springs. This book lets you know what facilities are available so you can plan your adventure according to the activity you are looking for.

Camping is a recreational use on district lands and is like no other camping experience in Florida. Since no one works at the gates the way they do at state and national parks and access to the property is always open, this means you are on your own for safety. Most times you must carry in your gear and food because vehicle access is not allowed. Most times you are alone in the woods, which can be scary for some, thrilling for others.

Primitive camping and primitive group camping are offered on many district lands, and camping is *free*. "Primitive" means no restrooms, no electricity, and no potable water are available, and designated camping sites are offered on a first-come, first-serve basis. Some sites have benches and fire rings at the site, and some have equestrian areas where trailer parking is offered with horse tie-up locations and wooden steps to dismount. Group sites may be offered, which means the site can be reserved in advance. These sites are typically still primitive; however, some may offer a pavilion with lights, grills, and a portable toilet. Visit the website of the water management district where you are looking to camp for their campsite reservation policy.

TRAIL TYPES

Most water management district trails are traditionally multiuse trails. This means that district recreation managers can manage one trail while providing recreation for hikers, bikers, equestrian users, runners, and wildlife viewers. This management style has less of an impact on natural resources as fewer clearings are needed for roads.

*Hiking Only*

Many districts offer hiking-only trails in partnership with the Florida National Scenic Trail (Florida Trail). Florida Trail volunteers have created a federally designated, nonmotorized recreational trail across approximately 1,000 miles in Florida. The path starts in the western panhandle of Florida at the beach in Fort Pickens State Park and heads north to meet the trail that begins at the Florida/Alabama state line and heads east through the middle of the Florida Panhandle. It heads south at Osceola National Forest west of Jacksonville, splits at Ocala National

Forest for a wide oval. It joins just north of Kissimmee River at Three Lakes Conservation Area and heads south to Lake Okeechobee. Here it splits again, bordering both sides of the lake. It joins again heading south to the Everglades through Big Cypress Preserve. You can find the latest ArcGIS map online at www.fs.usda.gov/main/fnst/about. This is the best way to see how the Florida Trail merges with district lands. With low district staffing, it is Florida Trail volunteers who ask for and help maintain this hiking-only trail while also partnering with district staff to maintain it.

## Auto Drives

Some district properties are open to vehicle access during certain periods of the day. These lands are typically large wetland restoration projects with many miles of levees, or large, thousand-acre timber properties that would take hours to hike or bike. On some of these lands, districts have provided auto-drive maps and guides. These take recreational users through areas they might not get to by foot, provide handicap-accessible recreation, highlight unique areas the user should see, and describe the area or management at designated stop points. On these drives hikers are also welcome to utilize the map and guide; however, hikers should beware of vehicles and move to the side of levees and roads when cars pass.

## Equestrian and Biking Trails

Many properties offer equestrian or biking trails or combine these into multiuse trails. Some equestrian trails have different entrances because of the need for larger parking areas to pull horse trailers in and out. Some biking trails feature tall hills (yes, tall hills in Florida!). A mountain biking trail can be found at Graham Swamp Conservation Area within St. Johns River Water Management District, resulting from historical piling of coquina rock, featuring large jumps, and wooden water crossings maintained by mountain biking partner groups. Hiking is typically welcome on these trails; however, hikers must follow trail guidelines to verify that hiking is allowed. Be safe on these multiuse trails.

## Paddling Trails

Some conservation areas host paddling trails. Lake Norris Conservation Area in St. Johns River WMD has a paddling trail accessible from the parking area. Hiking trails on the Suwannee River contain campsites that are available by reservation. If you have a canoe or kayak, bring it along because, per Marjorie Kinnan Rawlings' adventures on the St. Johns River, much of the Florida backcountry is accessed via its water.

## TRAIL BLAZE MARKINGS

Trail blaze markings are different in each district; trail maps, if provided, should be followed. Florida Trail markings are vertical orange rectangles and the trail is for hikers only. The district in which I worked, St. Johns River Water Management District, has diamond-shaped trail blazes. The blazes can be orange, white, red, yellow, or other bright colors.

There can be many different trails on a property, and each trail will have a different color blaze. For example, hikers can start out at a trailhead on the red trail, then turn off onto a loop where the trail is blazed yellow. Spur trails lead to another trail; the spurs have their own color. Spur trails will have a double diamond, one color on top for the trail color you are traveling to, and one color on the bottom for the one you just left. Two diamonds of the same color indicate a turn in the trail and to be on the lookout for an upcoming turn.

If you see a blue band painted around a tree in the St. Johns River Water Management District (other colors in other districts), it indicates you are hiking on a boundary. A white band indicates a tree that hosts a red-cockaded woodpecker nest.

Most trails do not have interior maps or signage so be sure to use your phone map and bring a printed map for guidance in case there is no cell coverage in these backcountry areas. Go back to the last diamond if you can't find the next one and look from there to find your way. You can always call the districts if you have a problem or 911 if you feel lost.

## Florida Hiking Tips: Being Country Savvy

Working or hiking in the backwoods requires unique skills and know-how. With years in the woods, including working alongside longtime land management staff at the St. Johns River Water Management District, I learned tips and tricks for becoming what longtime Recreational Land Manager Nels Parson calls *country savvy*. Becoming country savvy improves problem-solving skills and teaches independence and life lessons. I am a better person in the city and as a problem-solving mom because I know how to work in the woods, and it is an experience for which I will always be grateful.

The good news is you don't have to learn the hard way like I did! I've gathered some of what I learned about being country savvy on district lands, related to hiking, into these quick tips.

1. Park near the main road at the entrance where the car is completely visible to other drivers on the street. It will be less tempting for someone to steal or break into your car.
2. Always park your car facing your exit. That way if you have an emergency, you won't have to back up to get out.
3. If possible, park your car perpendicular to a trail. That way when you are returning after a long hike, you can see your car at the end of the trail and know you are on the right path to the exit. This advice applies only to sites you can drive to, of course, or if you are working in the woods, but still great advice I was taught by Crystal Morris, former Land Manager at St. Johns River Water Management District.
4. Flooded trails should be tested before crossing. Find a long stick to test the depth of the water and whether it has a hard bottom.
5. Be sure to look down to see snakes and step wide over downed logs and sticks, which is where snakes like to rest.
6. Hike with a friend.
7. Make noise to let bears know you are nearby.
8. Keep dogs on a leash for their safety. If a dog runs off into the woods, don't leave the trail to chase it as you can quickly become lost.
9. In the event you do become lost, be sure to enable GPS on your phone so helicopters can find you (see more tips below for hiking with technology).
10. Urinate facing uphill if you are female and downhill if you are male. You don't want anything flowing toward your feet! Also beware of mosquito bites on your exposed rear end, unless you've applied bug spray there! Funny restroom tip I learned firsthand

while working on a prescribed burn with helicopters in the air: Don't use the restroom behind a bush when a helicopter is flying nearby. You must find a tree to hide under! A bush will not hide you from a helicopter crew!

11. Don't sit on the ground, on a bed of leaves, or on a fallen tree, no matter how tired you get. Chiggers and ticks live in downed trees and fallen leaf litter. That short respite will leave your stomach itching for weeks with red spots, and ticks will quickly burrow into your ankles and waist area.

12. Tuck pants into socks to discourage ticks. Not a fashion statement, but this will prevent the problems in tip #11 above and is standard protocol for Florida hikers and land managers.

## HIKING WITH TECHNOLOGY

Whereas it is advised to print a trail map before you head into the woods (as many of the water management district properties are so backcountry and far from cell towers that you might not get service), it can be fun and helpful to use technology in the woods. Use a GPS to find geocache locations. Use your smart phone to follow the trail on a map opened on your screen. Download a compass map to help guide direction. Utilize Periscope, Snapchat, or Facebook Live to send out instant videos of your hike. Take a selfie and use hashtags to tag the district where you're hiking to be retweeted on Twitter or liked and shared on Facebook. Take photos and share on Instagram. Having a phone with you can also be good for safety. One girl ran after her dog, leaving the trail near the Gainesville Airport, and was lost for hours. A helicopter pilot homed in on the GPS in her phone and helped a search and rescue team find her. Use technology to assist you and to have fun in the woods, but be prepared to go it alone in case you do not get service or your phone battery drains.

## HIKING WITH KIDS

Taking children on a hike can be one of the most rewarding experiences. If they have all their necessities—food, water, comfortable clothes, diapers for changing—and it is not too hot or cold, they can enjoy exploring nature. It is amazing to see what interests them, from a pine cone to Spanish moss to an armadillo rummaging for food. Their wonder is contagious.

Get kids engaged on the trail by providing activities. Letterboxing (where you hide a box with prizes and then create clues leading to the box), doing an alphabet hike, where you find something that starts with the letter A, B, C, etc., or finding five things you hear, see, and feel, are all great ways to get them engaged on the trail. Be sure to know that if you make it only a few feet and they stop to play for awhile, you have succeeded. Also, the moment they get agitated, be prepared to head home. You don't want bad experiences or hikes that are too long for their age to cause them to dislike the woods.

Each property in this guide is marked to indicate whether trails are family friendly in the Uses and Restrictions sections. However, with a baby carrier or backpack carrier or where kids can run and play for a short distance, most of these hikes can be family friendly. Use your own judgment and safety and enjoy hiking with your family and guide their love of nature!

SAFETY

It is imperative that hikers maintain a high level of safety on these backcountry properties. Most of the sites are undeveloped, so that means there can be little to no shade or shelter, no provisions on site, and no drinking water sources. Be sure to bring enough water and food; wear protective gear like sunscreen, long pants, a hat, and hiking boots; and use bug spray. Always be on the lookout for snakes, make noises for Florida black bears, and never let children wade into creeks or rivers unsupervised, especially in the evenings, due to currents, snakes, and alligators. Do not hike during prescribed fire or wildfire. Beware of storms and lightning that come on quickly, and take shelter, where possible.

Let family know where you are going and how long you plan to be gone. Bring a phone, but also bring a printed map in case of no cell service. Do not hike in hunting areas during season. Check district websites before you hike to learn about trail closures due to construction, prescribed burns, or flooding. Be aware that trails can be rerouted frequently, so follow the blazes closely. Hikers are responsible for their own safety and for knowing the route.

# How to Use This Guide

This hiking guide is organized by each of the five water management districts (WMDs). You can pick the area of Florida you would like to hike, or if you are vacationing or live in a certain area of Florida, you can find your district and search for interesting hikes there. You can find descriptions of the district properties that host the Florida National Scenic Trail, property amenities, wildlife, trail features, and more throughout the guide.

## HOW TO FIND THE PROPERTIES

This book utilizes aerial imagery to locate GPS points, provides a link to the best map of the trails, and utilizes 911 addresses to assist in finding trailheads.

## FIND NATURAL COMMUNITIES

The description of each property includes a section on natural communities found on the property and wildlife you may view or encounter. If you'd like to see the rare upland scrub habitat or glades marsh and tree islands, you can find the properties that host those communities.

## FIND AMENITIES

Each property description includes a Uses and Restrictions section. From camping to picnicking, to horseback riding, to being kid friendly, find the amenities you are looking for.

## LEARN ABOUT THE PROPERTY

Each property has a specific purpose for being protected. The description sections show how each water body is connected to the next and the strategies for protecting the area.

## HIKING DESCRIPTION

Trail length, time it takes to hike, whether the trail is seasonally wet, and a description of what you will see on the hike are included. Each property description includes a trail highlight so you can be on the lookout for scenic vistas. Descriptions of hikes were created from hiking the property or by using aerial imagery of the site. Finally, there are descriptions of my personal experiences while managing or visiting the properties in my job as a female land management specialist in the Florida backcountry of the St. Johns River Water Management District.

## Whom to Call/District Websites

### NORTHWEST FLORIDA WATER MANAGEMENT DISTRICT

www.nwfwater.com (850) 539-5999
Facebook: @NWFWater
Twitter: @NWFWMD

### SUWANNEE RIVER WATER MANAGEMENT DISTRICT

www.mysuwanneeriver.com (386) 362-1001
Facebook: @SRWMD
Twitter: @SRWMD

### ST. JOHNS RIVER WATER MANAGEMENT DISTRICT

www.sjrwmd.com (386) 329-4500
Facebook: @SJRWMD
Instagram: @SJRWMD
Twitter: @FLORIDASWATER

### SOUTHWEST FLORIDA WATER MANAGEMENT DISTRICT

www.swfwmd.state.fl.us (352) 796-7211
Facebook: @WaterMatters
Instagram: @SWFWMD
Twitter: @SWFWMD

### SOUTH FLORIDA WATER MANAGEMENT DISTRICT

www.sfwmd.gov (561) 686-8800
Facebook: South Florida Water Management District
Twitter: @SFWMD

## FLORIDA FISH AND WILDLIFE CONSERVATION COMMISSION

www.myfwc.com (850) 488-4676
Facebook: @MyFWC
Instagram: @MyFWC
Twitter: @MYFWC

## FLORIDA FOREST SERVICE

www.freshfromflorida.com/Divisions-Offices/Florida-Forest-Service
Facebook: @FloridaAgriculture
Instagram: @FreshFromFlorida
Twitter: @FreshFromFlorida

## U.S. FISH AND WILDLIFE

www.fws.gov
Facebook: @USFWS
Instagram: @USFWS
Twitter: @USFWS

## U.S. FOREST SERVICE

www.fs.fed.us
Facebook: @USForestService
Instagram: @U.S.ForestService
Twitter: @ForestService

# 1

# Northwest District

The Northwest Florida Water Management District is the most rural of all five water management districts. From just east of Tallahassee west to the Florida/Alabama line, and from the Alabama and Georgia borders south to the Gulf of Mexico, its border is the panhandle of Florida, with 16 counties in its region. The district is 11,305 square miles in area, and conservation lands protect several major drainage basins: Perdido River and Bay System, Pensacola Bay System (Escambia, Blackwater, and Yellow rivers), Choctawhatchee River and Bay System, St. Andrew Bay System, Apalachicola River and Bay System, and St. Marks River Basin (Wakulla River). It hosts 270 of the more than 700 Florida springs, balances agriculture lands, promotes water conservation and reuse/reclaimed water systems, and provides flood protection maps and guidance to residents.

Although this district is low in population and development, it is not without its share of water resource issues. With water bodies crossing the borders of multiple states, the district works to manage water needs of Florida, Georgia, and Alabama in what have been historically deemed "water wars." For example, the Flint River and reservoir in Atlanta are utilized to provide drinking water for all of metro Atlanta; therefore, water resource managers in Atlanta are interested in holding back water for Atlanta residents. However, the reservoir outputs into the Flint River, which flows into Alabama, where water is needed for tourism. It flows on into Florida and out into the Apalachicola Bay, which needs a certain amount of freshwater for a delicate salinity balance to manage the huge shellfish industry on which those small businesses rely. This district helps manage those issues and others, including water quality, water supply, oil spills, and habitat loss in its quest to manage water for the people of the State of Florida.

Hiking in this region is hosted on long, linear properties that were purchased to protect the river systems. At the southernmost point of the Appalachian hills, properties may have some elevation, whitewater rapids, and hikes out to hidden lakes and along black-water streams, with water dyed black by decaying leaf litter. Natural communities here are a contrast to the south Florida glades marshes, hosting beech and magnolia forests, floodplain swamps, and hundreds of springs. Many of the hiking trails are managed by volunteers as part of the federally recognized Florida National Scenic Trail. Whether looking for long through-hikes or short park trails, you'll enjoy true rural Florida.

## Basics for the Northwest District

Be sure to note whether trails are seasonally flooded (typically in the summer rainy season) and whether there is hunting. Check www.myfwc .com for hunting dates prior to hiking.

Unless otherwise noted, all properties in this region are open from sunrise to sunset, free of charge. For any additional questions, contact the Northwest Florida Water Management District office at (850) 539-5999.

## Northwest Florida Water Management District Eastern Region

---

## 1. Elinor Klapp-Phipps Park Wildlife Management Area

**GPS:** Lat 30.536517, Long -84.280837
**Address:** 4750 N. Meridian Road, Tallahassee
**Trailhead Directions:** From Tallahassee, take North Meridian Road.
   Take a left on Miller Landing Road. Park at the soccer complex for one of the many trailheads within the park.
**Size:** 674 acres
**Trail Distance:** 17 miles
**Hiking Time:** 1 hour to day hike
**Difficulty:** Easy to strenuous

Florida Trail at Elinor Klapp-Phipps Park Wildlife Management Area

**Trail Surface:** Leaf litter, boardwalk
**Shade Level:** 0–25%
**Natural Communities:** Beech-magnolia and spruce-pine forests, seepage basin swamp, black-water stream, seepage stream
**Wildlife:** Bluebird, rare butterflies, fox squirrel, white-tailed deer, wild turkey, gopher tortoise
**Maps:** www.talgov.com/Uploads/Public/Documents/parks/pdf/phipps.pdf
**Uses and Restrictions:** Wildlife viewing, sports complexes, restrooms, playground, hiking, horseback riding, mountain biking, hunting. No ATVs allowed; motorized vehicles allowed on designated roads only. Be sure to check www.myfwc.com for hunting dates before hiking. Kid-friendly hiking on boardwalk. Family-friendly hiking encouraged.

**Trail Highlights:** Hikers will experience black-water streams and walk through beech-magnolia and spruce-pine forests. There is also a spur trail to a bat house.

**Additional Hiking:** Ochlockonee River Wildlife Management Area, Talquin Wildlife Management Area, Joe Budd Wildlife Management Area, Apalachicola National Forest

This park was purchased to protect Lake Jackson, which is a Florida Aquatic Preserve, a designated Florida outstanding water body, and a Surface Water Improvement and Management Act priority watershed. On the western border of Tallahassee, the property offers hiking, mountain biking, and horseback riding with 17 miles of multiuse trails. Some organized recreational facilities came with the purchase—ball fields, a park, and an athletic center—however, there is plenty of undeveloped hiking offered at this site close to the city of Tallahassee. Hikers will find a mix of easy to strenuous hiking in this lower red hills region. Hikers will walk along black-water streams, through beech-magnolia and spruce-magnolia forests, and through seepage swamps and will view giant cane, a stand of tulip poplars, the rare needle palm, and pinckneya. Hike as long or as short as you'd like, as this park has many options.

## Hike Details

Start at the trailhead marked at the entrance to the soccer complex or the trailhead marked at the equestrian entrance, both off Miller Landing Road. These trailheads lead to the orange-marked hiking-only Florida Trails: Coon Bottom Loop (1.5 miles), Swamp Forest Loop (1.8 miles), Creek Forest Trail (0.8 miles), and Oak Hammock Loop (2.5 miles) as well as the green-marked shared-use trails. The trailhead marked on Meridian Road, just south of the ball field complexes on that road, leads to the Coon Bottom Loop Trail, for hiking only. These approximately 7 miles of trails lead to another 11 miles of multiuse trails, marked in green on the map found at the link provided above. Also look for the Bluebird Trail, a series of 30 bluebird boxes built and installed along a path by an Eagle Scout.

## 2. Florida River Island Recreation Area: Apalachicola River

**GPS:** Lat 30.184587, Long -85.085421

**Trailhead Directions:** From the town of Bristol, travel 19 miles south on Highway 379. Take a right on Forest Road 188 and cross over the Florida River Bridge. Accessible only during times of normal to low water conditions.

**Size:** 5,806 acres

**Trail Distance:** 1.5 miles

**Hiking Time:** 2 hours

**Difficulty:** Easy

**Trail Surface:** Pavement, gravel, grass

**Shade Level:** 0–25%

**Natural Communities:** Floodplain

**Wildlife:** White-tailed deer, raccoon, eastern gray squirrel, opossum, various snakes, rabbit, more

**Maps:** www.nwfwater.com/system/assets/230/original/FL_Riv_Isl_inset_Final_z.jpg

**Uses and Restrictions:** Boating, camping, canoeing, fishing, hiking, hunting. No ATVs allowed; motorized vehicles allowed on designated roads only. Be sure to check www.myfwc.com for hunting dates before hiking. Not friendly for family hiking.

**Trail Highlights:** Hikers will enjoy views of Elsie Lake and an out-and-back hike to Greenback Lake. Be sure to bring a fishing pole (and license!) to try your luck at two fishing spots.

**Additional Hiking:** Apalachicola National Forest, Tate's Hell National Forest

Florida River Island Recreation Area is bordered on the west by the Apalachicola River and on the east and north by the Florida River, making it a true island. Hikers will enjoy views of Elsie Lake and Greenback Lake as well as beautifully maintained and healthy mesic flatwoods. The property protects the floodplains of these rivers, which flow into the Gulf of Mexico. There are no marked hiking trails; however, the mowed land-management roads are open to pedestrian use for exploring the Apalachicola River floodplain. Be sure to call ahead

Trailhead at Florida River Trail

for flood levels, as this area is accessible only during normal to low water conditions.

## Hike Details

After crossing Florida River Bridge, stay to the right and drive past Elsie Lake. Park at the fishing area on the lake. There are a few out-and-back hikes on grassy land-management roads. From the fishing area designated on the map, hike the road south and take a right to hike out and back to Greenback Lake. Or, after coming over the Florida River Bridge, turn south and park on the side of the road at the first mowed land-management road. Hike out and back to the southern point of Greenback Lake. Also be sure to drive all the way south to view Acorn Lake. There is a Florida River Island trail with signage and a boardwalk at the start, but this is not a maintained trail and the path is easy to lose. Also, the mosquitoes are a-plenty, so stick with winter hiking here.

### 3. Bellamy Bridge Heritage Trail: Upper Chipola Water Management Area

**GPS:** Lat 30.871242, Long -85.258026

**Trailhead Directions:** From I-10 east of Marianna, Florida, take SR 71 north. Head west on CR 162. The parking area is located 1/10 of a mile west of the western end of the Chipola River Bridge.

**Size:** 9,094 acres, 338 acres owned by the district

**Trail Distance:** 2 miles out and back

**Hiking Time:** 1 hour

**Difficulty:** Easy

**Trail Surface:** Sandy bottom

**Shade Level:** 25–50%

**Natural Communities:** Floodplain forest, hydric hammock, mesic flatwoods in planted pine

**Wildlife:** White-tailed deer, wild turkey, avian species

**Maps:** www.bellamybridge.org/

**Admission:** None

**Uses and Restrictions:** Hiking, wildlife viewing, hunting. No ATVs allowed; motorized vehicles allowed on designated roads only. Be sure to check www.myfwc.com for hunting dates before hiking. Family-friendly hiking.

**Contact:** Northwest Florida Water Management District, (850) 539-5999

**Trail Highlights:** Hikers will enjoy a majestic, peaceful, and sparkling view of the Bellamy Bridge as well as a view of the Chipola River.

**Additional Hiking:** Florida Caverns State Park, Look and Tremble

This trail is part of the Upper Chipola Water Management Area that protects both sides of Marshall Creek and Cowarts Creek, starting

Bellamy Bridge overlooking the Chipola River

at the Florida/Georgia border, and flowing into the Chipola River. The property consists of mostly floodplain swamp as well as planted pine in former mesic flatwoods habitat. This property has a historic structure, the Bellamy Bridge, that hikers can visit, but not cross. The bridge, built in 1851 and deemed obsolete in 1963, is considered the oldest in Florida. The bridge also has a unique haunted history; it is said that Elizabeth Jane Croom Bellamy can be seen near the bridge on spooky nights. In 2012 a trail was created through a partnership between Northwest Florida Water Management District and Jackson County so the public could hike in south of CR 162 and view the historic bridge as well as the natural habitat along the way.

My husband and I had a rare moment alone, sans kids, to hike to the Bellamy Bridge. It was an easy hike and we walked briskly under the shade of the trees of the floodplain swamp. Just as we began to wonder where the bridge was, we turned a curve to the left to see it. It was an amazing sight, such a large bridge in the middle of the woods. It was majestic and mighty, even though the bottom of the bridge was missing. We took a moment to enjoy this quiet and enchanted Florida historical spot, took multiple photos to keep our memories longer, and waited for the ghost to appear. Thankfully she spared us.

## Hike Details

The hike begins at the CR 162 parking area and heads southeast. Hikers will meander through hard-packed sandy soil. There are a few ups and downs through areas where the path has collapsed from flooding. Hikers will pass a wooden fence that blocks one path and guides to another. The bridge will come up on the left as mighty and ancient. Here it crosses the Chipola River. At this point hikers can marvel and then return to the parking area.

## 4. Look and Tremble: Chipola River

**GPS:** Lat 30.524885, Long -85.161778
**Address:** Altha, FL 32421
**Trailhead Directions:** From the town of Altha, take CR 274 southwest. Entry is at the intersection of CR 274 and Look and Tremble Road; however, the Florida National Scenic Trail is on the east side of the Chipola River.
**Size:** 9,045 acres within the Upper Chipola River Management Area
**Trail Distance:** 3.2 miles out and back
**Hiking Time:** 1 hour to day hike, depending on whether you continue on the Florida Trail when you leave the property
**Difficulty:** Easy to medium
**Trail Surface:** Leaf litter
**Shade Level:** 0–25%
**Natural Communities:** Floodplain forest and mesic flatwoods in planted pine

Overlooking the rapids of the Chipola River

**Wildlife:** White-tailed deer, wild turkey, gopher tortoise
**Maps:** www.nwfwater.com/system/assets/991/original/Lower_Chipola_
River_Final.jpg
**Uses and Restrictions:** Restrooms, fishing, canoe launch, canoeing,
wildlife viewing. No ATVs allowed; motorized vehicles allowed on
designated roads only. Not family friendly; however, every child
should experience the Look and Tremble rapids.
**Trail Highlights:** Hikers will find views of Class 1 rapids on the Chipola
River, a rare sight in Florida.
**Additional Hiking:** Torreya State Park, Econfina Wildlife Management
Area

Further south on the Chipola River, Look and Tremble adds more protection to the watershed, which eventually flows into the Apalachicola River and Apalachicola Bay. Water quality is of utmost importance here, as water flowing into Apalachicola Bay must be high quality to support the shellfish industry. Protection of this river through land conservation is key. The Chipola River at this point has limestone outcroppings and a drop in elevation, creating Class 1 rapids on the Chipola River. Hiking is on the east side of the river on the Florida National Scenic Trail. It is thrilling to hear the rapids at this spot on the river. If the water is low, the river is down at the bottom of the canyon, and bluff overlooks are amazing at this wild river with crystal blue water, yet with somewhat of a white, dusty sheen. The water is clear and extremely cold, even in summer. Hiking is on the east side of the river on the Florida National Scenic Trail.

In summer 2016 we drove to Look and Tremble. We crawled down a bank of the Chipola and my two-year-old son wanted all his clothes off to get in the water. He waded in and walked back and forth in the water, grabbing rocks to throw. Mosquitoes were biting him on his bare behind, but he didn't notice. He loved that river at first sight. When it was time to leave, he refused. I think we could have built a home there and stayed for the rest of our lives.

## Hike Details

From Look and Tremble Road, head east on CR 274 and cross the Chipola River. Take a right on the side road and head back west. Turn south onto the Florida National Scenic Trail. Here you will hike south on a meandering trail through floodplain swamp. East of the trail are views of mesic flatwoods in planted pine. The Look and Tremble Falls are slightly more than halfway down the length of the property. Spend a moment there enjoying the rapids and canoes paddling by. Veer to the east just north of Bauldree Branch Creek. Hike east past a cleared pasture and then continue east through mesic flatwoods. Hike along the branch of the Chipola following the creek until reaching the boundary of the district's Look and Tremble property. Turn back and retrace your steps to reach the parking area, or continue east on the road walk-path if you have a second car parked somewhere or are doing a through-hike.

## 5. Lafayette Creek Tract: Lafayette Wildlife Management Area

**GPS:** Lat 30.526613, Long -86.048613
**Trailhead Directions:** From the town of Freeport, Florida, take SR 20 west. Turn north on Joe Duggar Road. The road takes a 90-degree turn to the right; continue and head east. Turn north on J W Hollington Road, which runs through the property. The address is 3745 J W Hollington Road.
**Size:** 3,160 acres
**Trail Distance:** 10.1 miles
**Hiking Time:** Full-day hike
**Difficulty:** Easy
**Trail Surface:** Leaf and pine needle litter
**Shade Level:** 0–25%
**Natural Communities:** Sandhill
**Wildlife:** White-tailed deer, wild turkey, raccoon, opossum, gopher tortoise
**Maps:** www.myfwc.com/media/3037812/LAFAYETTE-CREEK-map.pdf
**Admission:** None
**Uses and Restrictions:** Camping, hiking, wildlife viewing, hunting. No ATVs allowed; motorized vehicles allowed on designated roads only. Be sure to check www.myfwc.com for hunting dates before hiking. Family-friendly hiking.
**Trail Highlights:** Hikers will cross Lafayette Creek, Wolf Creek, and Magnolia Creek as they follow the Florida Trail.
**Additional Hiking:** Choctawhatchee River Wildlife Management Area, Pine Log Wildlife Management Area, Apalachicola National Forest, Fitzhugh-Carter Tract Sandhill Lakes Mitigation Bank/Econfina Wildlife Management Area

This property traverses Lafayette Creek, Wolf Creek, and Magnolia Creek. The property was logged right up to the creek boundaries by previous owners; however, today, the Northwest Florida Water Management District has planted longleaf pine and wiregrass, restoring a "sea" of grass blowing in the winds. This trail is hiking only, as part of the Florida Trail, and hikers will ford three creeks as well as pass by a campsite.

## Hike Details

This property has access at the center point from J W Hollington Road. Therefore hikers can hike east, hike west, or enter the property from the Florida Trail, either east or west of the property. Hiking east from J W Hollington Road, take the trail through sandhill that has been logged. Continue hiking east to the tree line and enter a forested area of sandy soil. The trail emerges from the forested area, then enters it again. Cross Wolf Creek to the southeast and then two more creeks. A campsite is sited on an upland strand in the middle of Lafayette Creek. Continue hiking east until leaving the property, continuing on the Florida National Scenic Trail.

Or hike west from J W Hollington Road. You will cross Lafayette Creek and then head south following the west side of the creek boundary. Head due west along the boundary, hiking through floodplain swamp until reaching Magnolia Creek. From that point, hike north along the Magnolia Creek eastern boundary until leaving the property and continuing north on the Florida National Scenic Trail.

## 6. Fitzhugh-Carter Tract, Sandhill Lakes Mitigation Bank within Econfina Wildlife Management Area

**GPS:** Lat 30.497035, Long -85.670657

**Address:** 81 Water Management Drive, Havana, FL 32333

**Trailhead Directions:** From the town of Fountain, Florida, take SR 20 west. Head north on SR 77 and take a left on Chain Lake Road and a right onto Water Management Drive.

**Size:** 2,155 acres

**Hiking Time:** 2 hours to day hike

**Difficulty:** Easy

**Trail Surface:** Leaf litter

**Shade Level:** 0–75%

**Natural Communities:** Cypress bayheads, emergent wetlands, hydric pine wetlands, cypress wetlands, karst ponds, upland sandhill lakes, longleaf pine, wiregrass oak, pine forest communities

**Wildlife:** White-tailed deer, wild turkey, gopher tortoise, wading birds

**Maps:** www.myfwc.com/hunting/wma-brochures/nw/terrestrial

**Uses and Restrictions:** Picnicking, restrooms, handicap accessible, boat ramp, boating, fishing, hunting, canoe launch, canoeing, hiking, bicycling, wildlife viewing. No ATVs allowed; motorized vehicles allowed on designated roads only. Be sure to check www.myfwc.com for hunting dates before hiking. Family-friendly hiking.

**Trail Highlights:** Hikers will enjoy walking through wiregrass and longleaf pine habitats as well as past cypress-ringed wetlands with undisturbed, clear water and upland sandhill lakes.

**Additional Hiking:** Econfina Wildlife Management Area, Pine Log Wildlife Management Area, Choctawhatchee River Wildlife Management Area, Apalachicola National Forest

Sand Lakes Mitigation Bank, also known as the Fitzhugh-Carter Tract, is in the middle of the basin divide between the Choctawhatchee River and St. Andrew Bay watershed. It is named for its large sandy areas hosting sandhill habitat with longleaf pine and wiregrass as well as its cypress lined lakes. This mitigation bank is owned by Northwest Florida Water Management District and offers public hiking, rare for mitigation banks, which are typically privately owned. It was formerly managed as a fish camp until 2002. Isolated wetlands were connected in order to drain them, then upland longleaf pine were clear-cut and fast-growing sandpine were planted, moving water away from the property. Today the district accepts mitigation funding as credits for impacts to wetlands from nearby developments. This funding is utilized to restore wetlands on the property as well as longleaf pine uplands. Hiking will take you through longleaf pine and wiregrass restoration areas as well as cypress-lined aquatic habitats. The Northwest Florida Water Management District is a leader in wiregrass restoration, and hikers will see this in full effect at Sand Lakes Mitigation Bank.

I did a tour with the Northwest Florida Water Management District in 2011 to train on restoring wiregrass to areas where groundcover is degraded. This property's wetlands are stunning, and wiregrass natural communities are growing back through meticulous seed collection and transplanting methods as well as prescribed burn management.

## Hike Details

From Chain Lake Road and Dry Pond/Green Pond Road, hike northwest into the property on Dry Pond Road. Hikers will be traversing sandhill planted in longleaf pine and wiregrass. The property is in the middle of the basin divide between the Choctawhatchee River and St. Andrew Bay watershed. Veer to the left and hike on the south side of Deep Edge Pond through sandhill. Take a right and hike north through sandhill and between a small, perfectly circular sandhill lake on the left and Deep Edge Pond on the right. Hike north a short distance to see Black Pond at the canoe access, hiking through mesic flatwoods and hammock. Then hike northeast between Dykes Mill Pond and Black Pond through the hammock and pine. Hit Garrett Pond and head south on Green Pond Road back to the parking area through mesic flatwoods that are being restored. Cross Greenhead Branch Creek, and then hike southeast through sandhill to the entrance.

## 7. Florida Trail on Econfina Wildlife Management Area

**GPS:** Lat 30.428212, Long -85.609664

**Trailhead Directions:** From the town of Fountain, Florida, take CR 231 south. Head west on SR 20. Pass CC Road on the left and just east of Asphalt Plant Road is the small Florida National Scenic Trail parking area and trailhead.

**Size:** 41,000 acres

**Trail Distance:** 27.5 miles

**Hiking Time:** Half-day to overnight hiking opportunities

**Difficulty:** Medium to strenuous

**Trail Surface:** Leaf and pine needle litter, sandy soil, boardwalk

**Shade Level:** 0–50%

**Natural Communities:** Sandhill, floodplain forest, mesic hammock

Devil's Hole on the Florida Trail in Econfina Wildlife Management Area

**Wildlife:** White-tailed deer, wild turkey, raccoon, opossum, gopher tortoise

**Maps:** www.myfwc.com/hunting/wma-brochures/nw/Econfina-creek

**Uses and Restrictions:** Camping, hiking, biking, wildlife viewing, hunting. No ATVs allowed; motorized vehicles allowed on designated roads only. Be sure to check www.myfwc.com for hunting dates before hiking. Not friendly for family hikes.

**Trail Highlights:** Be sure to view Devil's Hole, a hidden circular spring that has a turquoise tint. It seems to have no bottom, causing visitors to think it flows straight down into the Devil's den.

**Additional Hiking:** Pitt and Sylvan springs, Ochlockonee River Wildlife Management Area, Talquin Wildlife Management Area, Joe Budd Wildlife Management Area, Apalachicola National Forest

Hiking this stretch of the Florida Trail can be hot and difficult because of the soft, sandy soil; however, the views of springs like Devil's Hole and Econfina Creek as well as a visit to Rattlesnake Lake make the hike worthwhile. Hikers I met while on the trail said that from the entrance and northeast to Porter Pond Road is tough; however, east of that road is extremely rewarding as you reach the Econfina Creek floodplain with views of the creek and also some shade. Be sure to bring plenty of water and snacks as this is a long trail with little shade.

## Hike Details

From SR 20, follow the orange rectangular blazes north and enjoy the rare longleaf pine and wiregrass habitat. Veer to the west and then curve around to the northeast through land that was once clear-cut. Heading due northeast, pass Mabel Porter Pond on the left before entering mesic flatwoods forest and then hike east toward Little Porter Lake through densely planted pine. Continue northeast to Swift Creek Swamp. When low, this wetland has a white sandy border. Continue hiking northeast through more dense pine forest until reaching a sandhill that was clear-cut around 2015. Hike northeast through this area, until reaching Porter Pond Road. Cross the road and continue hiking northeast along Econfina Creek in floodplain swamp. Pass through four campsites and stop at the Devil's Hole camp. Enjoy this clear teal spring shaped in a perfect circle. Continue hiking forested habitat until reaching Ten Mile Creek. At this point Econfina Wildlife Management Area boundary ends, but the Florida Trail continues.

## 8. Pitt Spring/Sylvan Spring in Econfina Wildlife Management Area

**GPS:** Lat 30.432718, Long -85.546503

**Trailhead Directions:** From the town of Fountain, just west of Blountstown, take I-75 south and head west on SR 20. The recreation area is just east of Strickland Road on the north side of SR 20.

**Size:** 10 acres

**Trail Distance:** About 1 mile, with opportunity to continue hiking on the Florida National Scenic Trail close by

**Hiking Time:** 2 hours

**Difficulty:** Medium to strenuous

**Trail Surface:** Leaf litter, boardwalk

**Shade Level:** 50–75%

**Natural Communities:** Floodplain swamp, hardwood/mixed forest

**Wildlife:** White-tailed deer, raccoon, birds

**Maps:** www.nwfwmd.com

**Uses and Restrictions:** Picnicking, restroom, handicap accessible, fishing, canoe launch, canoeing, hiking, wildlife viewing. No ATVs allowed; motorized vehicles allowed on designated roads only. Family-friendly hiking.

**Trail Highlights:** Hikers will find elevational changes, limestone outcroppings, views of Econfina Creek, and caves. Start and finish at springs.

**Additional Hiking:** Econfina Wildlife Management Area, Pine Log State Forest, Apalachicola National Forest

Pitt Spring is a 10-acre recreation area with trails and boardwalks. The property hosts an 11-foot-deep spring vent that creates a spring-water pool area before running 50 feet east to the Econfina Creek. Pit Spring trails are connected to Sylvan Spring by a trail and boardwalk. Sylvan Springs is a series of springs on the west side of the Econfina River. Hikers from around the world can partake in a leisurely hike before taking a dip in year-round 74-degree spring water.

While hiking there, our kids loved being in the spring pool. They also loved viewing the natural Florida Econfina River! There were canoes paddling by, fish to see in the clear water, overhanging trees, and white sandy soil. The whole family just stared in awe at the shallow water as we watched canoes mosey on past.

## Hike Details

Start at the Pitt Spring kiosk, which is at the restrooms in the parking area. Be sure to walk east to view Pitt Spring before hiking. Return to the kiosk. Take the boardwalk to the west through forested hardwoods. At the T-intersection, take a right to hike north to view the Econfina River. Hike back south, past the T-intersection, and continue further south toward a forested swamp area. Curve to the west and hike to Sylvan Springs through forested wetlands. The hike continues north, away from district land, through elevations that rise quickly through more strenuous terrain as you reach Williford Spring off the Econfina River.

## Northwest Florida Water Management District Western Region

### 9. Garcon North and Garcon South

**GPS:** Lat 30.459067, Long -87.092433

**Trailhead Directions:** From Pensacola, take I-10 west and turn south on SR 281. Head southwest on CR 191; the conservation area will be on your left.

**Size:** 3,245 acres

**Trail Distance:** Approximately 3 miles

**Hiking Time:** 2 hours

**Difficulty:** Easy

**Trail Surface:** Seasonally flooded trails with wet-prairie mowed plants

**Shade Level:** 0–25%

**Natural Communities:** Wet prairie and wet flatwoods

**Wildlife:** White-tailed deer, turkey, and avian species

**Maps:** www.nwfwater.com/system/assets/696/original/Garcon_Point_WMA_Map.jpg

**Uses and Restrictions:** Hiking, wildlife viewing. No ATVs allowed; motorized vehicles allowed on designated roads only. Family-friendly hiking.

**Trail Highlights:** Garcon Point North and South provide vast views of wet prairie and associated wildflowers and pitcher plants in bloom during season.

**Additional Hiking:** Old River Trail

This property was purchased to protect the wet prairie and salt marsh of the peninsula between Escambia Bay and Blackwater Bay. Because of its unique location between freshwater rivers and saltwater of the Gulf of Mexico, the property offers views of wet prairie freshwater flats, their associated seasonal wildflowers in bloom, spring blooms of the pitcher plant, and blooming plant species of the salt marsh.

## Hike Details

Start east of the intersection of Garcon Point Road and SR 281 at the Garcon Point North trailhead. Hike southeast and then curve to the south. Here the hike has sparse pine trees and views to the north of wet prairie. Be sure to look for pitcher plants along the path. Continue hiking south through pine flatwoods with the edge of the prairie on your east. The trail hits an intersection where you can either head west to the Garcon Point South trailhead or head east along a loop. Head east to continue through wet prairie and to head into wet flatwoods pine forest before curving back to the west. After a series of curves in the trail as it passes through pine flatwoods, conclude the hike at the Garcon Point South Trailhead.

## 10. Old River Trail

**GPS:** Lat 30.633859, Long -87.022426

**Trailhead Directions:** From the town of Milton, take SR 90 east and head north on Johnson Road. Veer north on Old River Road and dead-end in the conservation area.

**Size:** 5,800 acres

**Trail Distance:** 0.5 miles

**Hiking Time:** Day hike

**Difficulty:** Easy

**Trail Surface:** Leaf litter

**Shade Level:** 0–25%

**Natural Communities:** Floodplain swamp

**Wildlife:** White-tailed deer, wild turkey, fish species

**Maps:** www.nwfwater.com/system/assets/695/original/Blackwater_River_WMA_Map.jpg

**Admission:** None

**Hours:** Sunrise to sunset

**Uses and Restrictions:** Fishing, canoe launch, canoeing, hiking, boating, wildlife viewing, hunting. No ATVs allowed; motorized vehicles allowed on designated roads only. Be sure to check www.myfwc.com for hunting dates before hiking. Family-friendly hiking.

**Trail Highlights:** The trail takes hikers along a scenic view of the Blackwater River.

**Additional Hiking:** Whiting Park, Russell Harbor Landing Park, Blackwater Heritage Trail State Park, Blackwater River Water Management Area

Old River Trail property protects the wetlands of the Blackwater River. This river and the Yellow River flow into East Bay, which merges with Escambia Bay and then Pensacola Bay, just east of Pensacola. Pensacola Bay hits the barrier islands of Santa Rosa Sound before emptying into the Gulf of Mexico. This trail is a historical hiking trail that runs partially along the Blackwater River and partially along floodplain swamp. It is a short trail that connects two parks: Whiting Park, managed by the US Navy, and the Russell Harbor Landing Park, managed by the City of Milton. The short trail is utilized as a fitness path, has several benches along the way, and hosts interpretive signage. Hikers will enjoy views of the Blackwater River.

## Hike Details

Start at the end point of Hay Lo Drive and Old River Road. Hike west on the trail along the Blackwater River. Here you will be hiking through floodplain swamp. Turn southwest and hike the edge of a large wetland. Continue hiking until you reach Russell Harbor Landing Park. Continue hiking southwest on the east side of the park. Follow the edge of the park facilities on the boundary of the natural area and continue south until you reach the intersection of SR 90 and Blackwater River.

# 2

## Suwannee River District

Suwannee River Water Management District (SRWMD) is the smallest district of the five. However, what it lacks in size it makes up for in massive rivers, disappearing underground streams, waterfalls, rapids, and springs. In the eastern panhandle, the boundary runs from the Florida/Georgia border south to the Gulf of Mexico in the big bend area of Florida, east to Gainesville, and northeast to Bradford County, and the western border of Baker County almost to Jacksonville.

SRWMD hosts thirteen rivers, the major ones being the Suwannee River, Aucilla River, Santa Fe River, and Econfina River. It is home to many quaint small towns, including White Springs, Live Oak, Perry, and Lake City. Major issues in this district are water supply, sinkholes, flood control, and water quality. In fact, east Florida is quarreling with this district, which claims that pulling hundreds of thousands of gallons of water from the Floridan Aquifer in bustling Jacksonville is lowering the levels of water in north-central Florida springs, rivers, and lakes.

This area of the state has 300 documented springs. The high number of springs is related to the Cody Escarpment, an ancient shoreline that existed during a period of time when the sea level was much higher. East of the Cody Escarpment, a thick clay layer covers the limestone above the Floridan Aquifer. This clay slows down the flow of water through the ground and into the aquifer; however, west of the escarpment, in SRWMD, the clay layer has been eroded by ocean currents and wave action. Here the limestone is subject to dissolution, the process in which limestone is dissolved by water and chemicals, creating brittle holes in the limestone where water can easily flow through. The result is sinkholes, springs allowing water to flow up from the Floridan Aquifer, and rivers that disappear underground . . . and rise again further downstream.

Hikers will traverse miles of trails along rivers via the Florida National Scenic Trail. They will enjoy views of springs and waterfalls, and enjoy natural habitats that include floodplain forest and xeric hammock. There is plenty of elevational relief in this district boasting "high" bluffs (for Florida) overlooking rivers and whitewater rapids. This backcountry district and its springs and falls are visited by people from all over the world who want to dive in the clear, cool waters of the springs and view a more natural Florida of yesteryear.

## Basics for the Suwannee River District

Be sure to note whether trails are seasonally flooded (typically in the summer rainy season) and whether there is hunting. Check www.myfwc .com for hunting dates prior to hiking.

Unless otherwise noted, all properties in this region are open from sunrise to sunset, free of charge. For any additional questions, contact the Suwannee River Water Management District office at (904) 362-1001.

## Suwannee River Water Management District Northwest Region

---

## 11. Florida National Scenic Trail: Natural Well Branch along the Econfina River

**GPS:** Lat 30.241356, Long -83.692158

**Directions:** From Perry, travel north on US 19 to Tower Road and turn
left. Travel west a quarter of a mile and turn left on the first graded
road (Meatball Express Road). Travel south 2 miles; the tract entrance
is on the left. The hike begins at the lat/long above, off US Highway
19. Other options are to hike west on Meatball Express Road and then
travel south to cross the Econfina River or north at the Econfina to hike
west on the Florida Trail.

**Size:** 3,713 acres

**Trail Distance:** 4 miles
**Hiking Time:** Day hike
**Difficulty:** Easy
**Trail Surface:** Graded dirt road
**Shade Level:** 25–50%
**Natural Communities:** Mesic flatwoods, floodplain swamp
**Wildlife:** White-tailed deer, wild turkey, raccoon, avian species
**Maps:** www.srwmd.state.fl.us/DocumentCenter/View/10773
**Uses and Restrictions:** Hiking. No ATVs allowed; motorized vehicles allowed on designated roads only. Not friendly for family hiking.
**Trail Highlights:** Hikers will enjoy views of the Econfina River at the intersection of the river crossing.
**Additional Hiking:** Econfina River State Park, Middle Aucilla Conservation Area, Aucilla Wildlife Management Area, Flint Rock Wildlife Management Area, St. Marks National Wildlife Refuge, Big Bend Wildlife Management Area

This thin stretch of conservation land borders the Econfina River on both sides of the river. The river flows south through Econfina State Park and into the Apalachee Bay of the Gulf of Mexico. These lands are a mosaic of mesic flatwoods and strands of forested wetland swamp, protecting the waters of the Econfina River.

## Hike Details

The Florida Trail traverses this property at the southeastern border. From US Highway 19 at Mutt Road intersection, travel south on the western border of the highway. Then leave the highway and hike west on the southern boundary of the property, which is River Road. Here you will see mesic flatwoods of pine, cross strands of wetland swamps, and possibly encounter wildlife on the meandering 4-mile trek on dirt road. At just under the 4-mile point, head north to cross the Econfina River. Just past the river, the Florida Trail leaves the boundary and continues on a 12-mile stretch on the Foley Trail section of the Florida National Scenic Trail.

## 12. Florida National Scenic Trail: Cabbage Grove/ Jones Mill Creek: Aucilla Wildlife Management Area

**GPS:** Lat 30.200787, Long -83.922120

**Directions:** From Perry, travel west on US 98 to Highway 680. Travel north on Highway 680. Take a left on Highway 681. The entrance is on your right before reaching the Aucilla River.

**Size:** CABBAGE GROVE—2,047 acres

      JONES MILL CREEK—2,884 acres

**Trail Distance:** 7.9 miles

**Hiking Time:** Day hike

**Difficulty:** Easy

**Trail Surface:** Dirt trail

**Shade Level:** 25–50%

**Natural Communities:** Mesic flatwoods, floodplain swamp, wet hardwood hammock, cypress dome, freshwater marsh

**Wildlife:** White-tailed deer, wild turkey, raccoon, large list of avian species found on the SRWMD website, alligator, turtle, water snakes, river otter

**Maps:** www.srwmd.state.fl.us/DocumentCenter/View/10780

**Uses and Restrictions:** Hiking, biking, horseback riding, canoe and small boat access, fishing. Part of Aucilla Wildlife Management Area. Check www.myfwc.com before you hike for hunting dates. Not friendly for family hiking.

**Trail Highlights:** Enjoy views of limestone outcroppings, springs, and the Aucilla River on this stunning segment of the Florida National Scenic Trail.

**Additional Hiking:** Econfina River State Park, Econfina River Conservation Area, Aucilla Wildlife Management Area, Flint Rock Wildlife Management Area, St. Marks National Wildlife Refuge, Big Bend Wildlife Management Area

This property is the Middle Aucilla Conservation Area and protects land on both sides of the Aucilla River. The Aucilla River originates from springs in Georgia, flows underground and rises again in spots, and flows south into the Gulf of Mexico. The Aucilla River is a blackwater river, with tannins from decaying leaves leaching into the water and staining it a dark rust color. This property protects water quality in an area of extreme karst topography, where surface water can flow directly to the Floridan Aquifer. Hikers will experience the treasures of that topography: springs, sinkholes, and limestone outcrops on this Aucilla River Segment of the Florida Trail.

## Hike Details

From the entrance point, head west on Highway 681 and enter the Florida Trail heading northwest. Curve to the east and then cross the Aucilla River. The entire hike will follow the east side of the slowly meandering Aucilla River through floodplain forest. Hikers will pass O'Neal Grade Road and then a second road before heading west along the river edge. At the point of heading west, hikers will see the Aucilla Rapids. Be sure to stop and enjoy the view. There is a campsite just before reaching the northeast boundary of the property. Just past that point, at Ja Davis Road/Phelps Road, the Florida Trail leaves the property and continues west.

## Suwannee River Water Management District
## Northeast Region

---

## 13. Falling Creek Falls

**GPS:** Lat 30.258015, Long -82.668917
**Address:** 953 NW Falling Creek Road, Lake City, FL 32055
**Trailhead Directions:** From Lake City, travel north on SR 41. Pass under I-10 and turn right on NW Falling Creek Road. Travel one mile and the parking area is on the right before you cross the creek.
**Size:** 204
**Trail Distance:** 1 mile
**Hiking Time:** 1 hour
**Difficulty:** Easy
**Trail Surface:** Boardwalk
**Shade Level:** 50–75%

**Natural Communities:** Hardwood swamp

**Wildlife:** White-tailed deer, wild turkey, raccoon, avian species

**Maps:** www.srwmd.state.fl.us/index.aspx?nid=160

**Uses and Restrictions:** Picnic tables, historic building, boardwalk to falls, hiking, wildlife viewing. No motorized vehicles. Family-friendly hiking.

**Contact:** Columbia County, (386) 758-2123

**Trail Highlights:** Don't miss the view of a rare 10-foot waterfall in Florida!

**Additional Hiking:** Osceola National Forest, Big Shoals State Lands, Stephen Foster Folk Cultural Center State Park

A small property and a short hike, this property is worth the visit to see the big 10-foot-drop waterfall atypical for Florida. Northwest of Lake City, the property protects Falling Creek, which flows north and west to the Suwannee River. When water levels are at normal, drought-free conditions, water rages over the waterfall before going under Falling Creek Road through a deep ravine and then underground.

## Hike Details

From the parking area, head east for a loop trail hike through hydric hammock and floodplain swamp. At the northern end of the loop, take the boardwalk spur trail to Falling Creek Falls. Take a moment to enjoy the sound of the raging creek and the rare sight of a waterfall in Florida!

## 14. Big Shoals State Lands: Big Shoals, Falling Creek, Bell Springs, White Springs, Little Shoals, Gar Pond

**GPS:** Lat 30.352469, Long -82.688053

**Trailhead Directions:** Travel north on CR 135 from White Springs. Look for the Little Shoals entrance on the right. Or travel 2 more miles north of the Little Shoals entrance and take a right on SE 94th St., which ends at the entrance to Big Shoals.

**Size:** 5,884

**Trail Distance:** 28 miles of trails

**Hiking Time:** Day hike, or 1-hour hike to see Big Shoals

The rapids at Big Shoals State Lands

**Difficulty:** Medium. Big Shoals trail has roots and knobs along trail.

**Trail Surface:** Woodpecker Trail is paved, other trails are dirt paths.

**Shade Level:** 25–50%

**Natural Communities:** Hardwood hammock

**Wildlife:** White-tailed deer, raccoon, wild turkey

**Maps:** www.srwmd.state.fl.us/index.aspx?nid=161

**Admission:** $4.00/vehicle up to 5 passengers

**Hours:** Sunrise to sunset

**Uses and Restrictions:** Picnic tables, restrooms, canoe launch, hunting, hunt check station. Big Shoals Tract is part of the Big Shoals Wildlife Management Area. Be sure to check www.myfwc.com for hunting dates prior to hiking. Family-friendly hiking.

**Trail Highlights:** Hike on the border of the quiet but mighty Suwannee River on the way to roaring and raging Florida whitewater rapids!

**Additional Hiking:** Osceola National Forest, Falling Creek, Stephen Foster Folk Cultural Center State Park

This area is a conglomerate of properties owned by various state agencies and bound together in management to protect the Suwannee River. Hikers will follow a narrow footpath to Big Shoals along hammock bordering the Suwannee River. Forest clearings reveal views of the wide and mighty river, and excitement builds as you get closer to the falls. Finally hikers can hear the rushing river before reaching the overlook—you think you might be at Niagara Falls because of the loud nature of the water hitting the rocks. Savor the view as it is a rare one, and one that many native Floridians cannot say they have seen. Hikers can take in 28 miles of trails, including the paved Woodpecker Trail, as well as hiking on the Florida Trail. This area will take you back in time to the steamboat era, when visitors from up north vacationed in this backcountry area of "Old Florida."

## Hike Details

From the Big Shoals parking area due east of the entrance and next to the restrooms, hike due south. You will hike parallel to the Suwannee River through hammock and then on the edge of the river, with high bluffs creating scenic views. You will hear the whitewater before reaching the observation platform. Stop and enjoy this wide expanse of Florida whitewater! Continue hiking on the blue bike trails for additional adventure or return to the parking area.

From the Little Shoals entrance, follow the map and drive or hike to the interior restroom area. You can then hike the bottomlands toward the Little Shoals, hike up and over a bluff, and then down to the white sandy shores of the Suwannee River and the lesser, but no less amazing, Little Shoals Florida whitewater. No one is here; few have seen this. You are in a spot known only to avid hunters, adventuresome canoers, hardcore hikers, and those lucky enough to care for these lands. Hold it for yourself for a moment.

To pick up the Florida Trail, head east on CR 246 south of the property and head north on Morrell Road. There is a parking area where the road dead-ends into NW Hidden Drive. Hike north and then west where you pick up the southern border of the Suwannee River and then follow on the south side until you cross the river at CR 41. Follow the trail until it leaves the property and heads into the City of White Springs.

## 15. Florida National Scenic Trail: Swift Creek Conservation Area with Blue Sink, Rocky Sink, Swift Creek

**GPS:** Lat 30.342840, Long -82.822148

**Trailhead Directions:** From White Springs take CR 25A west. Pass SE 99th Way and then take a left just west of SE 100th Way. Travel south on this road to the parking area.

BLUE SINK TRACT—From White Springs travel southwest on SR 136. Turn right on 27th Road/McClurgh Lane. Drive through the entrance, veer to the left, and park at the parking area to see the sink.

**Size:** BLUE SINK—637 acres
ROCKY CREEK—251 acres
SWIFT CREEK—328 acres

**Trail Distance:** 2.5 miles

**Hiking Time:** Half-day hike

**Difficulty:** Medium

**Trail Surface:** Leaf litter

**Shade Level:** 50–75%

**Natural Communities:** Hammock

**Wildlife:** White-tailed deer, avian species, raccoon

**Maps:** www.srwmd.state.fl.us/DocumentCenter/View/10756

**Uses and Restrictions:** Hiking. No facilities. No motorized vehicles. Family-friendly hiking.

**Trail Highlights:** Scenic views of the Suwannee River while hiking on the Florida Trail.

**Additional Hiking:** Florida Trail, Big Shoals State Lands, Little Shoals, Stephen Foster Folk Cultural Center State Park, Osceola National Forest

This conservation area protects both sides, north and south, of the Suwannee River on its journey west and south to the Gulf of Mexico.

North of the Suwannee River is the Swift Creek Tract, which provides hiking through hammock along the river on the Florida Trail. The Blue Sink Tract is south of the river where a boardwalk path is provided for gazing at the waters. Hikers will find wonderful views of the river.

## Hike Details

From the entrance off CR 25A, drive to the parking area. From here you can join the Florida Trail and hike east or west along the beautiful waters of the Suwannee River. Hikers will traverse hammock overlooking the river, with a view of white sandy beaches during times of low water. Try the SR 136 entrance, which provides access to a parking area directly adjacent to the spring at Blue Sink.

## 16. Woods Ferry Conservation Area: Woods Ferry and Jerry Branch Tracts

**GPS:**
> JERRY BRANCH TRACT—Lat 30.364226, Long -82.855965
> WOODS FERRY TRACT—Lat 30.3433, Long -82.8550

**Address:** White Springs, FL 32096

**Trailhead Directions:**
> JERRY BRANCH TRACT TO THE FLORIDA TRAIL—From White Springs take US 41 north, take a left on CR 25A and travel all the way to I-75. Pass under I-75 and take an immediate left onto Southeast 134th Ave. Take a right at the second entrance for the closest trail to the Florida Trail.
>
> WOODS FERRY TRACT SOUTH OF THE RIVER TO ACCESS WOODS FERRY PATH—From White Springs, take CR 136 southwest, veer northwest onto CR 136A, take a right on 57th Drive and dead-end into the property. Drive back through Woods Ferry Path to the canoe launch.

**Size:** 1,578 acres

**Trail Distance:**
> FLORIDA TRAIL—2.7 miles
> WOODS FERRY PATH—~2 miles

**Hiking Time:** 2 hours
**Difficulty:** Easy
**Trail Surface:** Boardwalk
**Shade Level:** 25–50%
**Natural Communities:** Floodplain Swamp, mesic flatwoods, pasture
**Wildlife:** White-tailed deer, wild turkey, raccoon, avian species
**Maps:** www.mysuwanneeriver.com/DocumentCenter/View/10757
**Uses and Restrictions:** Hiking, biking, fishing, horseback riding, river
   camping, tent camping. No motorized vehicles. Family-friendly hiking.
**Trail Highlights:** Take in views of the Suwannee River on the Florida Trail.
**Additional Hiking:** Swift Creek Conservation Area, Big Shoals State
   Lands, Stephen Foster Folk Cultural Center State Park

These properties protect more of the weaving and winding Suwannee
River near White Springs. They host a 2.7-mile segment of the Florida
Trail that borders the Suwannee River on the north side. On the south
side of the river on the Woods Ferry Tract, the Woods Ferry Path offers
a canoe launch and more hiking. Access to the trail is either by crossing
under I-75 at the eastern end and hiking into the property or by entering from SRWMD land and making your way to the designated trail.
The Woods Ferry Tract is the first river camp on the Suwannee River
Wilderness Trail, with a canoe launch and 5 camping platforms. This
tract can be accessed off 57th Drive south of the river. The Suwannee
River is wide here and hikers can take in the scenic vistas provided by
the river.

## Hike Details

From the middle entrance off SE 134th Avenue, hike to the end of the
road and take an administrative road to reach the Florida Trail to the
southeast. Hike east through mesic flatwoods in planted pine, veer
south to hike on the edge of pasture and floodplain swamp, and continue southeast through planted pine and floodplain swamp. When
you reach the point where 62nd Street is opposite the trail on the
south side of the river, you are leaving public land and hiking private
land through floodplain swamp and under I-75 to continue hiking east.
From the parking area off 57th Drive and Woods Ferry Path, hike back

south toward 57th Drive. Head west and then south, following the trail through mesic flatwoods and floodplain swamp, across a creek, and through areas where frequent prescribed burns are conducted.

## 17. Florida National Scenic Trail: Camp Branch Conservation Area—Mattair Springs and Camp Branch

**GPS:**

CAMP BRANCH—Lat 30.378103, Long -82.879081

MATTAIR SPRINGS—Lat 30.369203, Long -82.908006

**Trailhead Directions:**

CAMP BRANCH ENTRANCE—From White Springs, travel west on CR 25A and cross under I-75. After the large curve to the north on 25A, look for the Camp Branch road sign. Turn left after the sign onto an unnamed road. Follow the road west approximately 1 mile to the parking area after taking one last left on the unnamed road.

MATTAIR SPRINGS ENTRANCE—From White Springs take CR 136 west. Veer north on CR 136A. Take a right on 71st Road and a left on Howell Road. Veer right onto 75th Drive and veer right into the entrance area. The parking area is in the property just off 75th Drive.

**Size:**

CAMP BRANCH—200 acres

MATTAIR SPRINGS—1,188 acres

**Trail Distance:**

MATTAIR SPRINGS—More than 10 miles

CAMP BRANCH—1 mile multiuse trail, approximately 2 miles of the Florida Trail on north side of the Suwannee River

**Hiking Time:** Half-day hike

**Difficulty:** Medium

**Trail Surface:** Dirt path

**Shade Level:** 25–50%

**Natural Communities:** Mesic flatwoods, floodplain swamp

**Wildlife:** White-tailed deer, wild turkey, gopher tortoise, snake species, avian species

**Maps:** www.srwmd.state.fl.us/DocumentCenter/View/10758

**Uses and Restrictions:** Hiking. No facilities. No motorized vehicles. Family-friendly hiking.

**Trail Highlights:** Enjoy hiking close to Camp Branch Creek and watching the waters fall into a Florida sinkhole.

**Additional Hiking:** Swift Creek Tracts, Jerry Branch Tracts, Big Shoals State Lands, Little Shoals, Stephen Foster Folk Cultural Center State Park

These properties protect the Suwannee River and Camp Branch, a creek north of the Suwannee River. The Camp Branch hike offers an exciting path along Camp Branch creek, where you can witness the creek entering a sinkhole and traveling underground. The trail joins the Florida Trail in two spots on this property where you can hike along the Suwannee River. The Mattair Springs property offers hiking and biking on marked equestrian trails and administrative roads. Hike through mesic flatwoods and wetland strands and bike along the edge of the Suwannee River.

## Hike Details

Camp Branch: From the parking area, head south along the hiking trail, on the eastern border of the property. You'll be hiking through mesic flatwoods that turn into floodplain swamp. Nearing the Suwannee River, there is a three-way intersection. Head south to join the Florida Trail or head due west to continue on the Camp Branch hiking trail. After a couple of jogs in the trail, you will reach a loop and turn northeast. Here the hiking is on the edge of the creek with cypress trees, leaf litter, and a slanted edge along the creek. Watch your step here and hike to the end of the creek where it flows down into a sinkhole. Take the loop back and at the Florida Trail, head east along the Suwannee River and back north to the parking area or head west on the Florida Trail and keep hiking on the north side of the Suwannee River.

Woods Ferry: Drive in through 75th Drive and park at the four-way intersection in the equestrian parking area, or take a right at the four-way intersection and then a left and drive straight to the Suwannee River and park there. From the Suwannee River parking area, head east along the fringe of the Suwannee River and mesic flatwoods and follow the edge of the river. At the first intersection you can veer right to follow the mesic flatwoods and do a shorter loop back to the parking area. Or you can hike a very long loop on the edge of the Suwannee River on the hammock bluffs along the south side of the river, then turn south and hike along the west side of the river, then east along the boundary of the property, leaving the river. It will take you through mixed upland forests and mesic flatwoods on the way back to the entrance of the property. Here you can take a second car and drive or hike on the road back north to the Suwannee River parking area, or continue hiking past the entrance, take a northwest turn to the right, and then turn right and hike north to hike the western boundary back to the Suwannee River. At the river, hike east to follow the river back to the parking area.

## 18. Florida National Scenic Trail: Linville, Sugar Creek, and Suwannee Springs

### GPS:
SUGAR CREEK TRACT FLORIDA TRAIL—Lat 30.400666, Long -82.941153
SUWANNEE SPRINGS/LINVILLE TRACT TRAILS—Lat 30.393374, Long -82.933986

### Trailhead Directions:
SUGAR CREEK TRACT FLORIDA TRAIL—From Live Oak take CR 129 north and cross the Suwannee River. Take the first left after the river onto SW 79th Terrace. The access is on the left under the power lines.
SUWANNEE SPRINGS/LINVILLE TRACT TRAILS—From Live Oak take CR 129 north, veer right onto 93rd Drive, and take a right onto 32nd Street. The parking area is at the end of 32nd Street.

### Size:
SUGAR CREEK—670 acres
SUWANNEE SPRINGS—135 acres
LINVILLE—173 acres

### Trail Distance:
FLORIDA TRAIL ON THE SUGAR CREEK PROPERTY—3.3 miles
SUWANNEE SPRINGS/LINVILLE CREEK—about 3 miles

**Hiking Time:** Half-day hike
**Difficulty:** Easy
**Trail Surface:** Dirt path
**Shade Level:** 25–50%
**Natural Communities:** Mesic flatwoods, floodplain swamp
**Wildlife:** White-tailed deer, wild turkey, gopher tortoise, snake species, avian species
**Maps:** www.mysuwanneeriver.com/DocumentCenter/View/10759
**Uses and Restrictions:** Hiking. Suwannee Springs Tract: restrooms, swimming, picnic tables, canoe launch. No motorized vehicles. Family-friendly hiking.
**Trail Highlights:** Hiking the Florida Trail along the Suwannee River and swimming in the river near the old Suwannee Springs house.
**Additional Hiking:** Camp Branch/Woods Ferry, Spirit of the Suwannee Music Park, Swift Creek properties

These properties protect both sides of the Suwannee River just north of Live Oak and east of privately owned Spirit of the Suwannee Music Park. A relatively untouched property, it boasts views of the Suwannee River as hikers traverse mesic flatwoods, hammock, and floodplains. The property hosts the Florida National Scenic Trail north of the river on the Sugar Creek property. South of the river, hikers can find a boundary trail and more hiking on the Linville and Suwannee Springs tracts. Be sure to stop at the old Suwannee Springs house. It was built in the 1800s around the sulphur springs. When the water is low there are white sandy beaches and you can picnic and swim in the water!

## Hike Details

Sugar Creek: From the access area under the power lines, hike east along the river into the property. Hikers will traverse hammock and mesic flatwoods past CR 129. The trail leaves the river, still moving in the southeast direction, before joining again at an oxbow in the river. Continue east on the river and hike through white sandy soil of scrubby flatwoods habitat before leaving the property, continuing on the Florida Trail.

Suwannee Springs/Linville Tract: From the parking area off 32nd St. at the river, explore the springs house and the river. Then hike west on the road, taking a left on the trail, to submerge yourself in the mesic flatwoods. When you reach the intersection of 91st Lane and the property boundary, take a left and hike east on the trail toward the Suwannee River. Follow the boundary of the river along hammock overlooking the water until you reach the eastern boundary of the property. At that point hike due west, following the property boundary through mesic flatwoods until leaving the boundary to hike northwest towards 91st Lane and returning to the parking area.

## 19. Florida National Scenic Trail: Fox Tail, Allardt

**GPS:**

ALLARDT TRACT—Lat 30.411157, Long -82.996664

FOX TRAIL—Lat 30.411369, Long -82.963168

**Trailhead Directions:**

ALLARDT TRACT—From Live Oak, take CR 129 north. Turn left and head west on CR 132/Stagecoach Road. Turn right on CR 795 and then take a right on Foxtail Road/24th St. The entrance road is on your left. Travel north on that road until reaching the parking area.

FOX TRAIL—From Live Oak, take CR 129 north. Turn left and head west on CR 132/Stagecoach Road. Turn right on CR 795 and then take a right on Foxtail Road/24th St. Take a left on 107th Road, then a right, and then a left into the property.

**Size:**

ALLARDT TRACT—443 acres

FOX TRAIL TRACT—199 acres

**Trail Distance:**

ALLARDT TRACT—~3 miles

FOX TRAIL TRACT—~2.5 miles

**Hiking Time:** Half-day hike

**Difficulty:** Easy

**Trail Surface:** Dirt path

**Shade Level:** 25–50%

**Natural Communities:** Mesic flatwoods, mixed upland forest, hammock

**Wildlife:** White-tailed deer, wild turkey, gopher tortoise, snake species, avian species

**Maps:** www.mysuwanneeriver.com/DocumentCenter/View/10760

**Uses and Restrictions:** Hiking, biking, equestrian trails, parking. No motorized vehicles. Family-friendly hiking.

**Trail Highlights:** Take in scenic views along the Suwannee River and "Old Florida" mesic flatwoods.

**Additional Hiking:** Camp Branch/Woods Ferry, Spirit of the Suwannee Music Park, Swift Creek properties, Holton Creek Wildlife Management Area

Northwest of White Springs and north of Live Oak, the Fox Trail and Allardt properties protect the Suwannee River on the south side of the river. Tiny tracts in comparison to traditional water management district properties, these are parts of a whole in the effort to protect the Suwannee River in a string of parcels along the river. Offering hiking and horseback riding, trails pass through mesic flatwoods and hammock on both tracts. The Florida Trail parallels the river on the north side with access to the trail east or west of these tracts.

## Hike Details

Allardt: From the parking area, hike north along the boundary through mesic flatwoods. Hike right (east) at the first intersection. Take the first right through the flatwoods for a shorter loop. Or continue east until reaching the southern boundary. At that point turn west and hike to the parking area.

Fox Trail: From the parking area, hike east along the hammock fringe, through mixed upland forest. Once nearing the river, veer southeast and enjoy views of the Suwannee. Follow the river's oxbow around and east to the eastern property boundary. Hike south until reaching the intersection. Hiking east will take you across the boundary and into Spirit of the Suwannee Music Park. Hiking west will take you along the property boundary, through a jog in the boundary, and back along the boundary. A hike west, north, west, and north will return hikers to the Suwannee River and the parking area/boat ramp.

## 20. Florida National Scenic Trail: Holton Creek Wildlife Management Area—Trillium Slopes, Holton Creek

**GPS:** Lat 30.438698, Long -83.058269

**Trailhead Directions:** From Live Oak, travel north on CR 249 and cross the Suwannee River. Turn right on CR 249; travel one mile, turn right on SW 64th Terrace into Holton Creek. Once on the property, drive past three parking areas to the end of the road for the closest parking area to the Suwannee River and the Florida Trail.

**Size:**

HOLTON CREEK—2,536 acres

**Trail Distance:** 8.1 miles

**Hiking Time:** Day hike

**Difficulty:** Easy

**Trail Surface:** Leaf litter

**Shade Level:** 50–75%

**Natural Communities:** Mesic flatwoods, mixed upland forest

**Wildlife:** Wild turkey, white-tailed deer, gray squirrel, rabbit, gopher tortoise, raccoon, American alligator, red-tailed hawk

**Maps:** www.srwmd.state.fl.us/DocumentCenter/View/10761

**Uses and Restrictions:** Hiking, equestrian trails, bicycling, fishing, camping, hunting, hunting for mobility impaired. The Holton Creek River Camp is on the Suwannee River Wilderness Trail and provides 5 screened shelters, a picnic pavilion, restrooms with hot showers, and a tent-camping area. For more information on the Suwannee River Wilderness Trail, call (800) 868-9914 or visit www.suwanneeriver.com. No motorized vehicles. Be sure to visit www.myfwc.com for hunting dates prior to hiking.

**Trail Highlights:** Experience scenic vistas that include cypress-lined bluffs overlooking the tannin waters of the Suwannee River, lined by white sand beach during times of low water.

**Additional Hiking:** Suwannee Ridge Wildlife and Environmental Area, Camp Branch/Woods Ferry, Spirit of the Suwannee Music Park, Swift Creek properties, Ellaville/Black/Anderson Springs/Mill Creek properties

The Holton Creek property protects the Suwannee River, limestone outcroppings, seepage slopes, and two first-magnitude springs of the total four springs that flow into the river. North of Live Oak, it is north-central Florida at its backcountry finest. When the river is low, it is framed with white sandy beaches. It meanders through multiple oxbows, helping in flood control by slowing the speed of water flow.

## Hike Details

From the Holton River Camp parking area, hike east or west on the Florida Trail. The hike will pass through mixed upland forest and hardwood-lined river bluffs overlooking the Suwannee River.

## 21. Florida National Scenic Trail: Twin Rivers State Forest—Ellaville, Black, Anderson Springs, Mill Creek North/South

**GPS:**

ELLAVILLE TRACT TRAIL/FLORIDA TRAIL—Lat 30.386931, Long 83.180682

ANDERSON SPRINGS—Lat 30.353255, Long -83.188643

SUWANNEE SPRINGS/LINVILLE TRACT TRAILS—Lat 30.393374, Long -82.933986

**Trailhead Directions:**

ELLAVILLE TRACT TRAIL/FLORIDA TRAIL—From Live Oak, travel west on US 90. Cross the Suwannee River. Just past Drew Way on your right, take a left into the entrance. Take an immediate left and drive to the parking area.

ANDERSON SPRINGS—From Live Oak, travel west on US 90. Turn left on River Road and travel south. Immediately after crossing over I-10, turn right into the entrance.

SUWANNEE SPRINGS/LINVILLE TRACT TRAILS—From Live Oak, take CR 129 north, veer right onto 93rd Drive and take a right onto 32nd Street. The parking area is at the end of 32nd Street.

**Size:**

TWIN RIVERS STATE FOREST—15,481 total acres

LINVILLE—173 acres

**Trail Distance:**
  ANDERSON ROAD—5.25 miles
**Hiking Time:** Half-day hike
**Difficulty:** Easy
**Trail Surface:** Dirt path or white sandy soil
**Shade Level:** 25–50%
**Natural Communities:** Floodplain swamp, sandhill
**Wildlife:** White-tailed deer, bobwhite quail, bobcat, river otter, beaver, American alligator, and wild turkey
**Maps:** www.freshfromflorida.com/Divisions-Offices/ Florida-Forest-Service/Our-Forests/State-Forests/ Twin-Rivers-State-Forest#features
**Uses and Restrictions:** Picnicking, hiking, bicycling, equestrian trails, canoeing, fishing, hunting. No motorized vehicles. Wildlife management area. Visit www.myfwc.com for hunting dates prior to hiking.
**Contact:** Florida Forest Service, Twin Rivers State Forest, (386) 208-1460
**Trail Highlights:** There is a sinkhole on the property, and hikers will gain views of Anderson Spring as it runs into the Suwannee River.
**Additional Hiking:** Suwannee River State Park, Camp Branch/Woods Ferry, Spirit of the Suwannee Music Park, Swift Creek properties

These parcels are owned by the Suwannee River Water Management District and managed by the Florida Forest Service as part of Twin Rivers State Forest. They were purchased to protect land at the confluence of the Withlacoochee River and the Suwannee River. It is at this point where the mighty Suwannee River takes a turn to the southwest on its journey toward the Gulf of Mexico on Florida's west coast. This area was once an important point of commerce where steamboats could be seen carrying goods along the rivers in the early 1800s. Today, hikers can visit Anderson Spring and hike through floodplain swamp and mesic flatwoods paralleling the Suwannee River or set out on this segment of the Florida Trail.

## Hike Details

Anderson Spring: From the trailhead take in the views of Anderson Spring. The clear waters hit the rust-colored Suwannee River as it flows past, but they don't mix with it at first, like oil not mixing with water. After enjoying the spring, hike south through the Suwannee River floodplain. At the first intersection, veer to the right, heading southwest along the Suwannee River. Follow the river along the fringe of the floodplain-sandhill ecotone. The hike is along the open sandhill with views of wiregrass and pine. Once hikers reach the bottom edge of the sandhill, the trail makes a 60-degree turn back north and then northeast to the parking area through various sections of sandhill, mesic flatwoods, and floodplain swamp.

Ellaville Tract/Florida Trail: From the parking area, hike southeast to join the Florida Trail. Hike south along the Suwannee River along the floodplain swamp. Past the power lines there is a bend in the river. It is here that you can take a right and hike west and then take a right and hike north for a shortcut between sandhill and floodplain and then between pine flatwoods and floodplain back to the parking area. Or continue hiking south until almost reaching I-10 before taking a right and hiking a loop back to the parking area.

## Suwannee River Water Management District Southeast Region

## 22. Poe Springs

**GPS:** Lat 29.821982, Long -82.652170
**Address:** 28800 NW 182nd Avenue, High Springs, FL 32643
**Trailhead Directions:** From High Springs, take SW 1st Avenue to the southwest and head west on SR 236/NW 182nd Avenue/CR 340. Turn right into Poe Springs Park.
**Size:** 100 acres
**Trail Distance:** 1.5 miles
**Hiking Time:** 1 hour
**Difficulty:** Easy
**Trail Surface:** Leaf litter
**Shade Level:** 50–75%
**Natural Communities:** Hydric hammock, floodplain swamp

Wading in the Santa Fe River next to Poe Springs

**Wildlife:** River otter, turtle, fish, white-tailed deer, raccoon, squirrel, avian species

**Maps:** www.srwmd.state.fl.us/DocumentCenter/View/10756

**Hours:** 9:00 am–6:00 pm, Thursday–Sunday

**Uses and Restrictions:** Boat ramp, spring access, swimming, lodge rental for parties/meetings, playground, park, picnic pavilions, ball fields, Santa Fe River access. Family-friendly hiking.

**Contact:** Alachua County, (352) 548-1210

**Trail Highlights:** Visit the clear waters of Poe Springs and see breathtaking "Old Florida" views of the Santa Fe River.

**Additional Hiking:** Ichetucknee State Park, River Rise Preserve State Park, San Felasco Hammock Preserve State Park, Paynes Prairie Preserve State Park

The Poe Springs Tract is owned by the Suwannee River Water Management District but managed as part of Alachua County's Poe Springs Park. The spring is a clear expanse with views of a limestone cave that leads down into the depths of the Floridan Aquifer. It has been modified to incorporate steps that allow the public to safely access the spring, with cypress trees and wetlands still present on one border. The short spring run is a peaceful wonder in north-central Florida. Hikers can walk the border of the spring run and watch the clear water hit the rust-colored tannin water of the Santa Fe River as it bullies past. Watch the kayaks float on by, stare as the waters seem to not mix. Return to the restroom area and note a floating dock you can climb down onto to watch the Santa Fe River and the Florida forest and wildlife while your feet hang in the water.

My family has been to Poe Springs several times. We love hopping in the spring and then walking in the spring run out to the Santa Fe River, looking for fish and turtles in the clear water. At the lodge on the river, our one-year-old daughter once walked up and down the edge, holding her dad's hands, unfearful of the dark water, the heavy current, the slippery rocks, or the large birds flying by. It was her river. It was as though she was a miniature Huckleberry Finn, ready to head out on adventure if we weren't holding her back. We will always appreciate the memories of taking our daughter to the springs at such an early age; with proper precautions and watchful adult attention, children can begin to forge their own appreciations of nature.

## Hike Details

When you drive in from the main road, travel to the right to park. Walk past the playground on your right and find the sign for the trailhead to the springs. The paved path takes you to a boardwalk that leads all the way to the spring swimming hole. Be sure to look for wildflowers on the left of the path on the way to the spring. Also beware of old hardwood trees falling over during wet periods. One person was fatally stricken by a falling limb on this boardwalk in 2015. At the spring, as you hike through ancient hardwoods of the Santa Fe floodplain, walk toward the picnic pavilions to view the Santa Fe River. Head back and walk to the restrooms to find the Hiking Trail sign. Hike east behind the restrooms, following the trail through the floodplain swamp of the Santa

Fe River. Enjoy views of buttressed knees, downed trees, and bits of light shining through the forest canopy on this shaded floodplain hike.

## 23. Santa Fe River Park: 47 Bridge

**GPS:** Lat 29.864331, Long -82.739914
FURTHER SOUTH ON CR 47—Lat 29.855934, Long -82.741824
**Trailhead Directions:** From Fort White, travel south on SR 47 and cross the Santa Fe River. Turn left into Santa Fe River County Park to start the hike, or travel a half mile further south for access to the seasonal road.
**Size:** 392 acres
**Trail Distance:** 1.5 miles
**Hiking Time:** 2 hours
**Difficulty:** Easy
**Trail Surface:** Leaf litter, seasonally flooded
**Shade Level:** 75–100%
**Natural Communities:** Floodplain swamp, sandhill, scrub, mesic flatwoods
**Wildlife:** Avian species, white-tailed deer, gopher tortoise, squirrel, wild turkey
**Maps:** www.mysuwanneeriver.com/DocumentCenter/View/10795
**Uses and Restrictions:** Hiking, biking, horseback riding, fishing, wildlife viewing. No motorized vehicles. Family-friendly hiking.
**Trail Highlights:** Take in views of the Old Florida Santa Fe River as you hike on the floodplain forest banks of the river.
**Additional Hiking:** River Rise Preserve State Park, Ichetucknee Springs State Park, Mallory Swamp Wildlife Management Area

Just south of the backcountry town of Fort White, this hike borders the southern edge of the Santa Fe River. Hiking in floodplain swamp, hikers will experience a path shaded by towering oaks and cypress trees. The view of the Santa Fe River is peaceful and undisturbed, and you can get to the river's edge at the boat ramp within Santa Fe River Park. There is also hiking on an unmarked seasonal road that traverses many upland natural communities throughout its route.

## Hike Details

From Santa Fe River Park, head directly east to the trailhead. Hike east through the floodplain swamp on the southern border of the Santa Fe River. Follow the river's south bank until the trail veers off to the south to follow a small creek channel. Once you reach the end of the trail on the creek channel, double back to the entrance. From the access south of the park on CR 47, hike east into the property. Here you are hiking on the fringe of a sandhill that is being restored on the north side of the trail and a scrub with white sandy soil and oaks on the south side of the trail. At the corner of the boundary, leave the scrub edge and hike southeast into the sandhill/mesic flatwoods fringe. Continue hiking southeast until the trail takes you to the boundary of the property. At that point, hike east until reaching the power lines. Hike north along the lines until leaving the lines to hike east through mesic flatwoods and floodplain swamp, almost reaching the Santa Fe River. This trail is out and back, so retrace your steps to return to the entrance.

## 24. Atsena Otie Key

**GPS:** Lat 29.124926, Long -83.035236
**Trailhead Directions:** Boat access only; from the Cedar Key beachfront park, travel southwest to the western dock and trailhead.
**Size:** 60 acres
**Trail Distance:** 2 miles
**Hiking Time:** 1 hour, not including boating to the island
**Difficulty:** Easy
**Trail Surface:** Leaf and pine needle litter
**Shade Level:** 25–50%
**Natural Communities:** Mesic hammock
**Wildlife:** Hundreds of avian species can be found on the dock leading to the trailhead, especially overwintering migratory birds.
**Maps:** www.mysuwanneeriver.com/DocumentCenter/View/10797
**Uses and Restrictions:** Restrooms, boat dock, canoe launch on beachy shore. No motorized vehicles. Family-friendly hiking.
**Contact:** US Fish and Wildlife Service, (352) 493-0238

Hiking the cemetery at Atsena Otie Key

**Trail Highlights:** Take a stroll on the beachfront and explore the old cemetery at the end of the hike.

**Additional Hiking**: Cedar Key Scrub State Reserve, Shell Mound at Lower Suwannee National Wildlife Refuge

Atsena Otie Key is an island located in the Cedar Keys National Wildlife Refuge system off the Gulf Coast of Florida near Cedar Key. Take a guided tour of the keys by local Cedar Keys charter to learn about all the islands. Or rent a kayak to paddle your way over. Once home to more than 250 inhabitants, the island was the original Cedar Key settlement, the name coming from the incorrectly identified juniper trees on the island. After a hurricane damaged the island, residents moved ashore to the current Cedar Key. The island is still home to the ruins of the Faber Mill, a lumber mill built to supply wood to make Faber pencils. Bricks from the mill can still be seen at the boat dock entrance to the island. The dock where charter boats are tied provides a stoop for hundreds of birds taking respite, and many different local and migratory avian species can be viewed here. Hikers will enjoy what seems like their own private island as well as viewing the gravestones in the cemetery at the end of the hike.

I have taken many Elder Hostel groups to hike the island. I never tire of watching dolphins swim and jump during the ride over. On one tour I was pregnant and the dolphins came right up to the boat. I was told they came to see me.

## Hike Details

This is an out-and-back hike. Start at the beachfront if you kayaked or the boat dock if you traveled by boat or charter. The kiosk at the end of the boat dock is the beginning of the hike. Travel southeast on the trail and hike through the mesic hammock with pines and saw palmetto. Absorb the peace of hiking an island and think of the Native Americans, war heroes, and inhabitants who once utilized the island. Pass by an old water cistern along the way. Continue along the path and end at an old cemetery. Take time to explore the historic site and read the graves. Continue on to the marsh and rest on a bench overlooking the other half of Atsena Otie Key. Backtrack on the trail and then explore the beachfront at the dock. Take in the views of the mainland and enjoy bird-watching while there.

# 3

## St. Johns River District

The St. Johns River Water Management District covers 18 counties in northeast and east-central Florida, from the Florida/Georgia border south to Vero Beach and west to Orlando. Major cities in this district (listed from the upper basin to the lower basin) include Palm Bay, Vero Beach, Orlando, and Jacksonville. This district covers the watershed of the St. Johns River, which is one of the few rivers in the northern hemisphere that flow north.

The major initiatives in this district include restoration of the Upper St. Johns River Basin, where the St. Johns River begins, flood protection, Indian River Lagoon water quality improvement, Northern Coastal Basin water quality improvement, and springs protection. Restoring Lake Apopka and managing the Ocklawaha River Basin, areas both drained for farming and ranching, are other large projects. Improving water quality for the St. Johns River from Orlando to Jacksonville is a major project, with scientists researching pollution issues and pollution reduction. Staffers work with agricultural partners to implement water management protection. Water initiatives in the various basins include water resource and water supply planning, conservation measures, and surface water use to protect dwindling Floridan Aquifer water supply, all to ensure water is available for ecosystems and wildlife and the citizens of the State of Florida for generations to come.

The St. Johns River Water Management District offers 40 properties providing trails. Natural communities that hikers will traverse range from massive marshes bound by levees in the Upper St. Johns River Basin in the south; to huge wilderness and timber management areas east and northeast of Orlando in east-central Florida; to smaller tracts of sandhill and mesic flatwoods on properties near Jacksonville. Recreation on these properties is guided by longtime State of Florida land manager Nels Parson. He takes great pride in his trails, having calculated and figured out locations for hundreds of miles of multiuse paths into St. Johns River wilderness for thousands to enjoy.

This is the district I was born and raised in, and where I worked for almost seven years. Though it has now been some time since I left, it seems like I am still part of the team. We spent time crawling through the woods in restoration work, slogging through wetlands up to our calves to mark and plan prescribed burns. The memory of the thrill of reporting to a wildfire with a barreling black plume of smoke, riding horses and ATVs to access hard-to-reach woods roads alongside a real-life Florida cowboy, working all night and freezing alongside wildfires, traveling to different backcountry cities each week for diverse assignments will forever stay with me. I climbed the pine trees of Hal Scot Preserve to prepare them for red-cockaded woodpecker nesting season, burned oak scrub with flames as tall as a two-story building, drove a bulldozer, counted longleaf pine seedlings hidden among thick palmetto, held an endangered Florida scrub jay, and have seen countless Florida black bear. I hope to share these forests and adventures with hikers and families far and wide.

## Basics for the St. Johns District

Be sure to note whether trails are seasonally flooded (typically in the summer rainy season) and whether there is hunting. Check www.myfwc .com for hunting dates prior to hiking.

Unless otherwise noted, all properties in this region are open from sunrise to sunset, free of charge. All maps can be found at www.sjr-wmd.com. For any additional questions, contact the St. Johns River Water Management District office at (386) 329-4404.

## St. Johns River Water Management District North Region

### 25. Bayard Conservation Area

**GPS:** Lat 29.976946, Long -81.63944

**Trailhead Directions:** From Jacksonville, take SR 16 South and cross the St. Johns River on the Shands Bridge. There are two entrances on the left just south of the bridge. Continue on SR 16 and head south when you reach US 17. Veer left onto CR 209 and take a left on CR 226 for two additional entrances.

**Size:** 10,371 acres

**Trail Distance:** 17 miles total

WHITE BLAZE TRAIL LOOP—7.0 miles; YELLOW BLAZE TRAIL—1.7 miles; RED BLAZE SPUR—1.5 miles; EAST TRAILHEAD TO OBSERVATION TOWER—1.1 miles; EAST TRAILHEAD TO WATER OAK BRANCH CROSSING—2.0 miles; WEST TRAILHEAD TO WATER OAK BRANCH CROSSING—1.7 miles

**Hiking Time:** Day hike

**Difficulty:** Easy

**Trail Surface:** Mostly old graded logging roads, dirt and grass for side trails; may be flooded in the rainy season

**Shade Level:** 0–25%

**Natural Communities:** Mesic flatwoods, wet flatwoods, floodplain swamp, sandhill

**Wildlife:** Wild turkey, white-tailed deer, gopher tortoise, bald eagle, little blue heron, eastern indigo snake

**Uses and Restrictions:** Hiking, picnic tables, restroom, primitive camping, canoe landing, canoe put-in, group camping, hunting. Only Area 1 (north of Bayard Road) is open to hiking during hunting season. Check www.myfwc.com for hunting dates. Family-friendly hiking.

**Trail Highlights:** The observation tower is a must. Get an eagle's-eye view of the forest where it's easy to spot deer and other wildlife. Davis Landing provides a view of the St. Johns River and primitive camping spot.

**Additional Hiking:** Belmore State Forest, Etoniah Creek State Forest, Black Creek Ravines

This former pine plantation near the country town of Green Cove Springs has been wonderfully restored through pine thinning and prescribed burns. Pack your camping bag for backcountry, primitive camping, or do some day hiking to the beautiful observation tower overlooking flatwoods as far as the eye can see. Take a water-based trip putting-in at the Shands Bridge. Canoe south on the St. Johns River to Davis Landing to camp and enjoy the undisturbed river as the Native Americans must have experienced it.

## Hike Details

This property boasts long hikes through miles of pine. Starting at SR 16 main entrance, take the main road and hike south. Take the first road east and the first trail to the south to view the observation tower. Or from the same entrance, take the main road all the way to the restrooms for a break. From there decide to hike east to the St. Johns River Davis Landing, continue and make a long loop back to the parking area, or turn around and head back.

## 26. Black Creek Ravines Conservation Area

**GPS:** Lat 30.058056, Long -81.846944

**Trailhead Directions:** From CR 218 in Penny Farms, take Green Road north until you come to the parking area.

**Size:** 964 acres

**Trail Distance:** 8 miles total
WHITE BLAZE TRAIL LOOP—2.3 miles; YELLOW BLAZE TRAIL LOOP—2.0 miles (starting from white trail and returning to white trail); YELLOW BLAZE SPUR TRAIL—0.7 miles (one way); RED BLAZE TRAIL LOOP—2.0 miles; WHITE/RED CONNECTOR TRAIL—0.9 miles; PARKING AREA TO BLACK CREEK BLUFF OBSERVATION POINT—2.5 miles; SHORTEST ROUTE FROM TRAILHEAD TO BLACK CREEK CAMPSITE—2.2 miles (one way)

**Hiking Time:** Half-day hike

**Difficulty:** Easy

**Trail Surface:** Deep sandy soils through the sandhills, dirt and grass/pine needles in the seepage slopes

**Shade Level:** 0–25%

**Natural Communities:** Sandhill, seepage slope

**Wildlife:** Gopher tortoise, roosting and wading birds, pine snake, bald eagle, river otter, white-tailed deer, woodpecker species, owl, bobcat, heron, egret, fox, raccoon, alligator

**Uses and Restrictions:** Hiking, primitive camping, group camping, ravine overlooks. Family-friendly hiking.

**Trail Highlights:** The views of the steep ravines created by the seepage slopes are a must-see as the elevation is extremely rare in Florida. Hiking along the red trail will garner views of sandhills restored through prescribed burning and lead to spectacular views of Black Creek from a tall bluff. The yellow loop and yellow spur will take you to a campsite on Black Creek.

**Additional Hiking:** Belmore State Forest, Etoniah Creek State Forest, Bayard Conservation Area, Branan Field Wildlife and Environmental Area

Seepage slopes, steep ravines, sandhills, and bluffs overlooking Black Creek—this property provides a nice display of rare and endangered Florida habitats. With elevations up to 90 feet along the creek in the sandhills, this property is prime building habitat as it is high and dry—rare in Florida and therefore highly sought for development. Thankfully, it has been preserved for listed species such as gopher tortoise and pitcher plants and for water quality, protecting the resources of Black Creek, a tributary of the St. Johns River.

I have been on this property many times, helping with many prescribed burns, legislative management tours, and solutions to erosion issues, as well as conducting one of my certified prescribed burn checkout burns. My favorite memory is camping overnight with no one else around. We hiked and found a one-dollar bill as well as a venomous pygmy rattlesnake.

## Hike Details

From the parking area, hike in on the white trail and take a left to hit the ravine overlooks. View dogwoods and other trees anchored to the sloping banks. Listen for the water coming up from the underground aquifer that is eroding the sandhills. These seepage streams are participating in a natural Florida process: as the water trickles out from the ground, erosion creates ravine slopes with plants that can survive in this strange habitat. Continue on to reach the yellow trail and hike the yellow trail loop through sandhill plants and wildlife as you head back to view the mighty Black Creek. Or hike the white trail to the white red spur until you reach the red loop. The red trail will take you through more sandhill that has been restored with the application of prescribed burning. It culminates in another spectacular view of Black Creek at a point high in elevation, and you'll stop to look in amazement at the height of the sandhills and also the valley the creek has carved into the creek bottom. This is Florida nature at its finest.

## 27. Deep Creek Conservation Area and Edgefield Tract

**GPS:**

NORTH TRACT—Lat 29.782641, Long -81.491662

WEST TRACT—Lat 29.706466, Long -81.483360

EDGEFIELD TRACT—Lat 29.695137, Long -81.575136

**Trailhead Directions:**

DEEP CREEK NORTH—From St. Augustine, take I-95 south to the SR 207 exit and head west. Turn north on CR 13 S. The property entrance will be on your left.

DEEP CREEK WEST—From St. Augustine, take I-95 south to the SR 206 exit and head west. Turn south onto Cowpen Branch Road. After a series of lefts and rights you will see the property entrance on your left, before you reach CR 13.

EDGEFIELD TRACT—From the SR 206 west exit off I-95, merge onto SR 207 and travel through Hastings. Turn north onto SR 207 A, and the property entrance will be on your left.

**Size:** 5,577 acres

**Trail Distance:** DEEP CREEK NORTH—2.7 miles round-trip

**Hiking Time:** Half-day if all three properties are hiked, not including driving

**Difficulty:** Easy

**Trail Surface:** Old logging road with compact soil and grass or leaf litter; levees at Edgefield tract

**Shade Level:** 0–25%

**Natural Communities:** Mesic flatwoods, floodplain swamp, water treatment ponds are present.

**Wildlife:** In the water treatment ponds of the Edgefield tract, a wide variety of wading and marsh birds can be observed. Hikers can view great blue heron, double-breasted cormorant, anhinga, common egret, tri-colored heron, boat-tailed grackle, and red-winged blackbird. White-tailed deer and wild turkey can be seen in the flatwoods near CR 13.

**Uses and Restrictions:** Hiking, boat launch, observation tower, handicapped access. No motorized vehicles. Family-friendly hiking.

**Trail Highlights:** Experience the mesic flatwoods of the North tract, some of the only uplands on the property. Bring your binoculars for birding at the Edgefield tract levee trail.

**Additional Hiking:** Moses Creek Conservation Area, Matanzas State Forest, Bayard Conservation Area

Deep Creek North and West tracts protect floodplains of Deep Creek, which flows directly into the St. Johns River. The Edgefield Tract is a stormwater treatment area comprising a system of water treatment ponds. The ponds catch water flowing from the Hasting tri-county farming areas and allow pesticides and fertilizers to settle to the bottom; clean water then moves on to the next step. Here, wetland plants extract more nutrients before water is released into a creek that flows into the St. Johns River. Hikers can experience uplands hiking in mesic flatwoods on the North and West tracts and hiking around the water treatment ponds to a lookout tower for bird-watching at the Edgefield tract.

During one prescribed burn at the Edgefield water treatment ponds, we trudged through heavy rough terrain and dragged our legs through thick briars as we went from pond to pond with our drip torches.

## Hike Details

The Deep Creek North tract crosses over a creek and through mesic flatwoods before making a loop and then backtracking. You can see fields to the north and wetland fringe to the south of the red trail. The Edgefield tract boasts views of the water treatment pond and a hike to a lookout tower. Here you can utilize binoculars to view wading birds. The Deep Creek West tract traverses mesic flatwoods, crossing two creeks and following two trail loops before backtracking to the entrance.

# 28. Dunns Creek Conservation Area

**GPS:** Lat 29.572778, Long -81.56

**Trailhead Directions:** From US 17 in Palatka, head south. Veer off onto CR 100/SR 20 east when you reach San Mateo. Turn right onto Tram Road; the property entrance will be on the south side of the road.

**Size:** 3,156 acres

**Trail Distance:** 5.3 total miles round-trip
WHITE BLAZE TRAIL—2.4 miles round-trip; YELLOW BLAZE AND YELLOW/WHITE CONNECTOR—2.9 miles round-trip

**Hiking Time:** Half-day hike

**Difficulty:** Easy

**Trail Surface:** Old logging roads with compact soil and grass or leaf litter; seasonally flooded

**Shade Level:** 25–50%

**Natural Communities:** Floodplain swamp, mesic flatwoods, basin marsh

**Wildlife:** The property plays host to numerous species of salamanders, toads, frogs, and snakes as well as American alligator, bobcat, raccoon, white-tailed deer, and gray fox. Many avian species may be present, such as yellow-crowned night heron, wood duck, swallow-tailed kite, red-shouldered hawk, barred owl, and woodpecker and warbler species.

**Uses and Restrictions:** Hiking, primitive camping, group camping, hunting, hunt check station. No motorized vehicles. Property is part of the Dunns Creek Wildlife Management Area. Be sure to check hunting dates at www.myfwc.com before you hike. Family-friendly hiking.

**Trail Highlights:** Hike across plywood walkways over extremely low points in the flatwoods where wetlands cross through them.

**Additional Hiking:** Dunns Creek State Park, Crescent Lake Conservation Area

Dunns Creek Conservation Area protects floodplains of Dunns Creek, a major tributary of the St. Johns River. Mostly floodplain swamp, but a sliver of mesic flatwoods peninsula provides a down-and-back hiking path with views of the cypress knees of the floodplain swamp. Get lost in the country feel of this old Florida property. I enjoyed working a prescribed burn on this smaller, yet peaceful property.

## Hike Details

The hike is down and back with three small loops off the main trail. Hike through areas planted in longleaf pine and over boardwalk paths through low-lying areas connecting mesic flatwoods through the wetlands.

## 29. Gourd Island Conservation Area

**GPS:** Lat 30.069584, Long -81.508826
**Address:** 10182 Russell Sampson Road, St. Johns, FL 32259
**Trailhead Directions:** From Jacksonville, take I-95 south; take exit 329 for CR 210 and head west. After a few hundred feet, take the first right on Russell Sampson Road. At the traffic circle, circle around and continue to the right on Russell Sampson Road. The parking area will be a few hundred feet on your right.

Gourd Island hiking trail

**Size:** 515 acres

**Trail Distance:** 4.1 miles

WHITE BLAZE ACCESS TO LOOP TRAIL—1.6 miles round-trip; RED BLAZE LOOP TRAIL—2.5 miles round-trip. Half-day trip.

**Hiking Time:** 1.5 hours, short hike

**Difficulty:** Easy

**Trail Surface:** The beginning of the white blaze trail is a wide road of sand and gravel; sandhill areas are truck trail paths. Areas near the creeks may be wet with dark, muddy soils.

**Shade Level:** 0–25%

**Natural Communities:** Sandhill, mesic flatwoods, wet flatwoods, floodplain swamp

**Wildlife:** Wild turkey, white-tailed deer

**Uses and Restrictions:** Hiking. No motorized vehicles. Family-friendly hiking.

**Trail Highlights:** The very center of the gourd-shaped upland underwent sandhill restoration around 2013. The slash pine was clear-cut, and prescribed burning is in the restoration plan. Hikers can appreciate the flowing wiregrass and towering longleaf pine coming in over the years. Also notice large old pine and cypress trees along Durbin Creek on the north side of the red trail—ancient nature right in the middle of sprawling south Jacksonville.

**Additional Hiking:** Julington Durbin Preserve, Bayard Conservation Area, 12 Mile Swamp Conservation Area, Guana Tolomato Matanzas National Estuarine Research Reserve

This is a relatively new conservation area, opened to recreation in summer 2012. The property was purchased to protect the waters of Sampson and Durbin creeks, both tributaries of the St. Johns River. The property namesake is the gourd-shaped uplands surrounded by Sampson and Durbin creeks. The hiking trail meanders through sandhill, floodplain swamp, and mesic and wet flatwoods to afford the hiker a mixture of natural communities to experience. Whereas the property is tiny compared with other St. Johns River Water Management District properties, the trail runs almost the entire perimeter of the property, creating maximum potential trail length.

## Hike Details

From the parking area, hike onto the main road north to the kiosk. Your instinct will be to hike the road straight back to the red loop; however, from the kiosk, hike a short distance on the road and almost immediately take a right into the sandhills. Follow the white trail heading east and then north until you cross the original entrance road. Continue hiking once you cross the road. The trail will come to a dead end at Sampson Creek. Take a left and hike the border along Sampson Creek. Cross Durbin Creek, and head north. You will then join the red loop trail and continue hiking north along Sampson Creek and enter the gourd-shaped uplands. Soon you will come to a four-way woods road intersection. Take the center road and continue heading north. After a couple of double-red left turns you will enter the mesic flatwoods and then the very center of the gourd within the sandhills sections of the hike. From this point on you will continue to follow the red blazes in a loop until you dead-end into the white trail. You will then follow the white trail south, back to the entrance.

## 30. Julington-Durbin Preserve

**GPS:** Lat 30.130278, Long -81.543333

**Trailhead Directions:** From Jacksonville, take I-95 south and exit west at Old St. Augustine Road. Take a left on Bartram Park Boulevard. After about half a mile, keep your eyes peeled for a blue and green sign on the right for Julington-Durbin Preserve as the entrance is easy to miss.

**Size:** 2,031 acres

**Trail Distance:**

> WHITE BLAZE TRAIL LOOP—3.9 miles round-trip; YELLOW AND WHITE BLAZE TRAIL LOOP—6.1 miles round-trip; PARKING AREA TO DURBIN CREEK LANDING (RED BLAZE SPUR TRAIL)—2.0 miles round-trip

**Hiking Time:** Half-day hike

**Difficulty:** Easy

**Trail Surface:** Sandy soil, compact soil with leaf litter

**Shade Level:** 0–25%

The flowing wiregrass at Julington-Durbin Preserve

**Natural Communities:** Sandhill, mesic flatwoods, scrub, wetlands, hardwood hammock, tidal marsh, floodplain swamp

**Wildlife:** Bald eagle, osprey, gopher tortoise, bobcat, wild turkey, white-tailed deer, and numerous species of wading and songbirds. Manatees seasonally swim in both creeks.

**Maps:** www.floridaswater.com/recreationguide/julington-durbin/

**Uses and Restrictions:** Picnic tables, hiking, biking, horseback riding, fishing. No motorized vehicles. Family-friendly hiking.

**Contact:** SJRWMD, (386) 329-4404

**Trail Highlights:** Hikers will enjoy the wildflowers of the sandhills, including the purple Bartram's Ixia, which can be found blooming in fire-blackened areas at the only time it will, post burn.

**Additional Hiking:** Gourd Island Conservation Area, Nocatee Preserve, Moses Creek Conservation Area, Guana Tolomato Matanzas National Estuarine Research Reserve

This property is on the south side of Jacksonville in the quickly growing area of Bartram Park. Land was set aside by the developer as part of permit approval and purchased for conservation by the district. District staff quickly came in to remove sand pine that had taken over, plant native longleaf pine, and then apply prescribed burns so the fuel loads (the density of the plants and brush) would be lower and wildfire risk would decrease. A plan was made to educate new families in the area about prescribed burns so they would understand and accept them. Development on the border of the preserve was rapid and dense, with homes and condos built right up to the edge of the conservation area. Today the district still manages with prescribed fire, and the sandhill and flatwoods natural communities are thriving. The property is an oasis amid a massive development, protecting Durbin and Julington creeks, tributaries of the St. Johns River. It provides wildlife habitat, water recharge, recreation and open space for residents, and is a training site for local high school cross-country teams. Hikers will be amazed that this large, natural conservation area with wildflowers, open space, and access to Durbin Creek is in the middle of Jacksonville.

I have enjoyed working burns many times at Julington-Durbin. At one burn I was photographed and published in the *Florida Times Union* local newspaper in my fire gear, shielding my face from the heat with my gloved hand. I also led a training burn as part of the process to become a Florida Certified burner. On that burn, a tree fell right in front of one of my team members, reminding us how careful we need to be in the woods. I later went on to create a Family Nature Hunt for Jacksonville families that guides them on a hike on the red trail with clues as they head to Durbin Creek. This hunt can be found online at www.fun4firstcoastkids.com if you would like to follow it. I also came back to burn on the property in May 2016 as a volunteer. Prescribed burners must do at least five burns and participate in fire education to keep their burn license. It was amazing to come back to this property with my friends and coworkers, the horses, the equipment, the smell of burning pine, and especially to see Danny Mills, my favorite Florida cowboy, after being absent from fire for four years. It was like a vacation compared with working from home with two kids aged four and two!

## Hike Details

For a short hike, take the white trail through the sandhill and take a left to get on the red trail. Hike through deep sandy soil to see turkey oaks, wiregrass, and wildflowers on the way to Durbin Creek. Notice how the vegetation changes to towering oaks and other tree species, the shade deepens to 100 percent, and the temperature drops when you move into the floodplain swamp. The mosquitoes come out in this area due to the pools of standing water, so bring insect repellent! Hike over two bridges until you reach Durbin Creek. There are remains of pilings from an old bridge and the creek moves peacefully here. During cold winters look for manatee that have come in from the Atlantic Ocean, moved through the St. Johns River, and into Durbin Creek. For a longer hike, take the white trail west, staying to the right. Hike due west and you will see sandhill on your left and mesic flatwoods that grade down into floodplain swamp as the elevation drops into the creek. There is a spur trail on the left that allows you to make the hike shorter, or continue west on the yellow trail. At the extreme western point of the yellow trail, follow it around for a U-turn and hike until you dead-end into the red trail. There you can take a right to view Durbin Creek or take a left and follow the red trail to the white trail and veer to the right back to the parking area.

## 31. Moses Creek Conservation Area

**GPS:** Lat 29.757222, Long -81.275556
**Trailhead Directions:** From I-95 in St. Augustine, take SR 206 east. There are two entrances on the north side of SR 206 west of the intracoastal waterway.
**Size:** 2,173 acres
**Trail Distance:**
   WHITE BLAZE TRAIL—1.35 miles; YELLOW BLAZE TRAIL—2.0

Meandering Moses Creek

miles; RED BLAZE TRAIL—3.7 miles; EAST TRAILHEAD TO GROUP
CAMP SITE—0.7 mile; EAST TRAILHEAD TO BLUFF OBSERVATION
POINT—1.5 miles; EAST TRAILHEAD TO MURATS POINT—5.7
miles; WEST TRAILHEAD TO MURATS POINT—5.7 miles

**Hiking Time:** 2 hours

**Difficulty:** Easy

**Trail Surface:** Sandy soil, compact soil with leaf litter

**Shade Level:** 50–75%

**Natural Communities:** Mesic flatwoods, scrub, wetlands, hardwood
hammock, tidal marsh

**Wildlife:** Wading birds such as great blue heron and egret, plus osprey,
hawk, gopher tortoise, white-tailed deer, river otter, and red fox

**Uses and Restrictions:** Hiking, picnic tables, shelter, group campsite, primitive campsite, restroom, observation point, security residence. No motorized vehicles. Family-friendly hiking.

**Trail Highlights:** Pick the east or west entrance to hike to the red trail. It will take you through many natural communities before you emerge on a bluff overlooking the tidal marshes of Moses Creek.

**Additional Hiking:** Guana Tolomato Matanzas National Estuarine Research Reserve, Twelve Mile Swamp, Stokes Landing

This property protects the tidal Moses Creek. It boasts views of many natural communities, including the flat areas of pine, the sugar white sand of scrub oaks, and the shaded jungle of hammocks with towering oaks and low palmetto, and culminates in an opening with vistas of the brackish-water marshes on Moses Creek from a high bluff. It is a glimpse of what St. Augustine, the oldest city in the nation, must have looked like to the Native Americans, pre-European conquest. The longer multiuse trails are perfect for horseback riding and biking as well as hiking.

I have burned many times on this property. Once the water on the red trail leading to Moses Creek was so high it was up to mid-wheel. On another burn I rode via horseback for the first time. Halfway through, the horse came up on a snake and jumped out of its skin . . . and so did I.

## Hike Details

Hike in from the east or west trailhead entrance until you reach the red trail at the power line. Beware the deep, soft, sandy soil of the power line! Cross the wetlands and continue north to one of the highest spots in the conservation area. Head south down the peninsula and choose to take a right to picnic on a peaceful, oak-lined spot, or continue on the red trail. The red trail guides hikers through the overhanging oaks and palmettos of the shady hammock leading to the marsh overlook of Moses Creek. Watch the creek slowly meander into the Matanzas River as you rest at a picnic table under the ancient oaks.

## 32. Murphy Creek Conservation Area

**GPS:** Lat 29.570278, Long -81.660278

**Trailhead Directions:** From Palatka, take US 17 south. After San Mateo, take a right on CR 309. The property entrance will be on the right, with the island accessible only by boat or canoe. To hike the island, use any nearby boat ramp, the closest being Brown's Landing Boat Ramp off Brown's Landing Road. Boat a little way west to the Murphy Island Boat Ramp across the St. Johns River.

**Size:** 4,755 acres

**Trail Distance:**

IN THE CONSERVATION AREA—1.8 miles round-trip

ON THE ISLAND—From boat dock and around loop trail and back to dock—2.7 miles; from boat dock to creek landing—0.8 mile

**Hiking Time:** 2 hours

**Difficulty:** Easy

**Trail Surface:** Old logging roads with compact soil and grass or leaf litter

**Shade Level:** 0–25%

**Natural Communities:** Floodplain swamp, sandhill, mesic flatwoods, hardwood hammock

**Wildlife:** Bald eagle, gopher tortoise, Virginia opossum, white-tailed deer, bobcat, fox. Numerous waterfowl and wading birds can be found in the wetlands.

**Uses and Restrictions:** Hiking, group camping area, restrooms, boat dock. No motorized vehicles. Family-friendly hiking.

**Trail Highlights:** The high bluffs on the island provide amazing views of the St. Johns River.

**Additional Hiking:** Dunns Creek Conservation Area, Dunns Creek State Park, Horseshoe Point Conservation Area, Marjorie Harris Carr Cross Florida Greenway, Ocala National Forest

This conservation area protects the floodplains of Murphy Creek and the St. Johns River, while also protecting an upland island on the St. Johns River. Hikers will traverse mesic flatwoods and sandhills on the mainland of the conservation area. Those with boat access can also experience hiking on a remote island in the St. Johns River with high bluffs providing views of the river.

## Hike Details

Hiking the conservation area includes passing through sandhill and mesic flatwoods on the white blazed trail. Notice gopher tortoise burrows and other signs of wildlife. If you can find boat or canoe access to Murphy Island, you can summit high bluffs that provide views of the St. Johns River.

## 33. Rice Creek Conservation Area

**GPS:** Lat 29.683056, Long -81.731111

**Trailhead Directions:** From Palatka, take SR 100 west. The property is on the south side of the road approximately 6 miles west of Palatka.

**Size:** 5,061 acres

**Trail Distance:** 4 miles total

MULTIUSE TRAIL (WHITE BLAZE)—2.1 miles; RICE PLANTATION LEVEE TRAIL (HIKING ONLY)—2.4 miles; BIKE TRAIL—1.6 miles

**Hiking Time:** Half-day hike

**Difficulty:** Easy

**Trail Surface:** Old logging roads with compact soil and grass or leaf litter

**Shade Level:** 50–75%

**Natural Communities:** Floodplain swamp, floodplain forest, mesic flatwoods, upland mixed forest

**Wildlife:** Florida black bear, white-tailed deer, wild turkey, river otter, wood duck, diverse migratory songbirds

**Uses and Restrictions:** Hiking, picnic area, inclement weather shelter, campsite, hunting. No motorized vehicles. The property is part of Etoniah Creek Wildlife Management Area. Hikers should check hunting dates at www.myfwc.com before hiking.

**Trail Highlights:** Hike the Florida National Scenic Trail to the levee trail, then follow the boardwalk out to one of the largest cypress trees in the state of Florida.

**Additional Hiking:** Marjorie Harris Carr Cross Florida Greenway, Etoniah Creek State Forest, Belmore State Forest

This property was once a rice and indigo plantation in the 1700s, as evidenced by remnant dikes. It protects Rice Creek, Little Rice Creek, the Rice Creek Swamp headwaters, and the floodplains of Rice Creek and Little Rice Creek, major tributaries to the St. Johns River. It conserves land that helps create a corridor between Belmore State Forest and Etoniah State Forest to the northwest, with the Cross Florida Greenway adjacent to the south, south of SR 20. This means wildlife have a greenway that provides cover, forage, and protection as they traverse from property to property. It hosts one of the largest cypress trees in the state, with a boardwalk path to the tree. It also plays host to the Florida National Scenic Trail, maintained by the Florida Trail Association as a hiking-only trail. This group installed a camping platform that is screened in and two stories, unique to northeast Florida. Hikers can take either the Florida Trail from SR 100 or the multiuse trail from the parking area. A bike trail is also found on the property.

This property is a few miles west of district headquarters in Palatka where I worked for four years. One day land management staff took a group trip to see the old rice plantation dikes and flood gates. Nels Parson was our tour guide and led us to the champion cypress tree he had found and confirmed and showed off the boardwalk he helped build with Florida Trail volunteers to provide access to the tree.

## Hike Details

From the parking area, take the bike path and then take a right onto the white trail. Dead-end into the Florida National Scenic Trail and hike southwest until you reach the levee trail. Hike south or take a right to hike the levee trail loop. In the southwest corner veer off the levee trail to hike the boardwalk to one of the largest cypress trees in the state.

## 34. Stokes Landing Conservation Area

**GPS:** Lat 30, Long -81.361111
**Trailhead Directions:** From the St. Augustine Airport on US 1, travel
north. Take a right on Venetian Boulevard, a right on Old Dixie Road,
and a left on Lakeshore Drive. The entrance will be on the right.

**Size:** 277 acres

**Trail Distance:** 2.5 miles total
WHITE BLAZE TRAIL LOOP—1.4 miles round-trip; YELLOW
BLAZE TRAIL—0.7 miles one way; YELLOW/WHITE CONNECTOR
TRAIL—0.4 mile

**Hiking Time:** 1 hour

**Difficulty:** Easy

**Trail Surface:** Dirt and grass/pine needles/leaves

**Shade Level:** 50–75%

**Natural Communities:** Hardwood hammock, marsh, mesic flatwoods

**Wildlife:** Wood stork, red-tailed hawk, wading birds, river otter

**Uses and Restrictions:** Hiking, picnic shelter, observation tower,
observation point, security residence. No motorized vehicles. Family-
friendly hiking.

**Trail Highlights:** Hike the white trail to the observation platform, built
by students, to take in scenic views of the marshes of Tolomato River.

**Additional Hiking:** Guana Tolomato Matanzas National Estuarine
Research Reserve, Moses Creek Conservation Area, 12 Mile Swamp

Bordering both sides of the Tolomato River, this property boasts scenic
views of squiggly shaped creeks through the marshes, tiptoeing wading
birds, ancient hardwood hammock with scraggly, overhanging oaks,
and marsh ecotones transitioning to upland vegetation. On this peaceful hike, you have your choice of an overlook tower, a picnic shelter, and
an observation point as destinations.

I once helped on a prescribed burn on this property, lighting palmettos 8 feet tall in a mesic flatwoods habitat, pushing the fire to the
marsh.

## Hike Details

From the parking area, hike in on the spur trail that leads to the white
trail. Take a left on the white trail and hike north until you reach the
intersection of 4 trails. Continue hiking straight through on the white
trail to reach the observation platform. Return to the intersection
and head south on the yellow/white trail to complete the loop, hiking
through mesic flatwoods with pine and palmetto.

## 35. Thomas Creek Conservation Area

**GPS:**

EAST TRAILHEAD—Lat 30.486633, Long -81.785871

WEST TRAILHEAD—Lat 30.486297, Long -81.786393

**Trailhead Directions:** Property is 20 minutes northwest of downtown Jacksonville. From Jacksonville, take I-10 west, exit at the I-295 North exit, and drive north. Exit at the US 1 North exit and drive north about 5 miles. There is no warning for the property until you drive right up to the gray sign and see the yellow gates. There are eastern and western parking areas for the east and west trailheads directly across from each other on US 1.

**Size:** 5,540 acres

**Trail Distance:**

EAST TRAILS—3.6 miles total

RED ACCESS TRAIL TO LOOP—0.6 miles round-trip; WHITE TRAIL—3-mile loop

WEST TRAILS—2 miles total

RED ACCESS TRAIL TO LOOP—0.6 miles round-trip; YELLOW TRAIL—1.4-mile loop

**Hiking Time:**

EAST TRAILS—1.5 hours

WEST TRAILS—30 minutes

**Difficulty:** Moderate. The trails are seasonally flooded in many areas along the trail, causing slower hiking and the need to take care not to slip. Watch for water moccasins in the water.

**Shade Level:** 0–25%

**Trail Surface:** Grassed surface with dark soils, extremely wet areas, bedded roads with grassed surface

**Natural Communities:** Mesic flatwoods, wet flatwoods

**Wildlife:** Wild turkey, red-tailed hawk, great blue heron, white-tailed deer

**Uses and Restrictions:** Hiking, no facilities. No motorized vehicles. Not for family hiking.

**Contact:** City of Jacksonville, Parks and Recreation Department, (904) 630-CITY

**Trail Highlights:** What this property lacks in scenic vistas it makes up for in the adventure of hiking flooded trails. Also, keep your eyes open for *Sarracenia minor*, hooded pitcher plant, in various places along the trails on both sides of the property.

**Additional Hiking:** Cary State Forest, Four Creeks State Forest

This property borders 10 miles of Thomas Creek, the largest tributary of the Nassau River, which runs into the Atlantic Ocean. The property consists of expansive areas of floodplain swamp that buffers Thomas Creek. The hiking trails meander entirely through wet flatwoods, a natural community consisting of pine, in this case planted slash pine, palmetto, gallberry, and other flatwoods plants.

This was one of the first properties I hiked in researching this guide. When I came to my first segment of flooded trail I thought I would quit on Day 1. Writing about all five water management districts in the state of Florida while holding the responsibilities of working from home *and* being a mother suddenly seemed daunting, as did getting through the massive pool of rainwater. I had no clue how deep the water was and I could not see if there were snakes. I texted my longtime friend and colleague, Jo Anna Emanuel. Supportive as usual, she said, "Just do it!" So I did and got wet up to my knees as I splashed through. It was fun and free and it felt exciting, the same feeling as going on an adventure into the Florida backcountry to research this book, something not many others have done before.

## Hike Details

Beginning at the east parking area, hike straight east on the red trail for 0.3 miles. At the dead end, take a left to begin the white trail loop. Continue hiking on the white trail until you see the borrow pit on the right. You will feel the need to keep going to the right, but the white trail heads to the left. Make sure you see the white blazes and take the left here. Continue on and you will come to a seasonally flooded area. Cross through on the ballast rock, which gives the wet area a hard bottom. Continue to watch for white blazes and hike until you dead-end into private property at a fence line and take a left. Again, watch for white blazes as you will want to continue straight ahead; however, pretty quickly you take a right at the fence corner and head along the fence line to the east. It is a bit uneven here and difficult to mow, so it is overgrown, watch your step. Don't get too comfortable because you will very quickly take a left into an overgrown area that is difficult to spot—again, watch for white blazes! You will go through another area that is under water seasonally and continue through a few more wet areas. You will come to another dead end that is not marked with white blazes in either direction! Take a left here and double-check for a white blaze a little farther on the trail. Continue hiking and at a certain point it gets a bit tricky. You will hit another dead end with no white blazes at the T. Take a left and you will see white blazes. Keep your eyes open for the blazes as you will take a right onto a tram road and an almost immediate left off of it. From this point you will continue on the white trail through various wet spots in wet flatwoods until you hit the red access trail again. Take a right to head back to the parking area.

West Trailhead: If you just hiked the east trail, move your car to the west parking area so people will know which side of the property you are hiking on. To do this, drive north on US 1 and then make the first U-turn you can and head south to the parking area directly across from the east parking area. Hike onto the red trail directly to the west for 0.3 miles. Continue straight back on the tram road until you hit the railroad. Take a left at the border at the railroad and head south. This area of the trail is not well maintained, but there is a worn path that is relatively free of weeds. Take notice of the double yellow blazed tree and take a left off the boundary and back toward the parking area. Follow this trail around through various wet areas until you dead-end into the red trail again. At the red trail, take a right back to the parking area.

## 36. Twelve Mile Swamp Recreation Area

**GPS:** Lat 30.01, Long -81.400278

**Trailhead Directions:**

ENTRANCE 1—From the St. Augustine Airport, take US 1 north. Take a left on SR 16 and the parking area will be on the right.

ENTRANCE 2—From the St. Augustine Airport, take US 1 north. Take a left on International Golf Parkway and the parking area will be on the right.

**Size:** 21,898 acres

**Trail Distance:**

INTERNATIONAL GOLF PARKWAY ENTRANCE—2.8 miles round-trip

SR 16 ENTRANCE—Less than 2 miles

**Hiking Time:** 1 hour

**Difficulty:** Easy

**Trail Surface:** Compact sandy soil, pine needles

**Shade Level:** 0–25%

**Natural Communities:** Mesic flatwoods planted in fast-growing slash pine, sand pine scrub, interspersed depressional wetlands

**Wildlife:** White-tailed deer, fox, songbirds, various species of snakes

**Uses and Restrictions:** Hiking, hunting. Wildlife management area. Be sure to check www.myfwc.com for hunting dates. Family-friendly hiking.

**Trail Highlights:** The planted pine forest still has remnant dune systems associated in a north/south direction. Notice the elevational changes of uplands and swales of wetlands that were once formed by the ocean pushing against the sandy soil.

**Additional Hiking:** Guana Tolomato Matanzas National Estuarine Research Reserve, Moses Creek Conservation Area, Stokes Landing

The St. Johns River Water Management District owns 378 acres of this massive conservation area. This portion is planted pine mesic flatwoods with the associated palmetto, gallberry, and other groundcover. This land is part of the larger conservation area that is mostly swamp systems that develop into creeks. These creeks let out into Stokes Creek, the Tolomato River, and the St. Johns River. Although they are not open to hiking, they preserve watersheds that help improve water quality of these rivers.

## Hike Details

Follow the interpretive trail guide created for the loop trail at the International Golf Parkway entrance. It stops at strategic points along the trail and has educational points at each stop. It talks of the forest management on the property and how pine is harvested and replanted. It describes how the high dunes and low swales were created on the property by wave action when sea level was higher in Florida, and it describes the sand pine scrub habitat whose sandy soils with poor nutritional value leave plants scraggly and short, supporting species adapted for dry areas. Interpretive trail map: www.sjrwmd.com/recreationguide/twelvemileswamp/

## St. Johns River Water Management District North Central Region

### 37. Pellicer Creek Conservation Area

**GPS:** Lat 29.6375, Long -81.257778

**Trailhead Directions:** From St. Augustine, take US 1 south. Turn east on Old Kings Road and pass I-95. Take a left into the preserve and the water management district parking area will be on the left.

**Size:** 3,057 acres

**Trail Distance:** 11.1 miles total
WHITE/RED BLAZE TRAIL LOOP FROM POWER LINE TRAILHEAD—5.7 miles; RED BLAZE TRAIL LOOP—3.8 miles; WHITE BLAZE SPUR TRAIL TO LAND BRIDGE ONE WAY—0.8 miles

**Hiking Time:** Day hike

**Difficulty:** Easy

**Trail Surface:** Sandy soil or soils covered in pine needle litter

**Shade Level:** 0–25%

**Natural Communities:** Sandhill, saltwater marsh, freshwater marsh, upland hardwood forest

**Wildlife:** Many endangered or threatened species have been spotted here, including southeastern American kestrel, gopher tortoise, creeping orchid, cinnamon fern, and East Coast coontie.

**Uses and Restrictions:** Hiking, fishing, restrooms, security residence, handicapped access. Princess Estate, an old hunting lodge purchased in 1886 and made of coquina, is the oldest building in Flagler County and home to Florida's first inground pool. To learn more about the lodge, visit here: www.flaglercounty.org/facilities/facility/details/18. No motorized vehicles. Family-friendly hiking.

**Trail Highlights:** The white trail bordering the bluffs of Pellicer Creek provide glimpses of the meandering creek. Taking the white trail to the west traverses dense, shaded sand pine and leads to a land bridge for hikers and wildlife to cross I-95.

**Additional Hiking:** Princess Place Preserve, Guana Tolomato Matanzas National Estuarine Research Reserve, Matanzas State Forest

This property protects 8 miles of Pellicer Creek shoreline. Hikers can experience high elevations and bluffs overlooking Pellicer Creek and its saltwater marshes caused by the ridges and swales found in the sandhills on the property. It is here that ocean waves pushed in dunes hundreds of years ago. The result is sandy soil that is high and dry and of poor nutritional value for plants. It plays host to sandhill habitat, with the associated open longleaf pine forest allowing plenty of light to penetrate to the forest floor, resulting in lush and diverse groundcover species, including wildflowers.

I helped monitor the clear-cut of the large sand pine plantation in 2011. The white/red trail passes through this clear-cut area. An offsite species, fast-growing sand pine was planted by a previous owner because it does well in sandy soil. It was removed to be replanted with native longleaf pine. I monitored the loggers to ensure they were moving along in progress while following best management practices, and also to help answer any questions. Post-harvest I installed and monitored vegetation survey transects throughout the clear-cut to track the regrowth of sand pine from seeds that had likely settled. This would help determine whether to plant longleaf pine and fight any sand pine regeneration, or let the area go back to sand pine. It was determined that sand pine were not an issue; managers have agreed to let the groundcover grow through prescribed fire and use the area for harvesting wiregrass, eventually planting longleaf pine.

## Hike Details

From the parking area at the power line off Old King's Road, take the white trail in and then veer off the power line, staying on the white trail. Continue to the left on the white trail until you hit the power line again. Head south and then west to hike the land bridge over I-95. Return and head north on the white trail along the power line. You can view Pellicer Creek here as it dead-ends into the creek. Then head east along Pellicer Creek and the high bluffs overlooking the creek. When you come to the red trail, you can hike directly south along longleaf pine sandhill and back to the parking area, or continue east on the red trail for a longer hike. After hiking, be sure to visit Princess Estate right next door, managed by Flagler County. Walk around the 1886 coquina lodge and Florida's first inground swimming pool. The house will be locked, but you can enjoy great views of the creek and peek in the windows, not to mention the waterfront campsites and nice restrooms adjacent to the lodge!

## 38. Crescent Lake Conservation Area

**GPS:** Lat 29.351590, Long -81.469996

**Trailhead Directions:** From US 17 in Palatka, head south. Turn east on Raulerson Road and dead-end into the property.

**Size:** 3,528 acres

**Trail Distance:**

OVERALL TRAIL LENGTH FROM TRAILHEAD, AROUND LOOP AND RETURN—3.5 miles

TRAILHEAD TO CAMPSITE—0.6 miles

**Hiking Time:** 2 hours

**Difficulty:** Easy

**Trail Surface:** Old logging roads with compact soil and grass or leaf litter

**Shade Level:** 0–25%

**Natural Communities:** Planted pine, mesic flatwoods, sandhill, floodplain marsh, floodplain swamp

**Wildlife:** Bald eagle, osprey, wading birds, waterfowl, white-tailed deer, Florida black bear

**Uses and Restrictions:** Hiking, picnic tables, group camping area with restrooms, shelter, and lights. No motorized vehicles. Family-friendly hiking.

**Trail Highlights:** The north end of the trail loop borders floodplain swamp. Explore the vegetation of the swamp as you hike on this path.

**Additional Hiking:** Lake George Conservation Area, Lake George State Forest, Haw Creek Preserve State Park, Haw Creek Preserve

This conservation area provides water resource protection for the floodplains of Crescent Lake, an oblong lake leading to the St. Johns River. The eastern 85 percent of the property is floodplain marsh and floodplain swamp that receive drainage from Haw Creek, Little Haw Creek, and Middle Haw Creek before releasing flows into Crescent Lake. The west side of the property hosts planted pine in old pasture grasses, mesic flatwoods planted in pine, and an upland campsite that hosts a shelter, restrooms, and lights, rare for the primitive characteristics of most district campsites. Hikers will find a loop trail that traverses most of the natural communities found on site.

## Hike Details

From the parking area, head directly east through planted pine that is now tall and luscious. It was planted in old cattle grass, which is extremely difficult to replace with natural groundcover, so it is still present. Take a right to hike on the white trail loop. As you head back northwest you will be on the border of the floodplain forest. Look into the forest for glimpses of wildlife.

## 39. Heart Island Conservation Area

**GPS:** Lat 29.205, Long -81.364722

**Trailhead Directions:** From the intersection of US 17 and SR 40 in Barberville, take SR 40 east. The property entrance off Bee Road is a little further east, before you reach CR 11, on the south side of the property. Continue heading south on Lake Winona Road to find marked hiking trails. The entrance is on the west side of Lake Winona Road.

**Size:** 14,246 acres

**Trail Distance:**

TOTAL—4.8 miles; option to hike all the graded roads on the property.
WHITE BLAZE TRAIL LOOP—1.1 miles; YELLOW BLAZE TRAIL
LOOP—1.8 miles; RED BLAZE TRAIL LOOP—1.9 miles

**Hiking Time:** Day hike

**Difficulty:** Easy

**Trail Surface:** Old logging roads with grassy or graded surface

**Shade Level:** 0–25%

**Natural Communities:** Mesic flatwoods, sandhill, strand swamp, planted
pine, floodplain swamp, dome swamp

**Wildlife:** Florida black bear, white-tailed deer, gopher tortoise, river
otter, woodpeckers, songbirds, fox, raccoon, American alligator, and a
variety of snakes and lizards have been observed.

**Uses and Restrictions:** Hiking, hunting, group campsite, cabin,
security residence. Heart Island is part of the Lake George Wildlife
Management Area. Review www.myfwc.com for hunting dates prior to
hiking. Family-friendly hiking.

**Trail Highlights:** Hike in from Lake Winona Road on the white trail to
reach the red trail. At the very western tip of the red trail you can
take the tram road north and hike directly across Deep Creek to the
northern side of the property. It is on this oak-lined tram road where
you will see evidence of Florida black bear, and you may even run into
one along the hike.

**Additional Hiking:** Lake George State Forest, Lake George
Conservation Area, Tiger Bay State Forest, Crescent Lake
Conservation Area, Clark Bay Conservation Area

Heart Island Conservation Area is a huge expanse of mesic flatwoods
that connects to Lake George Forest, which connects to the St. Johns
River just south of Lake George. These properties protect wetlands
and creeks of the St. Johns River. Former timber company land, the
conservation area was clear-cut before purchase by the district and
underwent heavy wildfire during extreme drought in the statewide
wildfires of 1998. The district has been working to replant pine and
introduce prescribed fire with the use of helicopter burns and burn-

ing by horseback to reach thousands of acres. I helped burn much of the north side of SR 40 in 2009 during great fire weather in a wetter period. I directed a survey of gopher tortoise and groundcover on the Lake Winona Road property in 2010 as part of the effort to restore sandhill there. I also helped with a prescribed burn on the Lake Winona Road property to prepare for longleaf pine, then surveyed the seedlings post-planting for survival. Hikers will have a chance to sight Florida black bear on the Lake Winona Road property south of SR 40. Be sure to grab a tasty, fresh grapefruit at the Lake Winona Road entrance at the parking area, built on a former orange and grapefruit grove. There is also the option to hike all the roads through the flatwoods and over creeks throughout the massive conservation area from the entrance off SR 40.

## Hike Details

In the marked trail system off Lake Winona Road, hike the white trail directly west, then have the choice of hiking the red trail along the newly planted longleaf pine. From the very western tip of the red trail you can take the tram road north and hike directly across Deep Creek to the northern side of the property. Or hike west on the white trail and take the yellow trail loop. This high-elevation area (70 feet above sea level, extremely rare in Florida) affords views of longleaf pine in the rare sandhill habitat. Look for gopher tortoise burrows and a sandhill upland lake, an old sinkhole connected to the aquifer, in this beautiful natural area.

## 40. Lake George Conservation Area

**GPS:** Lat 29.324167, Long -81.533333

**Trailhead Directions:** From Palatka, take SR 17 south. When you reach the town of Seville, take CR 305 west. Turn south when you see the Lake George Conservation Area sign. The trailhead parking area and campsite is down this road.

**Size:** 11,794 acres

**Trail Distance:** 8.0 miles round-trip, trailhead to Barrs Landing

**Hiking Time:** Day hike

**Difficulty:** Easy

**Trail Surface:** Old logging roads with grassed surface

**Shade Level:** 0–25%

**Natural Communities:** Mesic flatwoods, depression marsh, wet flatwoods, frontage on Lake George

**Wildlife:** Hikers may see Florida black bear. Sherman's fox squirrel, one of the area's largest concentrations of bald eagles, American alligator, gopher tortoise, bobcat, hawk, heron, river otter, owl, osprey, feral hog, and white-tailed deer.

**Uses and Restrictions:** Hiking, restrooms, hunting, hunt check station, canoe launch, boat launch, group campsites, security residence. Property is part of Lake George Wildlife Management Area. Be sure to check hunting dates at www.myfwc.com before you hike. Family-friendly hiking.

**Trail Highlights:** Enjoy a view of Lake George at the end of the hike at Barrs Landing. Stay for a moment and think of the Native Americans who once lived here, and of William Bartram who once passed through before there were roads. Picture Marjorie Kinnan Rawlings navigating the lake, without a smartphone or GPS.

**Additional Hiking:** Ocala National Forest, Lake George Forest, Crescent Lake, Heart Island Conservation Area, Tiger Bay State Forest

Lake George is the second largest lake in Florida, behind Lake Okeechobee, measuring nearly 6 miles wide and 11 miles long, with an average depth of 8 feet. Lake George is part of the St. Johns River, which flows into the lake at the south-central end and exits to the north. Salt Springs, Silver Glen Springs, and Juniper Springs all flow into the lake. Many wading birds and freshwater fish can be seen in the area. In 1773, William Bartram described his boat on the lake: "My vessel at once diminished to a nut shell on the swelling seas, and at the distance of a few miles, must appear to the surprised observer as some aquatic animal, at intervals emerging from its surface." In 1933, Marjorie Kinnan Rawlings and friend Dessie Prescott Smith wrote about their experience boating on the St. Johns River north through Lake George, saying they veered away from the safe haven of the western border of the lake and traveled through the center of the lake, only to find whitecaps and waves, to their detriment. Hikers may hear thunder while on the property on a clear day. But it is not thunder. The US military uses Lake George as a target-practice bombing range.

Lake George Conservation Area was owned by a timber company and planted in fast-growing pine. The district is managing the property to work toward a more natural forested state, harvesting timber to reduce pine density. This property underwent heavy wildfire during the extreme drought of 1998 and reforestation has occurred where trees were burned. Hikers will experience wildlife sightings, views of Lake George, and hiking through the peace and quiet of mesic flatwoods interspersed with wetlands.

I have burned extensively on this property via horseback, on helicopter burns and wildfires, by ATV, and by foot and spent many a day and night on wildfire duty. I have seen the elusive Florida black bear here early in the mornings, and many are prevalent here. It was on this property that, while I was conducting a burn on horseback, my horse took off toward the barn, his home. Danny Mills, the cowboy I worked with and who lives near this property, yelled, "Grab the reins, Terri," as my helmet flew off and I held on for dear life! Just as quickly as "Fat Joe" took off, however, he slowed to a trot and all was well.

## Hike Details

From the Pine Island group campsite, hike back out to the road and head west until you can hike north into the property. Take the loop to hike through many acres of mesic flatwoods interspersed with wetlands, scrub, and thousands of planted pine being thinned to a more natural forested state. When you reach Barrs Hammock group campsite, take the spur trail to Lake George for a spectacular view of the lake and possibly catch sight of a bald eagle diving for fish. Or park at Barrs Hammock group campsite and hike west to the lake. Also, while at the district, I rewrote the driving guide for Lake George Conservation Area, which you can obtain online or at each kiosk. Take this with you while hiking the roads, or drive the roads to see more of the property.

# 41. Clark Bay Conservation Area

**GPS:** Lat 29.075278, Long -81.249444

**Trailhead Directions:** From I-95 near Daytona, take SR 92 west. Veer off on Old Daytona Road and the conservation area will be almost immediately on the north side of the road.

**Size:** 4,795 acres

**Trail Distance:** White blaze trail is 5 miles round-trip.

**Hiking Time:** Half-day hike

**Difficulty:** Easy

**Trail Surface:** Old logging roads with grassy surface or deep white sandy soil

**Shade Level:** 0–25%

**Natural Communities:** Wet and mesic flatwoods, scrub, floodplain swamp

**Wildlife:** Florida black bear, bald eagle, sandhill crane, gopher tortoise, wood stork, white-tailed deer, wild turkey, migratory songbirds, swallow-tailed kite, heron, wood duck, and a variety of snakes and lizards

**Uses and Restrictions:** Hiking, hunting. This property is part of the Tiger Bay Wildlife Management Area. Be sure to check hunting dates at www.myfwc.com before you hike. No motorized vehicles. Family-friendly hiking.

**Trail Highlights:** Hikers will experience the extremely rare scrub natural community. There are species of scrub plants adapted to poor-nutrient, dry sandy soil here, including rosemary, myrtle oak, saw palmetto, rusty staggerbush, and other species. Pause a moment in this rare and delicate Florida habitat as it is high and dry, prime Florida real estate and extremely endangered, a habitat many Florida locals have never seen.

**Additional Hiking:** Tiger Bay State Forest, Heart Island Conservation Area, Lake George Conservation Area, Crescent Lake Conservation Area, Tomoka Wildlife Management Area

Clark Bay Conservation Area is unique in that it contains high-elevation scrub on the western boundary ridge along with floodplain swamp, which covers most of the property. The property protects Deep Creek and the Little Haw creeks, which flow into the Crescent Lake and Haw Creek drainage basins, respectively. These eventually flow to the St. Johns River. The wildfires of 1998 that ran across much of northeast and north-central Florida contributed to the death of many trees here, so the property is undergoing reforestation. While passing through the mesic flatwoods, take note of the extremely rare scrub habitat, complete with rosemary, open spots of blindingly white sandy soil, and scrub oak species.

## Hike Details

From the entrance, hike the white trail, which is also an old logging road, into the property. Continue west on the white trail as it leaves the road and enters the white sandy soil of the scrub. Take the white loop either way through the mesic flatwoods and be sure to view Deep Creek in the northwest corner of the white loop.

## St. Johns River Water Management District Northwest Region

## 42. Lochloosa Wildlife Management Area

**GPS:** Lat 29.570278, Long -81.660278

**Trailhead Directions:** From Gainesville, take SR 20 east. Turn south on CR 325. Pass CR 346, pass the Marjorie Kinnan Rawlings House, and the entrance will be 100 yards on your left, at the entrance of Cross Creek Fire Station.

**Size:** 10,338 acres

**Trail Distance:** The hiking trail is about 2 miles round-trip. You can hike any road on the property for miles of hiking. You can drive the property with the drive guide map and accompanying descriptions, and you can hike Burnt Island, which is about a 2-mile loop.

**Hiking Time:** Hiking trail is 1 hour, but hiking on roads and on Burnt Island can take a day.

**Difficulty:** Easy

**Trail Surface:** Hiking trail and Burnt Island are sandy to dirt soils that may be seasonally flooded. The remainder of the property is old logging roads, the large ones graded, with compact soil and grass or leaf litter.

**Shade Level:** 0–25%

**Natural Communities:** Mesic flatwoods

**Wildlife:** This area is of regional significance for large populations of bald eagles, ospreys, wading birds, and other wetland-dependent species. Eighteen listed species live within the area, including wood stork, sandhill crane, black bear, fox squirrel, and eastern indigo snake.

**Uses and Restrictions:** Hiking, restrooms, handicapped access, picnic area, picnic shelter, observation point, fishing, security residence. No motorized vehicles. Family-friendly hiking.

**Trail Highlights:** Hikers can take the trail from the Cross Creek Volunteer Fire Station and hike to the lookout tower over the lake, or drive in and park at the fishing location. From there you can see the lake and hike Burnt Island. Or take a look at the drive guide map that hikers can find online or onsite at the kiosk. Drive past spot #3 and, before you reach the outparcel shown in light blue, park and hike south to Lake Lochloosa just east of the creek that flows south into the lake. It is here that you will find one of the most secret, private spots in north-central Florida, with views of Lake Lochloosa, avian wildlife, and deer walking through to get a drink from the lake.

**Additional Hiking:** Longleaf Flatwoods Reserve, Newnans Lake Conservation Area, Tuscawilla Preserve, Paynes Prairie Preserve State Park

Lochloosa Wildlife Management Area is footsteps from Cross Creek, Marjorie Kinnan Rawlings country. The area is still rural with large home sites between Lake Lochloosa and Orange Lake. The management area was owned by a timber company before being taken over by district management, so much of it is planted in fast-growing slash pine. Managers are working to thin the densely planted pine and managing for a more natural mesic flatwoods. The property is home to Burnt Island, a Jurassic Park type of natural place where you emerge from the forest to spectacular views of Lake Lochloosa. This island has a large population of bald eagle nests and more mesic flatwoods. Hikers will enjoy a backcountry hike to the lookout tower overlooking a large expanse of marsh. And you can park at the shelter from the US 301 entrance and walk on the dock of Lake Lochloosa and hike the circle around Burnt Island.

In December 2010 I was called to a large wildfire at Lochloosa. We drove up to black smoke billowing wide and high into the clouds. We spent that entire cold night in the dark burning out the marsh. We would freeze when on lookout, and then sweat as we put fire on the ground. We spent two weeks over the Christmas holiday working that fire. One day, when the winds changed, many volunteers came out to remove pine needles from the Marjorie Kinnan Rawlings house and stand with water hoses to protect this historic home site and barn. Later, I monitored the restoration of those fire lines while pregnant with my daughter.

## Hike Details

From the Cross Creek Volunteer Fire Station, take the white trail east into the property. You will be hiking through mesic flatwoods in planted pine that is being managed to become a more natural forest, with fewer trees. This trail is seasonally flooded or muddy, so bring the proper attire. Hike to the observation tower and absorb the view of the Lake Lochloosa marsh. Or drive in and park at the fishing location. From there you can see the lake and hike Burnt Island.

## 43. Longleaf Flatwoods Reserve

**GPS:** Lat 29.565556, Long -82.188889

**Trailhead Directions:** From Gainesville, take SR 20 east. Turn south on CR 325. The property is 2 miles south of SR 20 on the west side of the road.

**Size:** 2,856 acres

**Trail Distance:** 6.15 miles total

WHITE BLAZE TRAIL LOOP—1.4 miles; YELLOW BLAZE TRAIL LOOP—1.6 miles; YELLOW BLAZE SPUR TRAIL—0.25 miles; RED BLAZE TRAIL LOOP—1.9 miles; RED/WHITE CONNECTOR TRAIL—0.7 miles one way; WHITE/YELLOW CONNECTOR TRAIL—0.3 miles one way

**Hiking Time:** Day hike

**Difficulty:** Easy

**Trail Surface:** Compact soil and leaf litter, sandy soil in the sandhills

**Shade Level:** 0–25%

**Natural Communities:** Sandhill, mesic flatwoods, basin swamp

**Wildlife:** The conservation area provides habitat for numerous wildlife species, including Sherman's fox squirrel, gopher tortoise, pine woods tree frog, Florida blue centipede, white-tailed deer, wood duck, and wild turkey.

**Maps:** www.sjrwmd.com

**Uses and Restrictions:** Hiking, group campsite, observation point, security residence. No motorized vehicles. Family-friendly hiking.

**Trail Highlights:** Hike the red trail loop for elevations at 90 feet, rare in Florida, and note the sandhill wildlife species and flowering plants in this natural community dominated by longleaf pine.

**Additional Hiking:** Lochloosa Wildlife Management Area, Newnans Lake Conservation Area, Tuscawilla Preserve, Paynes Prairie Preserve State Park

Only 5 miles north of Cross Creek, Marjorie Kinnan Rawlings' old stomping grounds, this property still displays the relaxed backcountry atmosphere of Florida's yesteryear, yet it is only a few short minutes from Gainesville and the University of Florida. Alachua County and St. Johns River Water Management District purchased the parcel, and they work hard to agree on resource management, protecting the resources of Orange Creek and Ocklawaha Basins, which flow to the St. Johns River. The south corners protect watershed to the River Styx, a river surrounded by swamp about which Marjorie Kinnan Rawlings wrote (and referred to as the depths of hell) in her memoir, *Cross Creek*. Today hikers can see it much as it was more than 60 years ago as well as enjoy hiking through mesic flatwoods, strand swamp, and longleaf pine sandhill on this beautiful property.

I was involved in many prescribed burns on this property on ATV, on horseback, and by foot. I was part of a management team monitoring a wildfire that had been put out already but had to have water sprayed on smoldering spots so it wouldn't reignite. It was during this exact time that Florida black bear had been sighted in the county. I was there by myself and you can imagine the number of times I heard sticks crack and had to look around in all directions for the bear, how I kept driving in circles so the ATV would make noise, the many times I checked in with my husband to let him know that I hadn't been eaten! Also, during one "bioblitz" on the property, top biologists in the district came together to identify its plant and wildlife species. A land manager was identifying plants in a dome swamp, a circular wetland with towering cypress trees that create a hollow domelike setting, when he came across a diamondback rattlesnake. His shrieks and the ensuing echoes ringing out through the dome as he ran in the opposite direction made us buckle in laughter, as we nervously checked for snakes around us before continuing to laugh. This is one of my favorite properties and areas of the St. Johns River Water Management District as I think of what it would be like to live here as Marjorie Kinnan Rawlings did, just down the way.

## Hike Details

From the trailhead off CR 325, take the white trail right, to the north. Note remainders of mesic flatwoods that were clear-cut because of a pine beetle outbreak killing the trees. This area has been allowed to regenerate naturally and has great groundcover and wildflowers. Continue to the red/white connector and enjoy more mesic flatwoods that were planted in longleaf pine. Prescribed burns have kept groundcover low and healthy, allowing the longleaf pine to spurt up tall, out of its grass stage, very quickly. When you reach the graded road, take a left and hike west to the back corner of the property (or take a left at the camping sign to see the primitive group campsite). Find some huge longleaf pine cones. They are the size of cinderblocks and are an indicator of how large full-grown trees become! Take the turn on the red trail heading south and hike through restored sandhill. Here, oaks used to grow, shading out the groundcover. These were removed, allowing wiregrass and wildflowers on the forest floor, forage for the gopher tortoise, a keystone species, to flourish. On your right, before you reach the yellow trail, you will see scrubby flatwoods and blindingly white sandy soil, an area thick with scrub oaks. This is a rare natural community that most likely supported the endangered Florida scrub jay at one time.

Take a right on the yellow trail and then a right on the yellow trail spur loop to the observation point clearing at Palatka Pond. Hike back and take a right on the yellow trail to continue around the loop. You will see many species of wildflowers as the yellow trail hits the white/yellow trail, and it is on this portion of the trail where you will be hiking through mesic flatwoods and seasonally flooded trails on the palmetto-lined path. Take a right on the white trail toward the parking area and hike the outer edge of the pine beetle pine clear-cut to close out a fantastic Old Florida hike.

## 44. Newnans Lake Conservation Area

**GPS:** Lat 29.693611, Long -82.193333

**Trailhead Directions:** From Gainesville, take SR 26 east. After the Hatchet Creek bridge, the entrance to Hatchet Creek Tract will be on your left. Continue east from this point and then south on CR 234 to reach the North Tract, where the entrance will be on your right. Continue south through the town of Windsor and take a right on SE 16th Ave. to visit the South Tract.

**Size:** 6,504 acres

**Trail Distance:**

HATCHET CREEK TRACT—8.7 miles total if you take the southern fringe of the red trail

RED/YELLOW CONNECTOR TRAIL—0.2 miles; RED/WHITE CONNECTOR TRAIL—0.7 miles; WHITE BLAZE TRAIL—1.5 miles one way; YELLOW BLAZE TRAIL LOOP—3.1 miles round-trip; RED BLAZE TRAIL LOOP—1.8 miles round-trip

NORTH TRACT

RED CONNECTOR TRAIL LOOP—1.3 miles one way; WHITE/RED CONNECTOR TRAIL—1.4 miles one way; WHITE BLAZE TRAIL LOOP—3.3 miles round-trip; YELLOW BLAZE TRAIL LOOP—2.6 miles round-trip (open only to groups with camping permit)

SOUTH TRACT

WHITE BLAZE TRAIL—2.2 miles

**Hiking Time:** Day hike

**Difficulty:** Easy

Newnans Lake footbridge over Hatchet Creek

**Trail Surface:** Compact soil and leaf litter, sandy soil in the sandhills, graded roads on the north tract and much of Hatchet Creek tract
**Shade Level:** 25–50%
**Natural Communities:** Mesic flatwoods, sandhill, floodplain swamp
**Wildlife:** Sherman's fox squirrel, gopher tortoise, pine woods tree frog, Florida blue centipede, white-tailed deer, wood duck, wild turkey
**Uses and Restrictions:**
   HATCHET CREEK TRACT—Family-friendly hiking
   NORTH TRACT—Hiking, group camping area, and picnic pavilion that backs up to the beautiful Little Hatchet Creek
   SOUTH TRACT—Hiking, restrooms, picnic pavilion, playground,

boat ramp. No motorized vehicles. This property is also managed as Newnans Lake Wildlife Management Area. The west side of the property is closed to recreation during hunting dates. Be sure to check www.myfwc.com for hunting dates before you hike; however, you can hike the east side of the property during times of hunting.

**Trail Highlights:** Hikers will hike over Hatchet Creek five times on five wooden bridges. During times of high water, be sure to roll up your pants and prepare to slog through mud as some of the bridges are not wide enough to cover the floodplains of this high-flow creek.

**Additional Hiking:** Gum Root Park, Palm Point Nature Park, Lochloosa Wildlife Management Area, Longleaf Flatwoods Reserve, Paynes Prairie Preserve State Park, Barr Hammock Preserve

Just east of the Gainesville Regional Airport, this property protects the watershed of Hatchet Creek and the floodplain swamp of Newnans Lake. Newnans Lake was once utilized by Native Americans, as evidenced by an Eastside High School class finding of 101 dugout canoes here. During a drought period in 2000, the canoes were exposed in the drying lake bed, and they ranged in age from 500 to 5,000 years old.

The conservation area offers hiking on three large swaths of land north and east of the lake. Hikers will find five wooden bridges on the north side of SR 26, miles of hiking through mesic flatwoods south of SR 26, and a loop trail starting at the Owens-Illinois Park entrance after enjoying views of the lake at the park. Be on the lookout for Florida black bear that frequent this property—one sometimes hangs out at the mailbox at the entrance to the Hatchet Creek Tract parking area off SR 26.

While hiking for research for this section, I was traversing the southern border of the yellow loop trail and deep in thought when all of a sudden I heard a huge rustling on the right edge of the trail. Frozen in shock, confusion, and fear, I heard heavy pounding only 5 feet away accompanied by fast rustling through the saw palmetto. It seemed as though the ground shook from the weight. It was a Florida black bear, and you better believe my heart was racing! I have also given tours for toddlers at the Hatchet Creek Tract.

## Hike Details

Hatchet Creek Tract: Take the yellow gate to the right at the parking area kiosk and start hiking on the white trail to the east and then north. When you reach Bee Creek, traverse the first wooden bridge, then at a three-way intersection, head left. This hike is on the fringe of the wetlands of Bee Creek on your left and mesic flatwoods on your right. Be on the lookout for woodpeckers high in the trees. Continue hiking this ecotone, the area between uplands and wetlands where the two natural communities meet, and take a left when you reach the graded road again. Here you will cross wooden bridge number 2 spanning Hatchet Creek. Enjoy views of the dark, leaf-stained tannin water over a bed of white sandy soil. For a shorter hike, start looking for a left at the yellow trail immediately following the bridge. If you take a left on the graded road, you are off the yellow trail and have gone too far. Take a right on the yellow trail for a hike through some sandhills over graded roads as well as trails through more mesic flatwoods. Whether you hike north for the long loop or south to head back on the yellow trail, when you get close to the intersection of the white/yellow trail, keep your eyes peeled for the east turn to cross the creek so you don't miss it. Then hike across three more wooden foot bridges over the meandering Hatchet Creek. Follow the white trail until you come to the T-intersection; take a right on the white trail to backtrack to the parking area.

North Tract: This hike has options to make it short or long. Take the red trail through mesic flatwoods, then a low water crossing, then cross a channelized drainage area over a bridge made by an Eagle Scout. Continue on and connect to the W/R trail connector. Take a left on the graded road, then head north along the eastern fringe of the floodplains of the lake. Here you will find many wet spots as you head north. When you reach the main graded road, continue across it to hike the white trail loop, or take a left and make a pit stop at a shaded picnic area and hike the loop in the western direction. You will be hiking through a mesic flatwoods that is a working forest by funding agreement with the Florida Forest Service. The entire hike was planted in longleaf pine around 2010. If you are camping on the property and taking the yellow trail loop, hike over Little Hatchet Creek. Hike through floodplain swamp, which is seasonally flooded, before reaching more mesic flatwoods, then hike south and back west through the floodplain swamp. It is in these flatwoods where massive swaths of flooded areas can be found during much of the year. If you're up for mud-bogging, go for it, and keep your eyes out for water moccasins! I loved it during my research for the hike. Otherwise, stick to hiking on the east side of the property.

South Tract: Take in views of Newnans Lake (bring your boat if you have one!) and then start hiking from the kiosk trailhead next to the boat ramp (across the street from the parking area). Hike around the loop through mesic flatwoods and then cross the street. Continue hiking through the yellow gate, then take a right through longleaf pine that was planted around 2011 (I personally did the survival survey of these seedlings that year). As you traverse the floodplain swamp after crossing the creek, be sure to keep your eye out for blazes on trees. They are not marked well here, and it feels easy to get lost. Head north and know that you are not far from the south side of the playground of Owens-Illinois Park and just east of the lake.

## 45. Orange Creek Restoration Area

**GPS:** Lat 29.43, Long -82.063056

**Trailhead Directions:** From US 301 in Island Grove, take SE 219 east and you will see the trail entrance on the south side of the road. From US 301 in Citra, take CR 318 east and the entrance will be on your left just east of NE 52nd Court.

**Size:** 3,524 acres

**Trail Distance:**
WHITE BLAZE LOOP TRAIL—2.7 miles; RED BLAZE LOOP TRAIL—3.6 miles round-trip; YELLOW BLAZE LOOP TRAIL—1.8 miles; WHITE, RED, AND YELLOW TRAIL AS ONE LONG LOOP—7.5 miles. Half-day trip.

**Hiking Time:** 2–2.5 hours South Hike, 1–1.5 hours North Hike, half-day hike

**Difficulty:** Easy

**Trail Surface:** Beginning of white blaze trail and portions of red trail are soft sandy fire line. Other trails are grassy roads or packed leaf litter.

Orange Creek Restoration Area

**Shade Level:** 0–25%

**Natural Communities:** Planted longleaf pine, mesic flatwoods, strand swamp

**Wildlife:** Wild turkey, white-tailed deer, yellow rat snake, black racer snake

**Uses and Restrictions:** Hiking, observation platform on the white trail overlooking Orange Creek. Not family friendly.

**Trail Highlights:** Hiking on the north trail will lead you into Old Florida country with tall palmettos, wetlands, and flatwoods. On the south trail, be sure to make your way to the observation point at the lake.

**Additional Hiking:** Longleaf Flatwoods Reserve, Paynes Prairie, Barr Hammock Preserve, Lochloosa Wildlife Management Area, Newnans Lake Conservation Area

This property protects wetlands in the Orange Creek Basin and borders the north and south sides of Orange Creek. Orange Creek flows to the Ocklawaha River, which flows northeast and into the St. Johns River. The property was drained for agricultural purposes in the 1940s and farmed until 1998, when the district purchased the property. Wetlands have been restored and longleaf pine was replanted following the end of a cattle lease around 2010. The property is now managed to preserve the creek and its associated uplands.

## Hike Details

From the kiosk, head west to the break in the fence and follow the trail until it heads north. This segment is boundary fire line and a bit soft. Hike into longleaf pine planted around 2010. Wind through hardwood hammock with sabal palmettos and oaks until you take a right just before the Orange Creek levee. You will shortly head south and pass the security residence. Stop and use the observation platform on your left past the storage area to overlook a deeper, open water area in the Orange Creek floodplain. Continuing on the white trail, you will hike a short distance on the main road before veering left to hike the levee of the Orange Creek floodplain. After turning east you will reach the beginning of the red trail, where you can hike the white loop back to the parking area or continue on the red trail. On the red trail, be sure to veer to the left at the fenced area to stay on the trail. The hike continues on for a good distance along hammock areas that border the Orange Creek wetlands.

With only one jog in the trail you will continue until you reach the yellow trail connector, where you can choose to take the red loop back to the parking area or continue on the yellow trail. At the yellow trail connector you will cross a wetland strand with a deeper wetland area on your right. Listen for frogs and stop to notice floating wetland plants. The trail continues east until you take a left to hike on a wide grassy path up to the levee. At the levee, stop to look out over the Orange Creek floodplains. This area was once farmland divided by dikes, levees, and ditches and is now functioning as a restored marsh. Take a right down the levee and continue on through an oak hammock and then a mesic flatwoods with pine, palmetto, and gallberry. Follow the loop around until you complete the loop back at the wetland area. You will rehike the yellow connector trail and then take a left onto the red trail to complete the red loop, heading back to the parking area. Stay to the left once you hit the white trail to continue to the parking area. This segment utilizes an old levee to cross a wetland area. Cross the main road once you reach it, then take the left to reach the parking area again.

North Trail: Head toward the kiosk to pick up a map if needed. Then choose which loop you'd like to hike first. I took a right to hike the red-blazed loop. This hike traverses low-lying shaded areas while winding in and out of higher planted longleaf pine areas of "Old Florida" cattle pasture. Once you reach the red/white connector trail, continue straight to hike onto the white loop trail. This trail takes you through more planted longleaf pine while meandering through various shaded sweetgum thickets. At the northernmost portion of the white trail you will cross an entrance road that leads to a campsite. Continue on and just before you reach the red/white connector trail again, you will notice a cemetery on your right. Take a right on the R/W connector and then another right onto the red trail to continue back to the parking area.

## St. Johns River Water Management District Southwest Region

### 46. Emeralda Marsh Conservation Area

**GPS:** Lat 28.886667, Long -81.790556
**Trailhead Directions:** From SR 19, just south of Ocala National Forest, take CR 452 west. Veer onto Goose Prairie Road and head west. After a series of 90-degree turns, the property entrance will be on your left.
**Size:** 7,068 acres
**Trail Distance:** Approximately 5 miles
**Hiking Time:** Day hike
**Difficulty:** Easy
**Trail Surface:** Graded levee roads
**Shade Level:** 0%

**Natural Communities:** Floodplain marsh and open water

**Wildlife:** Avian species are abundant here, both resident and migratory. For example, a population of eastern greater sandhill cranes winters in the area, and Florida sandhill crane residents can be found here. Thousands of ring-necked ducks and lesser numbers of wood ducks and hooded mergansers as well as large flocks of white pelicans and other waterfowl species can be seen in the area. Listed species include bald eagle, wood stork, limpkin, and snowy egret. The property plays host to one of the highest concentrations of alligators in central Florida.

**Uses and Restrictions:** Hiking, hunting, handicapped access, inclement weather shelter, observation platform, security residence. No motorized vehicles. The property is part of the Emeralda Marsh Public Small Game Hunt Area. Be sure to check www.myfwc.com for hunting dates prior to hiking. Not friendly for family hiking.

**Trail Highlights:** Hike to the observation tower to enjoy majestic views of Emeralda Marsh and waterfowl frequenting the area.

**Additional Hiking:** Ocala National Forest, Sunnyhill Restoration Area, Lake Apopka Restoration Area

Emeralda Marsh is found between Lake Griffin and Lake Yale along the Ocklawaha River. Historically the Emeralda Marsh consisted of 10,000 acres of wetlands that filtered water for the surrounding lakes, Haines Creek, and the Ocklawaha River. Farming operations drained the wetlands and utilized the nutrient-rich muck soils for crops. Pesticides, fertilizers, and oxidation-reduction of the muck soils caused degradation of the wetlands and the water. The St. Johns River Water Management District purchased almost half the area and is restoring the area through a system of plants cleaning the water, alum treatment where a chemical binds all the pesticides and fertilizers and the weight makes it fall to the bottom and out of the water column, and removal of the exotic plant, hydrilla, which clogs up the water column and shades the water. Wetland scientists once tested removal of hydrilla with a large piece of heavy equipment, called a loader, to remove its long roots and leaves from the water. They placed the hydrilla in a large sock which they placed on the bank in the hot sun to decompose. Hiking at Emeralda Marsh is on the levee and takes visitors out into the marsh to view thousands of avian species. This property has a guided interpretive map for driving for those in need of handicapped access and those interested in more information about the history of the property.

## Hike Details

This is a loop hike if you don't mind walking back to the beginning via the roadside, or take two cars with a partner. Hike in on the south entrance where there is a parking area. Hike the levee in a square fashion and be sure to stop at the observation tower for views of the marsh and Lake Griffin and the associated waterfowl, migrating and resident avian species, alligators, and other wildlife that may be on the levee.

## 47. Lake Apopka Restoration Area

**GPS:**

> CLAY ISLAND TRACT—Lat 28.674312, Long -81.707364
> NORTH SHORE TRAILHEAD—Lat 28.704448, Long -81.673086
> WILDLIFE DRIVE—Lat 28.669183, Long -81.561540
> MAGNOLIA PARK—Lat 28.635581, Long -81.550500

**Trailhead Directions:** To access the Clay Island entrance, from Orlando, take US 441 north to Zellwood; go west on Jones Avenue, then south on SR 448A to CR 48 and west on Ranch Road. If traveling from the town of Astatula, take CR 48 east to Ranch Road. Take Ranch Road south, then turn west on Peeples Drive, then south on Carolyn Lane to the parking area. See the latitude and longitude points for locations of all entrances.

**Size:** 20,009 acres

**Trail Distance:**

> MAGNOLIA PARK TRAILHEAD TO CLAY ISLAND TRAILHEAD—14.6 miles; MAGNOLIA PARK TRAILHEAD TO HISTORIC PUMP HOUSE—4.0 miles; NORTH SHORE TRAILHEAD TO HISTORIC PUMP HOUSE—7.5 miles; NORTH SHORE TRAILHEAD TO CLAY ISLAND TRAILHEAD—5.1 miles; CLAY ISLAND TRAIL LOOP (WHITE BLAZE)—5.8 miles. Longest hike/bike: 14.6 miles.

**Hiking Time:** Longer than a day hike if you hike through from east to west

**Difficulty:** Easy

**Trail Surface:** Levee roads

**Shade Level:** 0–25%

**Natural Communities:** Mostly managed marsh with some mesic flatwoods and pine plantation

**Wildlife:** Lake Apopka has improved so much in water quality that it has become one of the best birding areas in the state. A total of 362 birds are on the bird list here. Other wildlife include alligator, turtle, river otter, bobcat, and coyote.

**Uses and Restrictions:** Hiking, information kiosk, restrooms, picnic shelter, observation point, observation platform, field station. Motorized vehicles allowed only on the driving guide route. Be sure to follow length, speed limit, and trailer restrictions as noted in the drive guide on the SJRWMD website. Family-friendly biking or short out-and-back hikes.

**Trail Highlights:** From CR 48, drive in on Ranch Road to view endangered Florida scrub jays that may be seen sitting on the fence or grassy roadside. Continue to the Clay Island entrance to visit four observation towers on this loop hike through the marsh flow-way.

**Additional Hiking:** Sunnyhill Restoration Area, Emeralda Marsh Restoration Area, Ocklawaha Restoration Area, Wekiwa Springs State Park

Lake Apopka was once the bass fishing capital of the United States. Following World War II in the 1940s, farming was encouraged to help with reconstruction, and the north shore of Lake Apopka was one of the areas slated for farming. The marshes were cleared, drained, and diked to utilize nutritious muck soils for farming operations and to regulate water flow. After many years of farming, the lake turned a pea-green color from algal blooms resulting from pesticides and fertilizers flowing directly into the lake. Bass that create nurseries in the submergent vegetation could no longer live in the lake. Without the north shore floodplains to filter water flowing into the lake, the lake was essentially dying. The lake was one of the most polluted in the state.

In 1996, the St. Johns River Water Management District was mandated by the state to purchase the farmlands on the north shore. Each farm was purchased and taken out of production. The remaining soils were extremely toxic. Following research on soil remediation and implementing a plan, portions of the north shore were allowed to reflood. This caused toxic soils to be resuspended in the water column, and avian wildlife that flocked to this newly formed wetland ate fish from this extremely toxic area. A huge bird die-off ensued, jail time was considered, and water management district field staff witnessed thousands of birds dying slow deaths.

The shore was quickly drained again to dissuade the birds from coming. This time the soil was flipped so the toxic areas were buried before slowly being allowed to flood again. Today the north shore marsh continues to be treated through a series of marsh flow-ways where wetland plants soak up excess nutrients and alum is applied to allow nutrients to attract to each other and fall to the bottom. Other actions are being applied to manage the lake. The north shore wetlands are recovering, and avian wildlife have literally flocked to the area, with hundreds of birds visiting the area and overwintering here. A true wildlife success story.

In spring of 2015 a multiuse trail was completed, connecting the east shore to the west shore, bringing closure for wetland scientists and signaling a big victory for hikers, bikers, and nature enthusiasts alike.

I am honored to have written the management plan for this property, the first after the bird die-off. I have conducted legislative tours here as well as endangered plant surveys to restore scrub and scrub jay habitat and have also conducted prescribed burns here.

## Hike Details

Try a through-hike via foot or bike by starting at the Clay Island entrance, and view Florida scrub jays on your way in on Ranch Road. Hike east and visit the first observation tower before dead-ending into the lake. Hike north, east, then south before you head east and fringe the lake boundary. The hike will continue around to the east side of the lake until you exit at Magnolia Park trailhead. Try the white trail loop for a shorter hike.

## 48. Lake Norris Conservation Area

**GPS:** Lat 28.913333, Long -81.543611

**Trailhead Directions:** From SR 19 in Eustis, take CR 44 east. Travel north on CR 439 and then head east on CR 44A. From here travel north on Hart Ranch Road to the west entrance, or go farther east and travel north on Lake Norris Road for the eastern parking area.

**Size:** 3,660 acres

**Trail Distance:** 9.2 total miles

WHITE BLAZE TRAIL—5.6 miles round-trip; YELLOW BLAZE TRAIL—1.8 miles round-trip; RED CONNECTOR TRAIL—1.8 miles one way

**Hiking Time:** Day hike

**Difficulty:** Medium

**Trail Surface:** Sandy soil, compact soil with leaf litter

**Shade Level:** 25–50%

**Natural Communities:** Hardwood swamp, scrub, planted pine, improved pasture

**Wildlife:** Florida black bear, bald eagle, gopher tortoise, coyote, burrowing owl, osprey, alligator, snakes

**Uses and Restrictions:** Hiking, canoe launch, boat launch (with day permit), observation point, security residence. No motorized vehicles. Family-friendly hiking and canoeing.

**Contact:** Lake County Water Authority, including canoe rentals and camping reservations, (352) 343-3777

**Trail Highlights**: Hike from the eastern entrance on the white trail and view the peaceful flow of Black Water Creek. Continue on to the observation point at Lake Norris and hike out to the lake. Hikers will be rewarded with Old Florida views of the lake with its cypress-lined border and bald eagles nesting in season.

**Additional Hiking:** Ocala National Forest, Seminole State Forest, Lower Wekiva River Preserve State Park

Lake Norris Conservation Area is a motley mixture of Black Water Creek, Black Water Swamp, cattle pasture on a hill that reaches 95 feet in elevation, a mitigation bank restoration project, and an upland fringe reaching upward of 130 feet above sea level. Hikers will find spectacular views of Lake Norris and its Old Florida buttressed cypress trees on the lake border and also see Black Water Creek, a creek bordered by hardwood swamp that is a tributary of the Wekiva River. Be on the lookout for Florida black bear as this property is a travel corridor between the Ocala National Forest to the northwest and the Wekiva River conservation areas to the southwest.

## Hike Details

Bring two cars and hike from one side of the property to the other. From the eastern entrance, take the white trail. After taking in the quiet Black Water Creek, hike along the hardwood swamp wetlands until you reach Lake Norris. Hike out to the lake and bring your camera for classic Old Florida views of the cypress-bordered lake. You may see bald eagles and osprey. Canoes are available for rent here, and an old barn was made into a group camp shelter. Continue on the white trail and notice the planted pine and the cattle pasture. You may see cows and will see a beautifully manicured pasture, dotted with Russian thistle and cactus, managed by the cattle lessee. Merge onto the red trail at the end of the white trail loop.

At the red trail, hike along the bluff bordering the old phosphate mining borrow pit. Areas of forested mesic flatwoods will be on your right. Continue hiking south into old sandhill at an elevation of 130 feet, one of the highest points in Florida.

## 49. Ocklawaha Prairie Restoration Area

**GPS:** Lat 29.106944, Long -81.904722

**Trailhead Directions:**

MAIN ENTRANCE—From SR 19 in the Ocala National Forest, take SR 40 west. Head south on CR 314A and then take a right and head back northwest on SE 137th Avenue Road.

CHERNOBYL ENTRANCE—From SR 19 in the Ocala National Forest, take SR 40 west. Head south on CR 314A and take a right heading south on CR 464C. Head south a small distance and take a right into the parking area.

**Size:** 6,230 acres

**Trail Distance:** 6.7 total miles

UPLAND TRAIL LOOP (WHITE BLAZE)—3.4 miles; CHERNOBYL TRAIL (RED BLAZE)—3.8 miles

**Hiking Time:** Day hike

**Difficulty:** Easy

**Trail Surface:** Levee roads in the main entrance and white sandy soil with pine litter in Chernobyl Memorial Forest

**Shade Level:** 0–25%

**Natural Communities:** Floodplain marsh, planted pine, sandhill

**Wildlife:** The wetlands provide habitat for waterfowl and wading birds such as herons and egrets. The uplands provide habitat for the gopher tortoise, gray fox, bobcat, black bear, and resident and migrating sandhill crane.

**Uses and Restrictions:** Hiking, picnic area, restrooms, camping area, boat launch, hunting, hunt check station. No motorized vehicles. The property is part of the Ocklawaha Prairie Small Game Hunt Area. Hikers should check hunting dates at www.myfwc.com before hiking. Family-friendly hiking around the levee.

**Trail Highlights:** Hike the levee trail around the wetlands for majestic views of the marsh and the Kyle Young Canal, which is the diverted and channelized Ocklawaha River.

**Additional Hiking:** Sunnyhill Restoration Area, Emeralda Marsh Restoration Area, Lake Apopka Restoration Area, Ocala National Forest, Marjorie Harris Carr Greenway

The district purchased this property to restore wetlands within the Upper Ocklawaha River Basin. Similar to the other district properties in the chain of lakes area, Ocklawaha Prairie was drained and water diverted to the channelized Ocklawaha River for farming the nutrient-rich muck soils of the wetlands. After farm levees were graded down to field level, woody vegetation removed, muck dredged from old river channel, farm ditches filled, prescribed burning reintroduced, and wetlands connected to the channelized river, wetlands have been restored to a more natural level and waterfowl have returned. The area is so majestic and relaxing, a healing rehabilitation center has set up shop in the old farm worker houses, and patients can enjoy the quiet, peaceful scenery and hike on the levees of the Ocklawaha wetlands. Southwest of the main hiking area is the Chernobyl Memorial Forest, which provides upland hiking through planted pine and sandhill and is dedicated to those who lost their lives in the 1986 nuclear disaster in Ukraine. The planting of trees is said to symbolize rebirth, renewal, and restoration.

I wrote a management plan for this property, have conducted legislative tours here, and conducted prescribed burns.

## Hike Details

From the main entrance, hike on the white trail. At the first intersection, head north to hike the white trail loop. This upland trail traverses mesic flatwoods. Or from the first intersection in the white trail, take a left and head to the levee and the observation tower over the marsh. Here you can hike the levee trail around the marsh. At the Chernobyl entrance, hike in on the red trail through thickly planted longleaf pine. Hike north on the red trail; when you head slightly west away from the border line you will reach elevations of 65 feet above sea level to gain views of restored sandhill with swaying wiregrass. Head west at the dead end and hike along the floodplain swamp with swamp bay and other wetland trees. Hike south and enjoy the views as you return to the entrance.

## 50. Sunnyhill Restoration Area

**GPS:** Lat 28.992222, Long -81.8325 (main entrance at Sunnyhill Blue House)

**Trailhead Directions:**

MAIN ENTRANCE AT SUNNYHILL BLUE HOUSE—From SR 19 south of Ocala National Forest take CR 42 west. The property entrance will be on your right, before you reach the Ocklawaha River. Drive in and pass the first two buildings. Take a left and park behind the Blue House.

NORTH ENTRANCE—From SR 19 south of Ocala National Forest, take CR 42 west. Turn right on SE 182nd Avenue Road and travel north. The parking area will be the second parking area on your left.

SOUTH ENTRANCE—From SR 19 south of Ocala National Forest, take CR 42 west. Turn right on SE 182nd Avenue Road and travel north. The parking area will be the first parking area on your left.

MOSS BLUFF LOCK AND DAM ENTRANCE—North Entrance: From SR 19 south of Ocala National Forest take CR 42 west. Turn right on SE 182nd Avenue Road and travel north. Take a left on CR 314A. Take a left on 464C. Take a left into the Moss Bluff Lock and Dam County Park entrance.

**Size:** 4,191 acres

**Trail Distance:**

BLUE HOUSE TRAILHEAD TO OBSERVATION TOWER—0.8 miles; BLUE HOUSE TRAILHEAD TO SOUTH TRAILHEAD—3.0 miles; YELLOW TRAIL LOOP FROM RED TRAIL—3.6 miles; RED TRAIL LOOP FROM NORTH TRAILHEAD—4.0 miles; BLUE HOUSE TRAILHEAD TO MOSS BLUFF TRAILHEAD—7.4 miles; NORTH TRAILHEAD TO GROUP CAMPSITE—0.8 miles

**Hiking Time:** Day hike

**Difficulty:** Easy

**Trail Surface:** Levee with grass-covered trail, dirt paths covered with leaf litter

**Shade Level:** 0–25%

**Natural Communities:** Floodplain marsh, floodplain swamp, scrubby flatwoods, planted pine, sinkhole

**Wildlife:** Glossy and white ibis, little blue and tri-colored herons, great and snowy egrets, and many other wading birds. The area is a huge draw for migrating sandhill cranes. Red-tailed and red-shouldered hawks, osprey, and three owl species can be found at Sunnyhill. Florida black bear, river otter, and bobcat.

**Uses and Restrictions:** Hiking, picnic area, restrooms, observation platform, inclement weather shelter, group camping area, two boat launches, security residence. No motorized vehicles. Family-friendly hiking, but beware of lack of shade on the levee.

**Trail Highlights:** Hiking from the north entrance off SE 182nd Avenue Road will lead to oak- and palmetto-covered paths, and hikers are sure to see a Florida black bear. The Sunnyhill levee provides waterfront views of the channelized river and the historic Ocklawaha River floodplain.

**Additional Hiking:** Ocklawaha Prairie Restoration Area, Emeralda Marsh Restoration Area, Lake Apopka Restoration Area, Ocala National Forest

This property was purchased to restore wetlands associated with the Ocklawaha River. In the early 1940s, farmers drained the historic Ocklawaha River floodplain and actually diverted the river to a channel west of the river with an associated levee to prevent flooding of the farms and to utilize the nutrient-rich muck soils for farming. This conversion resulted in highly degraded wetlands, with poor water quality in the new river channel, which connects back to the original river channel on the north side of this property at Moss Bluff Lock and Dam. The district purchased the property in 2008. Water control–structure alterations and levee improvements allow water flow into the old river floodplains for better balance of wetlands and wildlife management with flood control and water storage. Hikers can follow the levee along the channelized river for waterfront and wetland views as well as hike in the upland areas that fringe the eastern border of the historic river channel.

I have written the land management plan for this property, conducted many prescribed burns, and given a legislative management tour. The Sunnyhill Blue House was once my home base and I hosted many recreational public meetings there. On one burn, a coworker and I were asked to take some equipment out to a burn. I thought we would be coming back to the Blue House and had no idea the fire location was miles and miles north. I had to embarrassingly ask that someone take me back to get my helmet and protective gear, holding up the start of the burn!

## Hike Details

From the Blue House, head west and up onto the levee to hike north. The levee is a wide grassy path that is stroller friendly. It takes you along the channelized Ocklawaha River and has views of the old Ocklawaha Riverbed wetlands to the east and the undeveloped SJRWMD Kohn Conservation Easement to the west, across the channel. Or hike east from behind the Blue House to the white shadowy path to the white trail that leads to the wide and grassy sinkhole. Or hike behind the Blue House to the white trail and then north on the white/yellow trail connector. It will lead to the yellow loop trail along an interior, smaller levee and into the pine plantation. From the yellow trail continue on to the red loop trail, through mesic hammock and scrubby flatwoods. The interior levee on the western boundary of the red loop overlooks floodplain swamp bordering the channelized Ocklawaha River.

## St. Johns River Water Management District
## South Central Region

### 51. Buck Lake Conservation Area

**GPS:** Lat 28.666111, Long -80.888889

**Trailhead Directions:** From I-95 take SR 46 west and then an almost immediate right for the first entrance. For the second entrance, continue on SR 46 past Hatbill Road; after the curve in the road the entrance will be on the right.

**Size:** 9,606 acres

**Trail Distance:**
EAST TO WEST TRAILHEAD, ONE WAY, LOWER ROUTE—7.6 miles; RED LOOP FROM WEST TRAILHEAD AND RETURN—8.4 miles; WHITE LOOP FROM EAST TRAILHEAD AND RETURN—8.6 miles; YELLOW LOOP—1.2 miles; YELLOW LOOP FROM EAST TRAILHEAD AND RETURN—2 miles; BUCK LAKE OBSERVATION TOWER FROM WEST TRAILHEAD AND RETURN—2 miles

**Hiking Time:** Half-day hike

**Difficulty:** Easy

**Trail Surface:** Dark soil that may be seasonally flooded on the west side of the property; deep sandy soil on the east side

**Shade Level:** 0–25%

**Natural Communities:** Floodplain marsh, salt flats, floodplain forest

**Wildlife:** Endangered Florida scrub jay, gopher tortoise, bald eagle, river otter, white-tailed deer, woodpecker, owl, bobcat, American alligator, wild turkey, heron, egret, and red fox

**Uses and Restrictions:** Hiking, group campsite, primitive campsite, boat ramp, observation platform, hunting. During hunting season, the property is managed as Buck Lake Wildlife Management Area. Be sure to check www.myfwc.com for hunting dates. Call ahead for drive-in permit to launch boat near observation platform. Family-friendly hiking.

**Trail Highlights:** Hike the 8.6 miles to the white trail loop and back to experience hiking through scrub and scrubby flatwoods. You may see some endangered Florida scrub jays coming out to see who is visiting their neighborhood! Or hike from the west trailhead 2 miles to the observation tower and visit Buck Lake and the surrounding wetlands.

**Additional Hiking:** Tosohatchee Wildlife Management Area, St. Johns National Wildlife Refuge, Seminole Ranch Conservation Area, Orlando Wetlands Park, Charles Bronson State Forest, Little Big Econ State Forest, Salt Lake Wildlife Management Area

Hikers are in for a treat while hiking Buck Lake Conservation Area. A mix of uplands due to a sandy ridge on the east side and wetlands on the west surrounding stunning, untouched Buck Lake, this property has much to see. The rare, endangered Florida scrub jay lives here and is closely managed by the district burning scrub and scrubby flatwoods on eight-year rotations. By this management strategy, trees won't grow tall enough to create perches for predatory birds and the oaks will be short, with open sandy spots between where the birds can cache their acorns. Gopher tortoise are also abundant here, their burrows supporting hundreds of species of animals, making them imperative to the ecosystem, a keystone species. The west side of the property boasts the wetland marshes of Buck Lake. Hikers can perch in the observation tower and witness white-tailed deer walking to and from the lake for water, a view nothing short of an African savanna.

This is one of my favorite properties because of the beauty of Buck Lake and the unique Florida scrub jay habitat. I also loved burning on a burn managed by Pete Henn, former land manager here. Surfer dude with a love of wildlife, he has done hundreds of careful and calculated burns to maintain habitat for wildlife, yet each of his burns seemed wild and untamed, as Central Florida nature can be. I have done vegetation surveys, pushing and climbing through scraggly, scratching oak scrub as high as my head, conducted legislative tours, and written a management plan for this property.

## Hike Details

If you have two cars, drop one off at the east trailhead and drive back to the west trailhead to park. Hike in on the red trail and stop to take in the view of Buck Lake at the observation tower. Continue on the red trail to the white trail and its scrubby flatwoods and scrub. Listen for the shushing of Florida scrub jays as you hike, and be on the lookout for gopher tortoise burrows. Continue hiking to the east trailhead through scrub for a nice half-day hike through many Florida natural communities!

## 52. Canaveral Marshes Conservation Area

**GPS:** Lat 28.545556, Long -80.896389

**Trailhead Directions:** From I-95 in Brevard County take SR 50 west. The parking area will be on the south side of SR 50 before you reach the St. Johns River.

**Size:** 12,644 acres

**Trail Distance:** Approximately 5 miles

**Hiking Time:** 2 hours

**Difficulty:** Easy

**Trail Surface:** Compact soil with leaf litter

**Shade Level:** 0–25%

**Natural Communities:** Floodplain marsh

**Wildlife:** Migratory and resident wading birds and waterfowl, American alligator

**Uses and Restrictions:** Hiking, picnic tables, shelter, group campsite, primitive campsite, restroom, observation point, security residence. No motorized vehicles. Not friendly for family hiking.

**Trail Highlights:** Experience the wide open space and big sky of the St. Johns River marshes.

**Additional Hiking:** Tosohatchee Wildlife Management Area, St. Johns National Wildlife Refuge, Seminole Ranch Conservation Area, Orlando Wetlands Park

Canaveral Marshes protects the floodplains of the St. Johns River as it continues to slowly meander north. Here the river is highly discernible, yet the river drops only 5 feet along this property's 25 miles of St. Johns River. Shoreline, marshes, and wetlands are still wide expanses. You may see land managers burning the marshes by helicopter and airboat on this property. There are uplands on the north side of the property off SR 50, and Florida Trail Association has established hiking-only trails here.

It was on this property that I did my first prescribed burn via airboat. We flowed out into the water and a helicopter dropped ping-pong balls of fire onto the marsh grasses above the water. We ensured the fire stayed within the fire line by boating along the edge of the line and pushing the vegetation down with a tool with a broomstick handle and rectangular rubber flap on the bottom. With black smoke rising into the shaded sky, the helicopter flying, radios buzzing, it was as though we were on a military operation in a war zone. Unbelievably exciting with no fear from this city girl!

## Hike Details

From the parking area the trail heads east then south, east and south for a long jog along the marsh before looping back.

## 53. Econlockhatchee Sandhills Conservation Area

**GPS:** Lat 28.587336, Long -81.155874
**Trailhead Directions:** From SR 50 in Christmas, in Orange County, head west. Turn north on Tanner Road. Take a right on CR 420 and the conservation area will be on the north side of the road.
**Size:** 706 acres

**Trail Distance:**
RED BLAZE TRAIL—0.8 miles one way; YELLOW BLAZE TRAIL
LOOP—1.7 miles
**Hiking Time:** 1 hour
**Difficulty:** Easy
**Trail Surface:** Sandy soil
**Shade Level:** 0–25%
**Natural Communities:** Sandhill, mesic flatwoods, xeric hammock,
floodplain forest
**Wildlife:** White-tailed deer, wild turkey, gopher tortoise, wide variety of
birds
**Uses and Restrictions:** Hiking. No motorized vehicles. Family-friendly
hiking.
**Trail Highlights:** Enjoy the carpet of wiregrass at the beginning of the
hike and the views of sandhill in the yellow loop. The fringe of the
yellow loop boasts views of the 50-foot-high xeric hammock of oaks
with carpet of deer lichen in this dry area that then grades down to
the Econlockhatchee River.
**Additional Hiking:** Hal Scott Regional Preserve and Park, Seminole
Ranch Conservation Area

The Econlockhatchee Sandhills property is small compared with other
District properties, but what it lacks in size, it makes up for in views.
The property protects two sides of the Econlockhatchee River and its
floodplains, and hikers can view the river at 20 feet above sea level and
then hike up to 50 feet above sea level in the sandhills and xeric hammock habitat. Millions of tourists and locals visit developed, touristy
Disney World each year, not knowing this natural, free adventure is just
a few miles east.

This property was purchased while I was a land resource planner. I
had the privilege of sitting at the table with the landowner's represen-
tative along with our own Robert Christianson, math genius and land
acquisition extraordinaire at the St. Johns River Water Management
District, as they negotiated the conservation/development boundary.
I sat silently and learned how he successfully negotiated, inch by inch,
using logic and simple explanation, for more land that would be forever

protected. I worked with the land manager to learn the property, learn the wildlife, develop the land management plan, write the board memo, and present the plan for management to the governing board, where it was approved for the next 10 years.

## Hike Details

Hike from the parking area along the meandering red trail through naturally regenerating longleaf pine. This area has a beautiful carpet of wiregrass on the forest floor, a prescribed burner's dream! Hike across the power line trail (watch your step) and transition to the yellow loop. The interior of this yellow loop was harvested for pine. It will be managed with prescribed burning to maintain the sandhill habitat and prevent oaks from moving in and preventing groundcover from growing on the forest floor. Be sure to stop at the two circular sandhill depressions filled with clear sparkling water flowing up from the Floridan Aquifer.

## 54. Hal Scott Regional Preserve and Park

**GPS:** Lat 28.619167, Long -80.964722

**Trailhead Directions:** From the intersection of SR 50 and CR 520 in Orange County, head south on CR 520. Take a right on Maxim Parkway, left on Bancroft Boulevard, right on Oberly Parkway, and south on Dallas Boulevard. The property entrance will be on the west side of Dallas Boulevard.

**Size:** 9,387 acres

**Trail Distance:**
WHITE BLAZE TRAIL LOOP—4.3 miles round-trip; YELLOW BLAZE TRAIL LOOP—6.3 miles round-trip (from Yellow/White trail intersect); RED BLAZE TRAIL LOOP—6.1 miles one way (from Red/ White trail intersect)

**Hiking Time:** Day hike or shorter

**Difficulty:** Easy

**Trail Surface:** Dark soil with pine needle and leaf litter

**Shade Level:** 0–25%

**Natural Communities:** Floodplain marsh, mesic flatwoods

**Wildlife:** The endangered red-cockaded woodpecker makes its home here in old longleaf pine, with the closely monitored help of district staff. Other wildlife sightings may include bald eagle, sandhill crane, gopher tortoise, bobcat, river otter, and indigo snake.

**Uses and Restrictions:** Hiking, group campsite, primitive campsite, security residence, inclement weather shelter. No motorized vehicles. Family-friendly hiking.

**Trail Highlights:** Experience what Old Florida looked like when buggies pulled by horses could easily traverse the forests because of the low groundcover and sparse trees. It was a time when wildfire was allowed to burn yearly and run to the nearest river or creek, and pines were yet to be planted densely in lines. Also be on the lookout for the shy red-cockaded woodpecker, a rare sighting in the state.

**Additional Hiking:** Long Branch Park, Pine Lily Preserve, Econlockhatchee Sandhills Conservation Area

Hal Scott is one of the most well-managed and well-manicured conservation areas in the state of Florida. Because the area is home to many families of endangered red-cockaded woodpeckers, prescribed burning must be conducted on a strict four-year rotation or less to keep underbrush down. This way wildfire can be prevented and the old longleaf pines, prime for heart rot and easy for the delicate woodpeckers to excavate for nests, will not burn. Hikers will see a mosaic of flatwoods and wetlands. Longleaf pine is scattered, many encircled with white paint to mark the trees housing woodpeckers.

In an effort to cross-train, I had the opportunity to help prepare for the endangered red-cockaded woodpecker nesting season on this property. I climbed one of the white-banded trees with a narrow metal ladder, a harness, and a type of rope that went around me and around the tree to help hold my body onto the tree while I climbed the ladder. It was a 40- or 50-foot, skinny, swaying pine. I climbed and climbed, not sure if I would live, especially when I reached the height of the nesting cavity and looked down. Maria Zondervan, endangered species manager extraordinaire, was down below. I trusted her with my life as I did all my coworkers. Upon reaching the top, I removed nests left by other species that had taken over. The tree was cleared and ready for the tiny birds to create a warm, cozy home in hopes that new eggs would result in viable juveniles. What a helpful activity for this rare bird and one of the most exciting/thrilling things I have ever done!

## Hike Details

Hike in on the white trail from Dallas Boulevard and head south and then west on the white trail. View the longleaf pine and flatwoods groundcover and take in any flatwoods wildflowers, something usually in bloom year-round. Take the yellow trail west and cross the mighty Econlockhatchee River. Stop to check for fish, frogs, or turtles in the river. Head south to check out the two primitive campsites and take the red loop around back to cross the Econlockhatchee. Head back to the parking area or continue hiking north on the red loop trail with more beautiful flatwoods and groundcover, then take the white trail back to the parking area.

## 55. Lake Jesup Conservation Area

**GPS:** Lat 28.719444, Long -81.188611

**Trailhead Directions:** From SR 46 in Sanford, take CR 415 south, then Cameron Avenue South for the North Cameron Tract entrance. Continue on CR 415 and head south on Snipes Avenue, south on South Mellonville Avenue and east on Oakway Lane to access the Marl Bed Flats Tract. Cross Lake Jesup on CR 417 heading south and get off on CR 419/434 heading east. Turn north on DeLeon Street, head east on Howard Avenue, and north on Elm Street to reach the East Lake Jesup Tract.

**Size:** 6,220 acres

**Trail Distance:**
NORTH CAMERON TRACT
    RED BLAZE TRAIL—1.2 miles round-trip
MARL BED FLATS TRACT
    RED BLAZE TRAIL—0.8 miles round-trip; YELLOW BLAZE
    TRAIL—0.5 miles round-trip
EAST LAKE JESUP TRACT
    WHITE BLAZE TRAIL—1.1 miles round-trip

**Hiking Time:** 2 hours

**Difficulty:** Easy

**Trail Surface:** Dark soil that may be seasonally flooded

**Shade Level:** 0–25%

**Natural Communities:** Floodplain marsh, hydric hammock

**Wildlife:** Hikers will see bald eagle, osprey, hawk, and American alligator around the shores of Lake Jesup, as well as numerous egrets, ibis, and great blue heron.

**Uses and Restrictions:** Hiking, observation platform, security residence. No motorized vehicles. Not friendly for family hiking.

**Trail Highlights:** Note the wide open space and big sky of Lake Jesup's marshes, view seasonal wetland wildflowers, observe birds, and imagine Old Florida as you hike through cattle country, Florida's third largest industry.

**Additional Hiking:** Lake Monroe Conservation Area, Econlockhatchee Conservation Area, Palm Bluff Conservation Area, Gemini Springs Addition

Lake Jesup is one of the many lakes connected to the St. Johns River in the South Central Region. The luscious grasses of the nutritious, mucky soils support cattle. The cattle lease here was held by Jimmy Lefils, the son of an old cattle rancher from France who originally settled Florida Cracker country. He talked many a time of cattle and fuel prices, the issue of ethanol making the price of corn as well as feedlot food for cattle increase. Once, when monitoring his cattle, I was required to ask how many cattle were on the property. He responded with a lighthearted country accent, "Well, that's like asking how much money I have in the bank!" With a red face I went on to the next question.

This property is mostly floodplain and hydric hammock, lands that hold St. Johns River floodwaters. Whereas the property historically burned by summer thunderstorm lightning fires, today it is surrounded by roads and is difficult to burn. The cattle lease is a great partnership for land management as the rancher gets more space to graze cattle and the cattle keep the grasses low, with the rancher mowing frequently to manage more area for cattle. The lease brings income to the district and allows the property to be managed where prescribed burns cannot.

With the construction of SR 46 crossing the tip of the lake at the St. Johns River, cutting off access of fresh, circulating water to the lake, Lake Jesup endured many years of degradation in water quality. Today, however, SR 46 has been lifted off the ground, allowing for better circulation of lake water. Wander through Old Florida cattle country and view the marshes of Lake Jesup and wetland wildflowers blooming at various times of the year.

## Hike Details

Pick one tract or all three to hike. Follow the trail maps for easy and short hiking. A favorite is the East Lake Jesup Tract to the observation tower. A shady quiet spot, the tower overlooks the marshes of Lake Jesup. This area is overgrown with willow; however, it is a great spot for observing birds flying, nesting, and hunting for fish. Watch out for spiders on the tower. I'll never forget Pete Henn, land manager on the property, and his high-pitched scream as a large, long-legged, yellow-and-black banana spider crawled across the brim of his hat after we climbed the tower! These tough woodsmen and their screams!

## 56. Lake Monroe Conservation Area

**GPS:** Lat 28.820278, Long -81.185278
**Trailhead Directions:** From the town of Sanford, take CR 415 east and then northeast across the St. Johns River. The main parking area is just off CR 415 on the east side of the road. A second entrance can be reached by taking a left onto Reed Ellis Road from CR 415. That entrance is on the south side of Reed Ellis Road, not far from CR 415.
**Size:** 7,473 acres
**Trail Distance:**
WHITE TRAIL LOOP—1.4 miles round-trip; YELLOW TRAIL LOOP FROM RED CONNECTOR—5.6 miles round-trip; RED TRAIL—1.9 miles one way
**Hiking Time:** Half-day hike
**Difficulty:** Easy
**Trail Surface:** Dark soil that may be seasonally flooded as well as deep sandy soil in the uplands

**Shade Level:** 25–50%

**Natural Communities:** Floodplain marsh

**Wildlife:** Numerous wildlife species can be found here, including the state threatened Florida black bear, Florida sandhill crane, gopher tortoise, the federally threatened Florida scrub jay, and eastern indigo snake.

**Uses and Restrictions:** Hiking, restrooms, inclement weather shelter, group campsite, primitive camping area, pitcher pump, hunting. The property is also managed as a wildlife management area. Be sure to check www.myfwc.com for Lake Monroe Wildlife Management Area hunting dates. No motorized vehicles. Not friendly for family hiking.

**Trail Highlights:** Hike south on the red trail for views of the St. Johns River as it meanders on by on its way to Lake Monroe. Cattle roaming the river are a reminder of being in cattle country and the tall and ancient cabbage palmettos are a reminder of Old Florida.

**Additional Hiking:** Lake Jesup Conservation Area, Palm Bluff Conservation Area, Gemini Springs Addition

Lake Monroe Conservation Area is on the flip side of the St. Johns River from Lake Jesup Conservation Area. The property has a long history of use, with Native American mounds excavated on the property. Later, ranchers diked and drained the property for grazing in the mucky, nutrient-rich soils of the floodplains. This severely altered water flow, causing wetlands to become degraded. The Florida Department of Transportation mitigation bank on the property has allowed for a more natural water flow, allowing water to stay on the property. Scrubby flatwoods are being carefully managed through fire to help maintain habitat for the federally threatened Florida scrub jay living here. Hikers will gain views of the St. Johns River and a bit of Old Florida cattle ranching in action along with hiking through the uplands and the chance to view Florida scrub jays.

## Hike Details

From the parking area on the Brickyard Slough Tract south of CR 415, hike south on the red trail. The hike will take you through shady hydric hammock and on to the floodplain marsh of the St. Johns River. Enjoy views of the river and watch cattle graze and utilize the river for drinking water. Hike back and take the yellow trail east to the yellow loop for views of the scrub, the upland habitat that supports the endangered Florida scrub jay.

## 57. Palm Bluff Conservation Area

**GPS:** Lat 28.890692, Long -81.140986

**Trailhead Directions:** From I-95 near New Smyrna Beach, take SR 44 West. Travel south on CR 415; the entrance is on the left side of CR 415.

**Size:** 3,321 acres

**Trail Distance:** 9.2 total miles
WHITE BLAZE TRAIL LOOP—1.0 mile; YELLOW BLAZE TRAIL LOOP—2.1 miles; RED BLAZE TRAIL LOOP—6.1 miles

**Hiking Time:** Day hike

**Difficulty:** Easy

**Trail Surface:** Old logging roads with grass

**Shade Level:** 0–25%

**Natural Communities:** Mesic flatwoods, depression marsh, wet flatwoods, pasture

**Wildlife:** Florida black bear, white-tailed deer, bluebird and brown-headed nuthatch, wild turkey, wading birds, and raptors

**Uses and Restrictions:** Hiking, group campsite, cabin, security residence. No motorized vehicles. Family-friendly hiking.

**Trail Highlights:** Hike the white trail and take a left when you reach the red trail to view a cabbage palm cabin at the crossing of Deep Creek. Built in the 1980s, it was a hunting/fishing cabin characteristic of the old cabins along the St. Johns River.

**Additional Hiking:** Lake Monroe Conservation Area

The front of this property was once protected by a conservation easement that I helped monitor to ensure the owners followed the conservation restrictions. Once the owners of the adjacent property east of the conservation easement realized that the easement would never be amended to allow for building a large road through the property, they gave up plans for dense development because of lack of access and sold the adjacent property. Today the property is preserved, but with special management considerations. Part of the property may be used as a water supply area; the east side of the property is a mitigation bank, which will afford extra funding for land management enhancement. The front of the property abutting CR 415 will always have the conservation easement, so it will be preserved for the Florida black bear and the Florida hiker for generations to come.

## Hike Details

Hiking at Palm Bluff is designed to allow for the option of short or long hikes. Start at the entrance and hike the 1-mile white loop through depression marsh and mesic flatwoods. Or continue along the red trail and cross Deep Creek. Take the red loop to hike south on the border of the creek and cross again on the southeast side of the property to hike back north along the border of the power lines and into mesic flatwoods interspersed with dome swamp. Hike the yellow loop from the red loop for 2 additional miles of hiking through mesic flatwoods, also bordering Deep Creek.

## 58. Seminole Ranch Conservation Area

**GPS:** Lat 28.619167, Long -80.964722

**Trailhead Directions:** From I-95 in Brevard County take SR 50 west and head north on CR 420, then take a right onto Wheeler Road. Or from I-95 in Brevard County, take SR 46 west and turn south onto Hatbill Road.

**Size:** 29,223 acres

**Trail Distance:** Approximately 10 miles

**Hiking Time:** Day hike or overnight

**Difficulty:** Easy

**Trail Surface:** Dark soil that may be seasonally flooded

**Shade Level:** 0–25%

**Natural Communities:** Floodplain marsh, salt flats, floodplain forest

**Wildlife:** Wading birds and waterfowl include white ibis, roseate spoonbill, white pelican, southern bald eagle, and sandhill crane. You may also spot white-tailed deer.

**Uses and Restrictions:** Hiking, group campsite, boat ramp, observation point, hunting. The hiking entrance off SR 50 is in a wildlife management area. Be sure to check www.myfwc.com for Seminole Ranch Wildlife Management Area hunting dates. No motorized vehicles. Family-friendly hiking.

**Trail Highlights:** Take in the wide open space and big sky of St. Johns River marshes along with wading bird sightings.

**Additional Hiking:** Tosohatchee Wildlife Management Area, St. Johns National Wildlife Refuge, Seminole Ranch Conservation Area, Orlando Wetlands Park, Charles Bronson State Forest, Little Big Econ State Forest, Buck Lake Wildlife Management Area, Salt Lake Wildlife Management Area

After Palm Bluff, Seminole Ranch is the next property heading north along the St. Johns River, protecting the river and its marshes. The river here is squiggly, with bends and turns that cause it to meander slowly. There are many lakes along the river and two of them, Puzzle Lake and Lake Harney, emit saltwater from underground springs. These springs are trapped ocean water from prehistoric times when ocean waves moved marine deposits to shape the landscape. Their presence has created salt flats on the northwest side of the property, with water holes where wading birds gather to harvest fish. Salt-tolerant plant and wildlife species are found here, like nowhere else on the St. Johns River. The flat nature of this part of the river has caused lakes to form, and within this property boundary are Lake Cone, Loughman Lake, and Salt Lake. Hiking from Hatbill Road off SR 46 includes seasonally wet trails with marsh views and old cabbage palm–lined paths. Hiking from SR 50 includes some forested wetlands and a hike to a primitive campsite.

## Hike Details

From Hatbill Road parking area, head west on the trail and then hike north and take the loop around, or continue hiking the second loop through floodplain trails. From the parking area off Wheeler Road, head east and then north to take the loop around and back to the parking area.

## 59. Little Big Econ State Forest

**GPS:** Lat 28.687528, Long -81.159436

**Trailhead Directions:** From Cocoa Beach, take I-95 north and exit west on SR 46. Take SR 46 west until reaching CR 426/Geneva Drive and head southwest. The Bar Street Trailhead entrance will be on your left.

**Size:** 10,236 acres

**Trail Distance:** Almost 30 miles of hiking, biking, and equestrian trails

**Hiking Time:** 2 hours to day/overnight

**Difficulty:** Easy

**Trail Surface:** Dirt paths and compact soil with leaf litter

**Shade Level:** 0–25%

**Natural Communities:** Mesic hammock, oak hammock, pasture, floodplain marsh, hydric hammock

**Wildlife:** Gray fox, river otter, white-tailed deer, wild turkey, bobcat, resident and migratory waterfowl, wood stork, wading birds, shorebirds, and numerous upland species. Other common sightings include sandhill crane, roseate spoonbill, bald eagle, osprey, and hawk.

**Maps:** www.freshfromflorida.com/Divisions-Offices/Florida-Forest-Service/Our-Forests/State-Forests/Little-Big-Econ-State-Forest

**Admission:** $4.00

**Hours:** Sunrise to sunset

**Uses and Restrictions:** Hiking, biking, equestrian trails, primitive camping, fishing, paddling, hunting, grill, picnic table. No motorized vehicles. The property is a wildlife management area. Hikers should visit www.myfwc.com for hunting dates prior to hiking. Family-friendly hiking.

**Contact:** Florida Forest Service Little Big Econ State Forest, (407) 971-3500

**Trail Highlights:** Hikers can follow the meandering Econlockhatchee River in this Old Florida natural backcountry.

**Additional Hiking:** Charles H. Bronson State Forest, Geneva Wilderness Preserve, Black Hammock Wilderness Area, Seminole Ranch Conservation Area

This property is part of east-central Florida's "Old Florida" nature at its best. The tract protects both sides of the Econlockhatchee River as it flows into the St. Johns River, and it connects the Econ Basin with Tosohatchee State Preserve in the southwest to other state lands along the St. Johns River to the east. The Econlockhatchee River is long, slow, and winding with sandy shores and lazy oaks overhanging bluffs. There are miles and miles of trails here, and the Florida Trail traverses the property and crosses the river. In 2010 the St. Johns River Water Management District added the Yarborough Conservation Easement to the property, and the family leases the property to continue their cattle operation. Black-and-white cattle will stare curiously as you hike to the river.

As cattle ranchers, participants in the third largest industry in Florida, the Yarboroughs are a longtime ranching family. In the early 2000s, Ed Yarborough sold a conservation easement, a protective legal agreement preventing sale of the land for development, to the St. Johns River Water Management District. His goal was to ensure there would be no development on the land and that his beloved ranch would stay preserved as a working farm. By the late 2000s, however, after his passing, the family, half of whom worked on the ranch and half of whom worked "in the city," came to a decision to sell the last of the remaining interest in the ranch to the district, keeping the family home on the fringe of the property. The family has created a way to live there, provide income for family members, continue using the land as a working cattle ranch, and preserve the land, just as their father wished. As an added benefit, the public can enjoy this "Old Florida" cattle ranch and its natural communities along the river.

I was the project manager monitoring the original conservation easement owned by the Yarboroughs. Every year I would head down with a staff member and meet the sons of the former landowner: huge, gruff Bo Yarborough, and his smaller but no less gruff brother. A gentle giant who was working the land as his father once did, Bo never seemed to mind taking time to show me the land once a year. We drove the property together and determined that no, there were no towering condos and no chemicals being poured into the river. I know where the initials of the family's young love interests are carved into their trees and where they used to camp along the river for family gatherings. Bo conducts prescribed burns to fertilize the pasture, works the cattle, and even loads them and drives them himself over to Texas to the feedlots before they return to Florida as beef.

One story he told was about the time a lightning strike on the land caused a wildfire. Since the property is bounded on three sides by water—the Econlockhatchee River to the north, a canal to the south, and the St. Johns River to the east—the Yarboroughs allow wildfires to burn slowly and safely to the waters' edges. However, the Florida Forest Service controversially is required to put all wildfires out to protect the people and the forested resources of the state of Florida. On the morning of the lightning strike, Bo's nephew, who worked for the Florida Forest Service at the time, showed up on the bulldozer to scrape the ground to install a fire line to stop the wildfire. This would have marked up the ground considerably, which was not necessary because the fire was going to run into the water and stop. Big Bo stood at one gate and his brother stood at the other, armed with shotguns. They would not let their forest service–employed nephew/son pass. The fire burned quietly into the river, the land was not marked up, and the fire fertilized the pasture just as nature would have done!

At the point the property was sold outright to the district in full fee, the district commissioned the University of Florida to visit the property for an oral history project. I was the project manager for the endeavor and traveled to the Yarborough ranch to record the families talking and reminiscing about growing up on the farm. It was the matriarch, Imogene Yarborough, who gave the interview. I was privileged to listen for hours as she described her family and her family's leadership in the agriculture industry of Florida and told stories about the farm. These recordings can be found online in the University of Florida oral history archives at www.ufl.edu, preserved for future generations to remember.

## Hike Details

From the Barr Street entrance, hike southeast on the Florida Trail. Traverse mesic flatwoods until you reach the Econlockhatchee River. Travel east and follow the winding river as it flows north and south on its way east. Once you reach the north-south Flagler Trail, there is an opportunity to cross the river and head south to continue on the

Florida Trail. Or you can visit the bridge, but then head north and take the loop trail north and then west. Here you will be hiking along mesic flatwoods/wet hammock fringe along your journey back to the Florida Trail and to the parking area. The Yarborough Tract is accessible from the Charles H. Bronson State Forest.

## 60. Charles H. Bronson State Forest

**GPS:** Lat 28.591414, Long -81.042221
**Address:** 3468 Phillips Road, Christmas, FL 32019
**Trailhead Directions:** From Titusville, take I-95 south and exit west onto SR 50. Head west and then turn right and head north on County Road 420. Veer to the right onto Phillips Road and follow the road until the property entrance.
**Size:** 10,941 acres
**Trail Distance:** Almost 50 miles of hiking and equestrian trails
**Hiking Time:** 2 hours to day/overnight
**Difficulty:** Easy
**Trail Surface:** Dirt paths and compact soil with leaf litter
**Shade Level:** 0–25%
**Natural Communities:** Floodplain marsh, sandhill, wet prairie, mesic flatwoods, cypress dome
**Wildlife:** American alligator, Sherman's fox squirrel, gopher tortoise, bald eagle, roseate spoonbill, sandhill crane, wood stork, Florida panther
**Maps:** www.freshfromflorida.com/Divisions-Offices/ Florida-Forest-Service/Our-Forests/State-Forests/ Charles-H.-Bronson-State-Forest
**Admission:** $4.00
**Uses and Restrictions:** Hiking, equestrian trails, primitive camping, fishing, hunting, grill, picnic table. No motorized vehicles. The property is a wildlife management area. Hikers should visit www. myfwc.com for hunting dates prior to hiking. Family-friendly hiking.
**Contact:** Florida Forest Service Little Big Econ State Forest, (407) 971-3500

**Trail Highlights:** Enjoy a shorter hike in the southern portion of the property through a mosaic of mesic flatwoods, cypress domes, and hammock. Or hike all the way north to connect to the Little Big Econ State Forest and hike the meandering Econlockhatchee River.

**Additional Hiking:** Little Big Econ State Forest, Geneva Wilderness Preserve, Black Hammock Wilderness Area, Seminole Ranch Conservation Area

This property is owned jointly by the St. Johns River Water Management District and Orange County but managed as a state forest by the Florida Forest Service. This is another part of east-central Florida's "Old Florida" nature at its best. Part of a large swath of conservation land protecting the St. Johns River marshes on the west side of the river, it sprawls from Little Big Econ State Forest south to Orlando Wetlands Park. This section of the St. Johns River winds and braids and sits and slows due to the flatness of the landscape. The area is host to four creeks that run through it. The property was once owned by the Lee family, an old-time Florida ranching family. The father sold the development rights to the St. Johns River Water Management District in the early 2000s to protect the land from development. His children operated the ranch after his retirement. In 2010 they sold it outright to the water management district and leased the land back to continue operating cattle. Today it is a working cattle ranch where hikers can traverse towering sabal palms while cows graze in this lazy, backcountry area far from the hustle and bustle of Disney and the coast.

I was the project manager for the conservation easement on the property and visited the land yearly. I met with David Lee, the son and manager, as we rode the property. He discussed oil prices, low cattle prices, and government decisions that affected cattle. He shared many personal stories about the land. When the land was sold to the district, I was the project manager on the oral history project through the University of Florida. I sat in on interviews with a graduate student recording David's father while the interviews were filmed by his forward-thinking middle school granddaughter. He spoke of miles of orange trees, and of climbing trees in his white church clothes before getting yelled at by his mother for soiling them. He talked about how his family had originally owned much more land, from the old two-headed palm tree east to the bend in the river, before selling it to a neighboring rancher. He talked of the great freezes of 1894 and 1895, when families who had given up everything to come to Florida to make it big in the orange business lost everything. With millions of dollars in frozen oranges left on the trees, many families just picked up and left, even leaving behind tables set for dinner. It was an honor to meet with him and listen and to have been on the property before it became state lands. The land is now protected, just as he wished, yet still functions as a working cattle ranch.

## Hike Details

From the Phillips Road entrance, hike the blue spur trail northeast through mesic flatwoods to pick up the Florida Trail. You can hike east or northwest. Hike northwest through mesic flatwoods and hydric hammock until reaching another spur trail. Hike west to head to the Chuluota Wilderness Park and pick up a car previously left to drive back to the Phillips entrance, or hike east. East will take you to the white trail, through a narrow swath of mesic flatwoods and hammock and to the north. Any gates you see, leave them as they are, open or closed, to manage the cattle fields. The white trail will lead you to the brown trail, an old road that heads north. When you reach the large east-west canal, you can hike west to a bridge and cross the canal. That bridge leads to a white/yellow/brown loop trail that follows the swirly boundary of the Econlockhatchee River. Loop back and return south to reach the original trailhead.

## 61. Wekiva River Buffer Conservation Area

**GPS:** Lat 28.711389, Long -81.410278

**Trailhead Directions:** From I-4 in Orlando, take the CR 434 exit and head west. Head north on Wekiva Springs Road and then take a right on Sabal Palm Drive. Take another right on Wilderness Drive and find a spot on the side of the road to park.

**Size:** 3,142 acres

**Trail Distance:** Approximately 2 miles round-trip

**Hiking Time:** 1 hour

**Difficulty:** Easy

**Trail Surface:** Dark soil with grass and leaf litter that may be seasonally flooded

**Shade Level:** 75–100%

**Natural Communities:** Floodplain swamp, hydric hammock

**Wildlife:** Florida black bear, ibis, wood stork, great blue heron, egret, river otter, barred owl, pileated woodpecker

**Uses and Restrictions:** Hiking. No motorized vehicles. Family-friendly hiking.

**Trail Highlights:** Leave the densely developed Orlando Sabal Palm Subdivision and walk into undisturbed peace as you hike under the oak- and palmetto-lined path toward the Little Wekiva River. Listen quietly for the birds flying overhead, but be loud enough to let the Florida black bears know you'd like to share their space for a while.

**Additional Hiking:** Wekiwa Springs State Park, Rock Springs Run State Reserve

This property is part of a chain of properties protecting the Wekiva River watershed and the wildlife habitat associated with this area. The property buffers the Little Wekiva River on the east and west sides of the river from the densely developed homes of Orlando's Markham Woods Road. It also protects habitat for the Florida black bear, which can frequently be seen roaming the property and the neighborhood streets as they travel from the Wekiva River to and from the Ocala National Forest. The property is mostly floodplain swamp, so hiking will be under oak and cabbage palm on fern-lined paths—a virtual Florida jungle path leading as far north toward the Little Wekiva River as a former logging road will take you.

I have visited this property and wrote the easy management plan.

## Hike Details

From the parking area off the street, hike directly north through the floodplain swamp. The trail is an old logging road so it will be mostly dry. This trail is out and back.

# St. Johns River Water Management District
## South Region

## 62. River Lakes Conservation Area

**GPS**: Lat 28.230649, Long -80.804104

**Trailhead Directions:** From I-95 in Cocoa Beach, head south and exit on CR 509, Wickham Road. Head west until you dead-end into the property.

**Size:** 39,663 acres

**Trail Distance:**
WHITE BLAZE TRAIL—2.5 miles one way; YELLOW BLAZE TRAIL—3.1 miles one way; RED BLAZE TRAIL LOOP—2.0 miles

**Hiking Time:** Half-day hike

**Difficulty:** Easy

**Trail Surface:** Trails may be seasonally flooded.

**Shade Level:** 0–25%

**Natural Communities:** Grasses that once supported ranch land, marsh

**Wildlife:** Many species of fish, several listed species: wood stork, bald eagle, Florida sandhill crane, river otter

**Uses and Restrictions:** Hiking, inclement weather shelters, camping platforms, boat launch, observation point, hunting. Property is part of the Upper St. Johns River Marsh Wildlife Management Area. Be sure to check www.myfwc.com for hunting dates before you go. Family-friendly hiking.

**Trail Highlights:** Enjoy the open space and peaceful nature of the upper basin of the St. Johns River.

**Additional Hiking:** Three Forks Conservation Area, Canaveral Marshes Conservation Area

Crossing US 192 from Three Forks Marsh into River Lakes Conservation Area, the St. Johns River turns into a more natural-looking, winding river, a far cry from the canal channels farther south. Protecting land around the St. Johns River and a series of nearby lakes, the aptly named River Lakes property plays host to the section of the river that flows in and out of Lake Washington, Lake Winder, and Lake Poinsette. This is an airboater's paradise, with wide open smooth sailing and well-worn airboat trails through the marshes. Many airboaters enjoy fishing and waterfowl hunting and run guided tour businesses. Park at Wickham Road and hike north or south for upland, grassy hiking trails. Leaving the ditched marshes and heading into wide plains once cleared for cattle ranching, hikers will traverse Florida hammock, complete with views of tall, swaying cabbage palms, saw palmetto, and squiggly branched oaks.

One of my early burns was at River Lakes. I remember one staffer asking me to put water on the ground and I just stared blankly at the engine, not knowing how to turn on their equipment, as the fire moved quickly. Ray Gibson helped me get the engine started and successfully draw water from the tank. Then I hopped on the back of an ATV with land manager, hunter socialite, yet military veteran and careful pre-scribed burner Doug Voltolina, and dropped fire from the drip torch from the side while he drove. Dropping fire . . . now that I could do! We created mile-long lines of fire through bahia grass (former ranch pasture) that would join together and move west toward the St. Johns River, the goal being to kill back some of the invasive willow. It was amazing to watch the two-story-tall flames with black smoke climbing into the sky. No one was present for miles except the busy cars on I-95 moving quietly in the distance. Prescribed burns on the large, wide expanses of the marshes of the St. Johns River are a thrilling experience.

## Hike Details

Choose to hike north, south, or both. Hiking is through former ranch-land grasses with little shade, but pause by the old oak trees and tall Florida palmettos. The destination view of the St. Johns River Marshes is worth the trek.

## 63. Three Forks Marsh Conservation Area

**GPS:** Lat 27.983056, Long -80.754722

**Trailhead Directions:** From I-95 in Palm Bay, take CR 514/Malabar Road exit and head west. Or take the CR 514 exit east and head south on CR 507. Then head west on Fellsmere Grade for the southernmost entrance.

**Size:** 47,529 acres

**Trail Distance:** 16.9 miles total

THOMAS O. LAWTON RECREATION AREA TO WILLOW
SHELTER—8.6 miles; WILLOW SHELTER TO FELLSMERE GRADE
RECREATION AREA—8.3 miles

**Hiking Time:** Hike as long as interested; however, watch for quick
changes in the weather as there is no shelter until mile 8.6.

**Difficulty:** Easy

**Trail Surface:** Graded levee

**Shade Level:** 0%

**Natural Communities:** Marsh

**Wildlife:** Waterfowl, wading birds, river otter, shorebirds

**Uses and Restrictions:** Hiking, handicapped access, picnic area,
inclement weather shelter, camping platforms, restrooms, boat launch,
canoe launch, hunting. Three Forks is part of the Upper St. Johns
River Marsh Wildlife Management Area. Be sure to view the hunting
brochure for dates at www.myfwc.com. Family-friendly hiking, but
beware of lack of shade on the long trail.

**Trail Highlights:** Experience the big air open space of the marsh down
in Florida ranch country. View wading birds and other critters that may
cross the levee. Notice a last remaining section of sawgrass near the
Thomas Lawton Recreation Area.

**Additional Hiking:** Herkey Huffman/Bull Creek Wildlife Management
Area, Blue Cypress Conservation Area, St. Sebastian Buffer Preserve
State Park

Three Forks Marsh is the third massive conservation area in the St.
Johns River Marsh as it continues north on its journey to Jacksonville.
Canal 54 and Fellsmere Grade separate this marsh from Blue Cypress
Conservation Area to the south and River Lakes Conservation Area.
Huge culverts control water flow from south to north into the marshes
for flood control. Managers must balance the delicate needs of the wetlands and wildlife with the heavy rains of summer and the dry periods
of winter. Too much water in the marsh could cause the need to "put
water to tide." Water from Three Forks could be discharged into Canal
54, but this threatens the oyster and clam waters of the coast, as too
much freshwater dilutes the salinity required by these species.

It is here that St. Johns River Marsh forms three forks of creeks, the namesake of the property, that discharge into the very beginning of the St. Johns River. Here the river passes through the first of many lakes along its journey to Jacksonville: Lake Hell N' Blazes and Sawgrass Lake. Hiking is only on the levee and there is no shade; however, it is worth it to view wading birds, see wildlife, breathe in the fresh air of the marsh, and experience the wide open space far from the hustle and bustle of the highly populated Florida east coast that is the St. Johns River Upper Basin.

## Hike Details

Park at Thomas Lawton Recreation Area and hike south on the levee to hike the loop. Or take a left on the levee and follow it south to Willow Shelter out and back. See the wide open space of the marsh and the remnant sawgrass near the recreation pad. View wildlife crossing the trail and wading birds in the marsh.

## 64. Blue Cypress Conservation Area

**GPS:** FELLSMERE GRADE (STICK MARSH ENTRANCE)—Lat 27.823056, Long -80.707222
CR 512 SITE—Lat 27.6625, Long -80.643889

**Trailhead Directions:** From I-95 in Palm Bay, take CR 507 south. Head west on Fellsmere Grade. Continue south on CR 507 and head west on CR 512 to reach the parking areas at the CR 512 area.

**Size:** 61,574 acres

**Trail Distance:** Levee Trail—around 20 miles

**Hiking Time:** Day hike

**Difficulty:** Easy

**Trail Surface:** Sandy soil, compact soil with leaf litter

**Shade Level:** 0%

**Natural Communities:** Marsh

**Wildlife:** Great blue heron, white ibis, snowy egret, limpkin, night heron. Other species include wood stork, osprey, bald eagle.

**Uses and Restrictions:** Hiking, restrooms, handicapped access, boat ramp, camping platforms, picnic area, canoe launch, inclement weather shelter. Not friendly for family hiking.

**Trail Highlights:** The only uplands on the property are the levee. Use the levees as a vantage point to view large expanses of water and marsh as you hike south from Canal 54. Consider hiring an airboat guide to take you through the massive marsh.

**Additional Hiking:** Three Forks Conservation Area, Fort Drum Conservation Area, St. Sebastian River Buffer Preserve State Park

South of Three Forks, Blue Cypress is the next preserve heading south on this journey to the headwaters of the St. Johns River. Another flood-plain marsh formerly converted to drained farmland, Blue Cypress is now undergoing restoration. Nicknamed the Stick Marsh or Farm 13, the large St. Johns Water Management Area was once a farm with palm trees in the fields. When the soil was turned to bury the fertilizers and pesticides, it was time to return water to the former marsh. The palms and other trees were left and stood for many years in the middle of the marsh before falling, creating some of the best bass fishing in Florida. Through all the destruction to make way for farming, this conservation area still manages to have some astonishing aspects. Blue Cypress Lake is a massive, natural cypress-lined lake on the eastern side of the conservation area, making for breathtaking paddling. The area east of CR 512 has been reflooded from various farming and citrus groves and is an airboater's heaven. With marsh and lily pads as far as the eye can see, one would never know this was a former farm field if not for the surrounding, protective exterior levees.

On this property I was touring the Blue Cypress Marshes east of CR 512 to understand the property while writing the management plan. We headed east into the marshes on an airboat, always a fun adventure! We viewed an old orange grove surrounded by water that was undergoing remediation before being flooded and reconnected to the marsh. As we turned back, passing over old farm levees at airboat crossings, hardware fell off the boat. It must have been an important piece of the boat because the airboat engine stopped. We were far out with no cell service! What a beautiful view if you had to be stuck somewhere! We paddled until we had service and someone drove to pick us up and brought out another airboat. Out of three airboat rides, I've fallen out or been stuck twice!

## Hike Details

This is an out-and-back levee hike heading south on the eastern border of the conservation area. View the stick marsh on your right/west and listen to the airboats buzzing by, the john boats meandering, looking for a good fishing spot. Think of the Native Americans who made their home here on the prolific marshes of the St. Johns River headwaters. As you hike, picture yourself as a rancher or farmer who wanted to utilize the luscious muck soils for farming and found ways to drain the soil and levee the exterior to keep the water out. Think of the wildlife who search for clean water to survive in this large expanse of wild. Think of the water managers who try to balance all of the above and protect those farms and homes that now border the mighty marshes.

## 65. St. Sebastian River Preserve State Park

**GPS:** Lat 27.824291, Long -80.607518

**Address:** 1000 Buffer Preserve Drive, Fellsmere, FL 32940

**Trailhead Directions:** From Palm Bay, take I-95 south and exit onto Malabar Road. Head east and then turn an immediate south onto Babcock Street Southeast. Take a left onto Buffer Preserve Drive and take a left into the parking area at the visitor's center.

**Size:** 22,000 acres

**Trail Distance:** 60 miles

**Hiking Time:** Day hike or overnight

**Difficulty:** Easy

**Trail Surface:** Dirt path

**Shade Level:** 0–25%

**Natural Communities:** Mesic flatwoods, cypress domes, scrubby flatwoods, sandhills, strand swamp, mangrove

**Wildlife:** Manatee, red-cockaded woodpecker, Florida scrub jay, Bachman's sparrow, bald eagle, white-tailed deer, coyote, bobcat, wild turkey, quail, eastern indigo snake, gopher tortoise, alligator

**Maps:** www.floridastateparks.org/park/St-Sebastian-River

**Hours:** 8:00 am to sunset, visitor center open Thursday through Sunday 10:00 am–4:30 pm

**Uses and Restrictions:** Hiking, bicycling, boating, equestrian camping, primitive camping, group camping, canoe/kayak launch, fishing, geocaching, equestrian trails, interpretive kiosk, picnic pavilion, restrooms, interpretive tours, education center, handicap accessibility. No motorized vehicles. Family-friendly hiking.

**Contact:** Florida State Parks, (321) 953-5005

**Trail Highlights:** Experience the mesic flatwoods through miles of backcountry trails and visit the manatees in the C-54 canal in winter.

**Additional Hiking:** Blue Cypress Conservation Area, Fort Drum Conservation Area

This property is a story of nature that has overcome fragmentation of the Florida landscape by highway and canal. Rare swaths of longleaf pine ecosystems not only survive here but thrive despite I-95 breaking the property into east and west halves and Canal C-54 further cutting the property in half north to south. Yet even with the disruption, the property still manages to provide habitat for 74 protected plant and wildlife species. In the winter, manatees seeking warm water swim into the C-54 canal from the ocean. Red-cockaded woodpeckers inhabit the mesic flatwood areas in the northeast quadrant; Florida scrub jays inhabit the scrubby flatwoods in the southeast quadrant. Hikers will be amazed to hike longleaf pine forests, walk along the St. Sebastian River on the southeast border of the property, and wander through miles and miles of trails with wildlife abounding.

I have visited the property many times to assist with photos for image development, to help manage collegiate regattas that utilize the C-54 canal for racing, and to work with recreation managers from all five water management districts. We designed and wrote a pamphlet describing the components of district recreation and the many opportunities provided by backcountry Florida district land in order to illustrate the value of recreational land to politicians. As project manager, I coordinated the language, layout, design, and installation of educational panels, computers, and materials for the visitor's center. I worked with district and park staff in Palatka, Tallahassee, and Fellsmere to create this fun and educational center.

## Hike Details

Choose from one or more of the four quadrants. View scrub jays in the southeast or visit the manatee viewing area in the northwest quadrant. View red-cockaded woodpecker in the northeast quadrant. Notice the longleaf pine mesic flatwoods and the many other natural communities on the property as you follow the trails.

## 66. Fort Drum Marsh Conservation Area

**GPS:** Lat 27.641389, Long -80.766389

**Trailhead Directions:** From I-95 in the Vero Beach area, take the SR 60 exit west. Fort Drum entrance will be on the south side of the road.

**Size:** 20,862 acres

**Trail Distance**
RED BLAZE TRAIL LOOP (MULTIUSE)—3.4 miles; WHITE BLAZE TRAIL LOOP (HIKING)—0.6 miles; YELLOW BLAZE TRAIL LOOP (HIKING)—1.2 miles; LEVEE TRAIL—more than 10 miles

**Hiking Time:** 2 hours–half-day

**Difficulty:** Easy

**Trail Surface:** Dark soil covered in grass or pine needles in flatwoods; graded road on levee

**Shade Level:** 0–25%

**Natural Communities:** Mesic flatwoods, marsh

**Wildlife:** Florida sandhill crane, wood stork, crested caracara, bald eagle, white-tailed deer, wild turkey, and a large population of feral hogs

**Uses and Restrictions:** Hiking, picnic tables, restrooms, canoe launch, fishing, primitive camping, group campsite, hunt check station. Hunting during winter season. Be sure to check www.myfwc.com for hunting dates. Family-friendly hiking.

**Trail Highlights:** Take the red trail south from the parking area and turn right at the first intersection. Take the next left to hike over the infamous palmetto-lined boardwalk to Hog Island. This island is where ranchers once kept cattle grazing in what little uplands there were in this area, but now where feral hogs roam free—as you will see, from soil uprooted by hungry snouts. Feral hogs, brought by the Europeans, are kept under control by hog trappers and hunting as part of the plan for the wildlife management area.

**Additional Hiking:** Blue Cypress Conservation Area, St. Sebastian Buffer Preserve State Park, Kissimmee Prairie Preserve State Park

Fort Drum Marsh is in the St. Johns River headwaters and the southernmost reach of the St. Johns River Water Management District. Its origins were once a wide expanse of marsh where water flowed in from Fort Drum Creek and released into a wide expanse of floodplain. Drained and diked to allow for ranching, the property is now bordered on all four sides of its square layout by dikes and levees, on the south by the Florida Turnpike and on the north by SR 60. The property is part of what is known to restoration ecologists and water managers as the Upper Basin Project. The project aims to restore water flow, wetlands, and wildlife habitat by filling canals and interior ditches and removing exotic ranch grass species, while still maintaining flood protection to neighboring landowners with border levees. A mighty feat, but managers have worked to balance wetlands and flood protection, and they have even found ways to include recreation in the uplands.

## Hike Details

Hike the red trail south to the shaded boardwalk path lined with palmetto around ancient Hog Island. Then head west to leave the island and hike the red trail loop in the mesic flatwoods uplands. This area is a peaceful hike and you are sure to see wildlife. Don't forget to stop at Horseshoe Lake near the parking area on the way in or out!

# 4

## Southwest Florida District

The Southwest Florida Water Management District (with the initials SWFWMD, creating the endearing nickname, "Swift Mud") is in west-central Florida. The district comprises 16 counties with more than 4 million inhabitants. The boundary runs from Levy and Marion Counties southwest of Gainesville, down through Tampa Bay and south of Sarasota on the Gulf of Mexico and east to Polk County. The largest cities here are Tampa/St. Petersburg and Sarasota. The district is home to Homosassa Springs and Crystal River with manatees, Weeki Wachee Springs with swimmers dressed as mermaids, and the infamous Tampa desalinization plant.

Major issues in this more clustered, less developed area of Florida include aquatic plant management to improve fish nurseries and decrease invasive/exotic plants, clam habitat and stormwater treatment improvement, and farm incentives to strive for best management practices in agriculture. Water supply planning research is conducted and permits researched. Minimum flows and levels are maintained to ensure enough water for habitat and river/springs health, springs protection and management, water conservation, surface water quality improvement, and more.

Hiking in this region includes traversing tributaries, swamps, and hammocks, sandhill ridges, and mesic flatwoods. The trails here track around flatlands with water—large expanses of marsh with levees or old trails, huge sloughs, and massive swamps. The lands in this region were purchased to protect the major river systems, lakes, and swamps and include the Alafia River, Myakka River, Green Swamp, Little Manatee River, Lake Panasoffkee, and more. Hikers will enjoy the clear rivers and springs, glimpses of manatees, and wide expanses of marsh in this backcountry section of Florida.

## Basics for the Southwest Florida District

Be sure to note whether trails are seasonally flooded (typically in the summer rainy season) and whether there is hunting. Check www.myfwc.com for hunting dates prior to hiking.

Unless otherwise noted, all properties in this region are open from sunrise to sunset, free of charge. For any additional questions, contact the Southwest Florida Water Management District office at (356) 796-7211.

## 67. Alafia River Corridor

**GPS:** Lat 27.826803, Long -82.129696
**Address:** 931 Old Welcome Road, Lithia, FL 33547
**Trailhead Directions:** From Tampa, take SR 60 east. Veer off onto CR 640/Lithia Pinecrest Road and head southeast. Find the northern hiking trailhead by traveling north on CR 39; the parking area will be a few miles north on your right. Find the southern equestrian trailhead by traveling south on CR 39 from CR 640/Lithia Pinecrest Road and traveling east on Old Welcome Road. Turn south on Old Welcome Road and dead-end into the parking area.
**Size:** 2,963 acres
**Trail Distance:** 3-mile hiking trail, 8-mile hike on equestrian trail
**Hiking Time:** 2 hours to day hike
**Difficulty:** Easy
**Trail Surface:** Floodplain soils and leaf litter in oak hammock
**Shade Level:** 25–50%
**Natural Communities:** Hardwood swamp, upland hammock, old phosphate mines that have been revegetated, pasture, oak hammock, riverine swamp
**Wildlife:** White-tailed deer, avian species, wild turkey
**Maps:** www.swfwmd.state.fl.us/recreation/areas/alafiarivercorridor.html
**Hours:** Daily, 8:00 am–5:00 pm, when park gates close
**Uses and Restrictions:** Hiking, primitive camping, group camping (letter of authorization required from Hillsborough County Parks, Recreation and Conservation Department), equestrian trails, picnic

shelter, restrooms available at adjacent Alderman's Ford Park during
park hours. No motorized vehicles. Family-friendly hiking.

**Contact:** Hillsborough County Parks, Recreation and Conservation
Department, (813) 672-7876

**Trail Highlights:** Hikers have the chance to cross the Alafia River North
Prong. Note especially the leaning, ancient live oaks overtaken by
resurrection fern.

**Additional Hiking:** Alafia River State Park, Alderman's Ford Park,
Alderman's Nature Preserve, English Creek Environmental Studies
Center, Lithia Springs Park, Edward Medard Park and Reservoir

This property protects the watershed of the Alafia River, its north
prong, West Branch, Mizelle Creek, Owens Branch, its south prong, and
Chito Branch, which are the creeks leading into the Alafia River. These
creeks, and the resulting Alafia River, flow into Tampa Bay. Protection of these tributaries and watershed is important for water quality,
wildlife habitat, and the health of Tampa Bay. Hikers will cross creeks
and experience hiking in floodplain swamp and oak hammock uplands
during a 3-mile hike. Hikers can also utilize the southern equestrian
trailhead for 8 additional miles of hiking.

## Hike Details

From the northern border of the Pinecrest Sports Complex, head east
onto the trail. Hike across the Alafia River North Prong and then follow
the border of the property along the railroad to the southeast. Leave
the border at the next intersection to hike southwest to a loop trail.
This trail loops around upland hammock. If you hike northwest, you
can then head south and take an oval loop to the west through revegetated pasture. If you hike southeast, you can then hike south and then
take the next possible left to hike east. This path will lead you north
and then west to a fishing spot. For 8 more miles of hiking, enter the
property from the Old Welcome Road equestrian entrance. Head south
and then east toward the Alafia River South Prong. Cross the creek and
continue hiking east to find a picnic shelter on the Alafia River. This
long hike on the equestrian trails hosts several loop trails and creek
crossings through Old Florida.

## 68. Alston Tract at Upper Hillsborough Preserve

**GPS:** Lat 28.175175, Long -82.122362

**Address:** 42144 Deems Road, Zephyrhills, FL 33540

**Trailhead Directions:** From Tampa, get on I-4 and head east. Exit on CR 39A then head north, merge into CR 39 and continue north. Take a right on Florida Avenue, take a left on Saunders Road, and a right on Deems Road. The conservation area will be on your right before you take a 90-degree north turn on Deems Road.

**Size:** 2,983 acres

**Trail Distance:** 12 miles of multiuse designated trails

**Hiking Time:** Day hike

**Difficulty:** Easy

**Trail Surface:** Dirt or white sandy soil trails that are seasonally flooded or seasonally dry sugar sand

**Shade Level:** 0–25%

**Natural Communities:** Mesic flatwoods, strand swamp, floodplain forest

**Wildlife:** Osprey, Florida black bear, Florida panther

**Maps:** www.swfwmd.state.fl.us/recreation/areas/uh-alston_tract.html

**Uses and Restrictions:** Hiking, camping, equestrian use, restrooms, picnic tables, grills/fire rings, nonpotable water. No motorized vehicles. Family-friendly hiking.

**Trail Highlights:** Hikers will enjoy open expanses of pine flatwoods that include rare longleaf pine overstory. Mixed throughout are wetland swamps that are forested.

**Additional Hiking:** Green Swamp Wilderness Preserve, Blackwater Creek Preserve (Hillsborough County owned), Upper Hillsborough Preserve-Upper Hillsborough Tract, Lower Hillsborough Wilderness Preserve, Flatwoods Wilderness Park

This tract of the Upper Hillsborough Preserve is a special find for hikers. Preserving wide expanses of Florida pine flatwoods, this property is interspersed with wavy strands of swamp and draped with cypress and other water-loving trees. The tract is part of the upper reaches of the Hillsborough River and protects floodplains for the river, storing water during rain events. It also protects a wildlife corridor from the Green Swamp down to the Polk/Pasco County line. Hikers will take off for 12 miles of hiking in this Old Florida gem.

## Hike Details

From the Deems Road trailhead, hike east and follow the squiggly trail along the northern edge of a strand swamp, then through an area of large live oaks and a patch of sandy soil. Following another squiggle to the south, you'll enter a mesic flatwoods area with few trees. Follow the trail south and then to the northeast, where you will bisect a wetland strand. Head to the northern boundary and skirt the edge of a circular wetland swamp and continue heading east. You will come to a T-intersection. It is here where the hiker must decide whether to walk north or east through Florida mesic flatwoods and wetland strand swamp heaven. There are a series of five oblong loops to make the hike as short or as long as you'd like. Take the first loop and then head back to the parking area for the shortest distance. Or take the exterior of all the loops for the longest distance. Regardless of the path taken, you'll have about 10 miles to enjoy being in your own private, backcountry Florida wilderness!

## 69. Upper Hillsborough Tract at Upper Hillsborough Preserve

**GPS:** Lat 28.235177, Long -82.146943

**Address:** 41404 CR 54, Zephyrhills, FL 33540

**Trailhead Directions:** From Zephyrhills, take CR 535/Chancy Road to the east. Veer around the long curve and head north. The entrance will be on your right on the border and just north of the Zephyrhills Municipal Airport.

**Size:** 6,978 acres

**Trail Distance:** 12 miles of multiuse designated trails, 3.5 miles of hiking-only trails maintained by the Florida Trail Association, 24 miles of interior roads available

**Hiking Time:** Day hike

**Difficulty:** Easy

**Trail Surface:** Dirt or white sandy soil, two track trails that are seasonally flooded or seasonally dry sugar sand

**Shade Level:** 0–25%

**Natural Communities:** Mesic flatwoods, strand swamp, floodplain forest

**Wildlife:** Osprey, Florida black bear, Florida panther

**Maps:** www.swfwmd.state.fl.us/recreation/areas/uh-upperhill.html

**Uses and Restrictions:** Bicycling, hiking, camping, equestrian use, fishing and frogging, hunting. No motorized vehicles. This property is a wildlife management area. Property north of CR 54 is not included in the wildlife management area and is open to hiking and multiuse year-round. Family-friendly hiking.

**Trail Highlights:** Hikers will enjoy the untouched mesic flatwoods and strand swamp wetlands that make this a truly Florida backcountry hike.

**Additional Hiking:** Green Swamp Wilderness Preserve, Blackwater Creek Preserve (Hillsborough County owned), Upper Hillsborough Preserve-Alston Tract, Lower Hillsborough Wilderness Preserve, Flatwoods Wilderness Park

This tract of the Upper Hillsborough Preserve is another exciting find for hikers that is contiguous and similar in natural communities to the Alston Tract of the Upper Hillsborough Preserve to the south. The property maintains wide, almost untouched expanses of Florida pine flatwoods interspersed with strands of forested swamp. This property is bisected by the Hillsborough River and the associated tributaries that drain into it. There is no bridge to make the crossing at Cedar Ford, so be ready to get your feet wet! The tract is part of the upper reaches of the Hillsborough River and protects floodplains for the river and stores water during rain events. It also protects a wildlife corridor, from the Green Swamp down to the Polk/Pasco County line. The parcel north of CR 54 is closed to hunting year-round, making the property open and safe for hiking during the best time of the year: cool weather months. Hikers have the opportunity for 12 miles of multiuse hiking and 3.5 miles of hiking-only trails maintained by the Florida Trail Association.

## Hike Details

From the main entrance off CR 535, head east through flatwoods and head south at every intersection you reach, skirting two large dome swamp wetlands until you reach the Cedar Ford Crossing of the Hillsborough River. Head east and then south at the next intersection to dead-end into River Run Trail. Head north at this T-intersection and hike through flatwoods until you dead-end into another T-intersection. Take a left here to cross back over the Hillsborough River, or take a right and then a left to hike north along the boundary and ultimately the railroad tracks to make a large loop through flatwoods and wetlands. If the Cedar Ford is not crossable due to high water, from the main entrance hike north for a choice of two loops, West Loop Road or East Loop Road, making your way toward Flat Ford Road. Hikers can continue across the railroad tracks (use caution when crossing) to hike the few uplands surrounded by wetlands associated with the Hillsborough River floodplains. Park at the CR 54 entrance for hiking unimpeded by hunting.

## 70. Conner Preserve

**GPS:** Lat 28.321688, Long -82.444250
**Address:** 22500 SR 52, Land O'Lakes, FL 34637
**Trailhead Directions:** From Tampa, take SR 41 north past Land O'Lakes until you reach CR 52. Head east on CR 52 and the preserve will be on the south side of the road.
**Size:** 2,980 acres
**Trail Distance:** 16 miles of hiking-only trails plus several miles of multiuse wooded roads
**Hiking Time:** Day hike
**Difficulty:** Easy
**Trail Surface:** Dirt or white sandy soil trails that are seasonally flooded or seasonally dry sugar sand
**Shade Level:** 0–25%
**Natural Communities:** Sandhills, marshes, cypress sloughs, mesic flatwoods
**Wildlife:** Osprey, Florida black bear, Florida panther

**Maps:** www.swfwmd.state.fl.us/recreation/areas/conner.html

**Uses and Restrictions:** Hiking, unpaved bicycling, primitive campsite, equestrian trails (day use pass required), model airplane flying field, picnic table. No motorized vehicles. Family-friendly hiking.

**Trail Highlights:** Hikers will see mesic flatwoods and wetlands and also travel along sandhill ridges.

**Additional Hiking:** Weeki Wachee Springs State Park, Green Swamp Wilderness Preserve, Werner-Boyce Salt Springs State Park, Jay B. Starkey Wilderness Park, Cypress Creek Preserve/Flood Detention Area, Upper Hillsborough Preserve, Lower Hillsborough Wilderness Preserve

Conner Preserve is a mixture of natural communities with a mosaic of mesic flatwoods and upland sandhill ridges mixed with wetland marshes and cypress sloughs. The property is a key wildlife habitat corridor between the Starkey Wilderness Preserve and the Cypress Creek Preserve, making a contiguous swath of conservation land for the region. The property was a cattle ranch prior to district ownership, and hikers will appreciate the progress of restoration converting the pasture grasses to natural areas.

## Hike Details

At the entrance, hike south and then immediately veer to the right to hike through sandhill ridges. Here you will find white sandy soil, groundcover of wiregrass and seasonal wildflowers, and sparse pine overstory. Enjoy a series of two loops through the sandhills. A third long loop will take you through mesic flatwoods intermixed with extensive marsh wetlands. Or, from the entrance, hike south and veer to the left to take in a series of loops through mesic flatwoods and marshes.

## 71. Deep Creek Preserve

**GPS:** Lat 27.060977, Long -82.021001

**Address:** 10787 SW Peace River Street, Arcadia, FL 34269

**Trailhead Directions:** From Punta Gorda, take I-75 north and exit on CR 769, heading north. Take a right on Peace River St. and the entrance to the conservation area will be on the south side of the road.

Deep Creek Preserve. Photo courtesy Southwest Florida Water Management District.

**Size:** 2,000 acres

**Trail Distance:** 9-mile network of multiuse trails and roads

**Hiking Time:** Day hike

**Difficulty:** Easy

**Trail Surface:** Dirt with pine needle–covered trails that may be seasonally flooded

**Shade Level:** 0–25%

**Natural Communities:** Mesic flatwoods dominated by longleaf pine, freshwater marsh, wet prairie, oak scrub and scrubby flatwoods, tidal swamp, salt marsh, mangrove forest

**Wildlife:** Osprey, Florida black bear, Florida panther

**Maps:** www.swfwmd.state.fl.us/recreation/areas/deepcreek.html

**Uses and Restrictions:** Boating and paddling available at the adjacent Deep Creek Park (east of the Deep Creek Preserve entrance), equestrian, group, and primitive camping, portable restroom, nonpotable water, equestrian use, fishing, multiuse trails, picnic facilities at campsite with pavilion available at the adjacent Deep Creek Park. No motorized vehicles. Family-friendly hiking.

**Trail Highlights:** Hike directly to the banks of Deep Creek, a prominent branch of the highly braided Peace River.

**Additional Hiking:** Deer Prairie Creek, Myakka River State Park, Myakka State Forest, Charlotte Harbor Preserve State Park, Gasparilla Sound Charlotte Harbor Aquatic Preserve, Cape Haze Aquatic Preserve, Cecil M. Webb State Wildlife Management Area, Babcock Ranch Preserve, Bob Janes Preserve, Yucca Pens Unit State Wildlife Management Area, Prairie Pines Preserve

There are many creeks historically named "Deep Creek" in Florida, but this one runs along the highly braided Peace River. It is a tidal creek due to proximity to Gasparilla Sound-Charlotte Harbor, which opens to the Gulf of Mexico at Port Charlotte/Punta Gorda, just north of Naples. The property consists of a wealth of natural communities, the dominant being mesic flatwoods. The pine forest is interspersed with depressional marshes with a wide open expanse of scenic views and fresh air. Deep Creek and the Peace River with its associated braided creeks form the eastern border of the property and play host to salt marsh and mangrove forest created by the tidal nature of the creek. Hikers will see the open nature of the mesic flatwoods forest and can hike directly to the banks of Deep Creek.

## Hike Details

From the entrance, hike south through pasture until you reach mesic flatwoods and a four-way intersection. (Take a right and hike the loop for a shorter path option.) Continue hiking south at this intersection and slowly veer to the east to hike to the banks of Deep Creek, and be sure to make a reservation to do some peaceful backcountry camping on the banks of the creek. There are plenty of loops available here to achieve more hiking miles.

## 72. Edward W. Chance Reserve—Coker Prairie Tract

**GPS:** Lat 27.463890, Long -82.188855

**Address:** 34300 East State Road 64, Myakka City, FL 34251

**Trailhead Directions:** From Tampa, take I-75 south. In Bradenton, take CR 64 east. The entrance will be on the south side of the property, just east of Bill Parrish Road.

**Size:** 2,100 acres

**Trail Distance:** 6 miles of interior roads

**Hiking Time:** Day hike

**Difficulty:** Easy

**Trail Surface:** Sandy soils and old roadbed. Trails may be seasonally flooded at creeks.

**Shade Level:** 0–25%

**Natural Communities:** Pine flatwoods, scrubby flatwoods, scrub, freshwater marsh, hardwood hammock

**Wildlife:** Osprey, Florida black bear, Florida panther

**Maps:** www.swfwmd.state.fl.us/recreation/areas/edwardchance-coker.html

**Uses and Restrictions:** Parking, hiking. No motorized vehicles. Family-friendly hiking.

**Trail Highlights:** Hikers will enjoy hiking through the endangered scrub and scrubby flatwoods habitat.

**Additional Hiking:** Edward W. Chance Reserve—Gilley Creek Tract, Lake Manatee State Park, Duetter Park, Rye Wilderness Park, Myakka River State Park, Upper Myakka River Watershed

The Coker Prairie Tract has rare splotches of scrub and scrubby flatwoods. These habitats comprise open sandy soil, oaks that are short and stunted as a result of poor-nutrient soils that quickly drain water, and few pines. The habitat once supported the Florida scrub jay, which nests in the prickly oaks, far from pine tree perches, and caches acorns in the white sandy soil. Years of fire suppression have caused many of these areas to become overgrown, allowing trees to grow too tall and dense for the jays to survive. This habitat is also prime for Florida development because it is high and dry, a rare occurrence in the state. Jays have found refuge on well-maintained islands of state and private lands, but they are no longer found here. Hikers will love seeing the endangered and rare sandy soil–adapted plants and also crossing creeks and hiking through the mesic flatwoods of Coker Prairie.

## Hike Details

From the entrance, hike due west. Hike directly through the scrub habitat and make a loop and head back to the parking area or continue hiking west. Take a short jaunt south out of the scrub and then hike west again, back "uphill" to the scrub. From here you can do another loop and head back or continue west to cross Webb Branch creek. Take the first left west of the creek to hike a loop around scrub and then scrubby flatwoods on the fringe of the creek. Or take the second left west of the creek to hike an old roadbed through scrub and scrubby flatwoods. From the old roadbed after passing the loops, veer east through a mesic flatwoods spur, also known as Coker Prairie, or continue on the roadbed south across a creek to a last scrub loop, or hit the southern boundary and head back.

## 73. Edward W. Chance Reserve—Gilley Creek Tract

**GPS**: Lat 27.497987, Long -82.312229
**Address:** 22310 CR 675, Parrish, FL 34219
**Trailhead Directions:** From Tampa, take I-75 south. In Bradenton, take CR 64 east. Just past Lake Manatee, take CR 675 north. Just past the creek the entrance will be on your right off CR 675.
**Size:** 5,800 acres
**Trail Distance:** 12 miles of marked, multiuse, interior roads
**Hiking Time:** Day hike
**Difficulty:** Easy
**Trail Surface:** Dirt with pine needle–covered trails that may be seasonally flooded
**Shade Level:** 0–25%
**Natural Communities:** Hardwood hammocks, Florida palmetto prairie, mesic flatwoods, scrubby flatwoods
**Wildlife:** Osprey, Florida black bear, Florida panther
**Maps:** www.swfwmd.state.fl.us/recreation/areas/edwardchance-gilley.html

**Uses and Restrictions:** Bicycling, hiking, equestrian, fishing. No motorized vehicles. Family-friendly hiking.

**Trail Highlights:** Hikers will enjoy viewing Old Florida from a rancher's perspective, complete with cattle, open spaces, mesic flatwoods, and backcountry creeks.

**Additional Hiking:** Lake Manatee State Park, Duetter Park, Rye Wilderness Park, Myakka River State Park, Upper Myakka River Watershed

Surrounded by farmland, this property protects Gilley Creek, a major tributary of the Manatee River. Hardwood hammocks are found along the creek bed; however, much of the area is former row crops converted to pasture. Prescribed fire is utilized to maintain any natural areas, and lofty goals of restoring scrub habitat to the point of supporting the federally endangered Florida scrub jay are being undertaken. Hikers will walk through Old Florida cattle pasture and mesic flatwoods and cross three creeks.

## Hike Details

From the entrance, hike east and take a loop around mesic flatwoods for a shorter hike. Continue east from the loop on an old ranching road straddling mesic flatwoods on the south and pasture on the north until you dead-end into hammock bordering Gilley Creek. Head north through pasture, crossing Oak Noll Road. Travel northeast toward the tree line. Here you can cross through a branch of a tributary of Gilley Creek and head north to hike a large loop, or cross the tributary itself and hike to the east on the border of the property around the large loop to the east. Pasture and open space are in the middle of the loop. At the extreme eastern edge of this large loop you can continue on for three more loops to the east, or simply continue on the large loop to cross the creek again and backtrack to the entrance.

## 74. Flying Eagle Preserve

**GPS:** Lat 28.821656, Long -82.252888
**Address:** 11080 E Moccasin Slough Road, Inverness, FL 34450

**Trailhead Directions:** From the town of Inverness, take SR 44 west and immediately veer south on SR 41. Take a left and head east on Eden Drive, which turns into East Moccasin Slough. Follow this for many miles until the road dead-ends at Tsala Apopka Lake. Use the second entrance, which will be on the south side of the road.

**Size:** 10,950 acres

**Trail Distance:** 13 miles of designated or marked, unpaved trails

**Hiking Time:** Day hike

**Difficulty:** Easy

**Trail Surface:** Levee trail

**Shade Level:** 0–25%

**Natural Communities:** Lakes, depression marshes, floodplain swamp, scattered islands of forested swamp

**Wildlife:** Osprey, Florida black bear, Florida panther, and be on the look out for eagles. Located on western section of the Great Florida Birding and Wildlife Trail.

**Maps:** www.swfwmd.state.fl.us/recreation/areas/flyingeagle.html

**Uses and Restrictions:** Hiking, bicycling, Site 56 for bird-watching on the Great Florida Birding Trail, equestrian/group and primitive camping, 9 miles of equestrian trails, fishing, hunting, picnic tables. No motorized vehicles. Property is a wildlife management area. Be sure to visit www.myfwc.com for hunting dates before visiting. Family-friendly hiking.

**Trail Highlights:** Hikers will see scattered uplands mixed with marshes.

**Additional Hiking:** Lake Panasoffkee, Fort Cooper State Park, Citrus Wildlife Management Area, Ross Prairie State Forest, Halpata Tastanaki Preserve, Crystal River Preserve State Park, Chassahowitzka Wildlife Refuge and Wildlife Management Area

This massive property includes the Tsala Apopka Chain of Lakes and is a neighbor to the Apopka Chain of Lakes, farther east. This lake series is connected to the Floridan Aquifer and is an important aquifer recharge area. In this mosaic of small lakes, marshes, and swamps, hiking is on the levee trail that straddles the preserve and the adjacent McGregor Smith Boy Scout Reservation. Hikers will love the open space and fresh air of this large preservation area.

## Hike Details

From the entrance, head east on the trail and cross the creek. Continue to head east and then hike a short loop to the east and head back for a short hike. Or head south and take North Dead End Trail to the west, Main Road to South Dead End Trail to the west, Main Road to Dike Road to the east, or Main Road and even farther south to Tsala Trail.

## Green Swamp Wilderness Area

This preserve is made up of five different management units. Green Swamp is an important physiographic feature of Florida as it is a plateau above surrounding areas, yet it contains 560,000 acres of wetlands and flatlands along with ridgelines. Rainwater drains across the surface to create the headwaters of four major rivers: the Withlacoochee, Ocklawaha, Hillsborough, and Peace. It is also a place of groundwater recharge as water trickles down through the soil. Therefore this area is vital to protecting the quality and quantity of Florida's water supply, and this purchase was a big win for land conservation in Florida. In 1974 the state of Florida designated 322,000 acres of the area as an Area of Critical Concern, and land purchase for preservation began in the early 1970s. Hiking in the area is extensive and the Florida National Scenic Trail bisects the area. The area has been preserved in its natural state, and hikers will be amazed at this example of Florida's natural wonders. Three Green Swamp management units that offer hiking are represented here.

## 75. Green Swamp—East Tract

**GPS:** Lat 28.303069, Long -81.924567
**Address:** 17764 Rockridge Road, Polk City, FL 33868
**Trailhead Directions:** From Polk City, take CR 33 north. Take a left on Rockridge Road. The entrance will be on your right.
**Size:** 51,149 acres
**Trail Distance:** 32 miles of hiking on the Florida National Scenic Trail, which bisects the property in an east-west direction, also a 13.9-mile overnight loop, and a 7.7-mile day loop

**Hiking Time:** Day hike or overnight

**Difficulty:** Easy

**Trail Surface:** Dirt trails, seasonally flooded

**Shade Level:** 0–25%

**Natural Communities:** Wetlands, floodplain swamp, freshwater marsh, upland ridges

**Wildlife:** Avian species, other wildlife

**Maps:** www.swfwmd.state.fl.us/recreation/areas/greenswamp-east_tract.html

**Uses and Restrictions:** Hiking, bicycling, camping (with reservation), fishing and frogging, hunting. No motorized vehicles except for fishing on weekends on Rock Ridge Road in May and June. Hunting is allowed on the property. Visit www.myfwc.com for hunting dates before hiking. Family-friendly hiking.

**Contact:** Southwest Florida Water Management District, (352) 796-7211 ext. 4470

**Trail Highlights:** Hikers can experience the Florida National Scenic Trail in backcountry wetlands preserved in a natural state.

**Additional Hiking:** Colt Creek State Park, Green Swamp—Hampton Tract, Green Swamp—Little Withlacoochee Tract, Green Swamp—West Tract

Green Swamp East Tract is part of the Green Swamp Wilderness Area. This property is in the middle of the wilderness area and is the largest of the five management units within the 110,000-acre preserve. The Withlacoochee River runs through the parcel, which is characterized by wetlands, wetlands, and more wetlands. However, old road grades run throughout the property, allowing for more than 50 miles of hiking, including 32 miles of Florida National Scenic Trail. Be prepared for wet hiking, as the wild wetlands create seasonally flooded paths.

## Hike Details

From the Rock Ridge Road entrance, hike north on the Main Grade of the Florida National Scenic Trail. Hike through mesic flatwoods and wetlands and cross the Withlacoochee River. Hike west on the grade to continue on the Florida trail onto Main Line Road. The trail continues west through wetlands until you reach Trial Ford Camp, where the path crosses CR 471 and leaves the parcel to enter the Green Swamp—West Tract. Other roads are available for hiking from the Rock Ridge Road entrance that run through wetlands throughout this large property.

## 76. Green Swamp—West Tract

**GPS:** Lat 28.352323, Long -82.127514
**Address:** 13347 Ranch Road, Dade City, FL 33525
**Trailhead Directions:**

> MAIN ENTRANCE—From Dade City, take Sumner Lake Road and head east. Turn southeast onto River Road. Dead-end into the main parking area.

Green Swamp West Tract. Photo courtesy Southwest Florida Water Management District.

SOUTH ENTRANCE—From Dade City, take SR 98 southeast. Turn north onto CR 471. Just south of the Withlacoochee River and past Colt Creek State Park is the parking area.

**Size:** 37,350 acres

**Trail Distance:** 32.4 miles of Florida National Scenic Trail on Green Swamp East and West tracts, 60 miles of additional marked trails, 1.5-mile side trail connecting to Withlacoochee River Park

**Hiking Time:** Day hike or overnight

**Difficulty:** Easy

**Trail Surface:** Dirt trails with leaf litter, seasonally flooded

**Shade Level:** 0–25%

**Natural Communities:** Wetlands, floodplain swamp, freshwater marsh, upland ridges

**Wildlife:** Avian species, other wildlife

**Maps:** www.swfwmd.state.fl.us/recreation/areas/greenswamp-west.html

**Hours:** Daily from sunrise to sunset

**Uses and Restrictions:** Bicycling, bird-watching, boating and paddling (boat ramp off River Road), equestrian trails, camping, fishing, hiking, Florida National Scenic Trail, hunting, picnic facilities, handicap access and facilities available, restroom at campground, nonpotable water available at main entrance at River Road. No motorized vehicles. Property is part of wildlife management area. Be sure to visit www.myfwc.com for hunting dates prior to hiking.

**Trail Highlights:** Hikers will cross the Withlacoochee River and walk through wetlands bordering the river as they hike on the Florida National Scenic Trail.

**Additional Hiking:** Colt Creek State Park, Green Swamp—Hampton Tract, Green Swamp—Little Withlacoochee Tract, Green Swamp—West Tract

Green Swamp West Tract is part of the 110,000-acre Green Swamp Wilderness Preserve. The property is a mixture of wetlands and floodplain swamp bordering the Withlacoochee River as well as scrubby uplands that bisect the property southeast to northwest. Hikers will enjoy crossing the river and hiking alongside its floodplain swamp as well as many more miles of trails with campsites that allow for overnight hikes. The Florida National Scenic Trail continues through this property from Green Swamp East Tract and into Withlacoochee State Forest for a hiking-only paradise.

## Hike Details

From the main entrance off River Road, hike across the Withlacoochee River and north through pasture on Ranch Road. Take a left on the path with the orange blazes to get on the Florida Trail. Hike through mesic flatwoods and wetlands. The Florida Trail goes east of Foster Bridge Camp before joining a former woods road. Here it borders the Withlacoochee River floodplain swamp before eventually crossing Main Line Road and heading into scrub habitat. At High Bluff Campsite it crosses the border into Withlacoochee State Forest. Hikers can walk more of the Florida Trail on this tract by entering off CR 471 at McNeill Entrance. There are many miles of trails on this property. A unique route on Main Line Road will send you through sandy soil uplands that are part of the characteristic ridge within Green Swamp Wilderness Area, rare among the thousands of acres of wetlands.

## 77. Green Swamp—Hampton Tract

**GPS:** Lat 28.259268, Long -81.958491

**Address:** 18490 Rock Ridge Road, Lakeland, FL 33809

**Trailhead Directions:** From Dade City, take SR 98/US 301 South and veer off to the southeast on SR 98. Turn to the north on Rockridge Road; the property entrance is at the intersection of Rockridge Road and Deen Still Road West.

**Size:** 11,052 acres

**Trail Distance:** 28 miles of multiuse trails

**Hiking Time:** Day hike or overnight

**Difficulty:** Easy

**Trail Surface:** Dirt trails, seasonally flooded

**Shade Level:** 0–25%

**Natural Communities:** Wetlands, floodplain swamp, freshwater marsh, upland ridges

**Wildlife:** Avian species, other wildlife

**Maps:** www.swfwmd.state.fl.us/recreation/areas/greenswamp-hampton_tract.html

**Uses and Restrictions:** Bicycling, camping, equestrian use, fishing, hiking, picnic facilities, handicap access and facilities available. No motorized vehicles.

**Trail Highlights:** Hikers can cross creeks at eight different points on this property.

**Additional Hiking:** Colt Creek State Park, Green Swamp—Hampton Tract, Green Swamp—Little Withlacoochee Tract, Green Swamp—West Tract

This parcel is part of the Green Swamp Wilderness Preserve. It is east of Colt Creek State Park and southwest of Green Swamp East Tract. It hosts Colt Creek, Gator Creek, and Bee Tree Drain along with the associated wetlands of those creeks. Hiking is along a series of old grades and levees traversing mesic flatwoods and wetland strands.

## Hike Details

From the Hampton Gate at the main entrance, hike northwest through mesic flatwoods and wetlands. Stay on Buddy Sutton Grade to cross Colt Creek and reach a fishing area. From here hike west across Colt Creek and then south on Levee Grade. Here you will hike across Gator Creek and through miles and miles of mesic flatwoods and wetland strands before heading east on a loop back to the trailhead. There are many miles of hiking on this property to explore. Simply take the map and some provisions for a long hike or overnight camping for a true Florida backcountry experience.

## 78. Half Moon–Gum Slough in Half Moon Wildlife Management Area

**GPS:** Lat 28.869571, Long -82.218177

**Address:** 8864 CR 247, Lake Panasoffkee, FL 33538

**Trailhead Directions:** From Ocala, take I-75 south and turn east on SR 44. Turn north on CR 247/Half Moon Ranch Road, just before the

Withlacoochee River. Just past CR 248 there is a parking area on CR 247.

**Size:** 9,480 acres

**Trail Distance:** 24 miles of designated or marked multiuse trails

**Hiking Time:** Day hike

**Difficulty:** Easy

**Trail Surface**: Dirt path

**Shade Level:** 0–25%

**Natural Communities:** Springs, sloughs, mesic flatwoods, wet flatwoods, hydric hammock

**Wildlife:** Osprey, Florida black bear, Florida panther

**Maps:** www.swfwmd.state.fl.us/recreation/areas/gumslough.html

**Admission:** None

**Hours:** Daily from sunrise to sunset

**Uses and Restrictions:** Trails for hiking, bicycling, and equestrian use, freshwater ponds open for fishing (with license), hunting, picnic facilities, handicap access and facilities available, restrooms and water available at hunt check station. No motorized vehicles. Property is a wildlife management area. Be sure to visit www.myfwc.com for hunting dates before visiting the property. Family-friendly hiking.

**Trail Highlights:** Hikers can walk along the edge of floodplain swamp that borders the floodplains of the Withlacoochee River.

**Additional Hiking:** Lake Panasoffkee, Potts Preserve, Flying Eagle Preserve, Halpata Tastanaki Preserve, Two Mile Prairie, Withlacoochee State Forest, Half Moon-Gum Slough Wildlife Management Area

Half Moon-Gum Slough is a property bordering the Withlacoochee River. It protects the river and its wetlands, including Gum Slough that flows into it. Gum Slough is a 4-mile spring run formed from several springs. The area affords 24 miles of hiking trails through floodplain swamp edge, mesic flatwoods, and hydric hammock.

## Hike Details

From the entrance, hike north. Follow the trail until you come to an intersection with a choice of left or right; take a right. Hike left and then south into the Half Moon-Gum Slough property. Then hike west and then north along the floodplain edge. You will be able to follow this path until you can take a right at the next intersection and make a loop back to the entrance. Or you can follow this trail for many miles to the north until you reach the border of Gum Slough floodplains, with many opportunities to loop back along the route to follow the trail south through the Half Moon Wildlife Management Area property and back to the parking area.

## 79. Lake Panasoffkee

**GPS:** Lat 28.869571, Long -82.218177
**Address:** 7519 NW 18th Way, Wildwood, FL 34785
**Trailhead Directions:** From Orlando, take US 27 northwest toward I-75. Travel north on I-75 and immediately exit on SR 44 west. After going around a curve, take a left into the parking area on NW 18th Way.
**Size:** 9,911 acres
**Trail Distance:** 18 miles of marked trails
**Hiking Time:** Day hike
**Difficulty:** Easy
**Trail Surface:** Grassed roads
**Shade Level:** 25–75%
**Natural Communities:** Floodplain forest, scrub, sandhills, mesic flatwoods
**Wildlife:** Alligator, osprey, Florida black bear, Florida panther
**Maps:** www.swfwmd.state.fl.us/recreation/areas/lakepanasoffkee.html
**Uses and Restrictions:** Bicycling on 8 miles of marked trails, hiking and equestrian use on 18 miles of multiuse trails, equestrian/group/ primitive camping, nonpotable water, restrooms, fishing at Little Jones Creek and two borrow pits, hunting, picnic facilities. No motorized vehicles. Property is a wildlife management area. Be sure to visit www. myfwc.com for hunting dates before visiting the property. Family-friendly hiking.
**Trail Highlights:** Hikers will enjoy crossing Little Jones Creek as well as the opportunity to hike a long distance through floodplain swamp.

**Additional Hiking:** Flying Eagle Preserve, Half Moon-Gum Slough Wildlife Management Area, Half Moon-Gum Slough, Panasoffkee Outlet, Jumper Creek Wildlife Management Area, Citrus Wildlife Management Area, Emeralda Marsh Conservation Area, Lake Apopka Restoration Area, Crystal River Preserve State Park

This property was preserved to protect the wetlands associated with Lake Panasoffkee. The property protects Little Jones Creek and Big Jones Creek and thousands of acres of floodplain forest that filter water flowing into Lake Panasoffkee. The property offers 18 miles of trails that can be shortened through loops or hiked through by utilizing two cars: one parked at the main entrance off SR 44 and one at the southeast entrance off CR 514. Hikers will get to cross the bridge at Little Jones Creek and wander through miles of undisturbed mesic flatwoods and floodplain forest.

## Hike Details

Hike south into the property on Jones Creek Trail. Walk through pasture, then skirt the edge of a depression marsh, and walk through pasture again. When you reach the first intersection, take a left, heading east to hike the loop trail. Hike a sinuous path along the edge of floodplain swamp until you reach the bridge at Little Jones Creek. Cross the creek to view the swamp and then turn back if you would like to cut the hike off here and return via the western side of the loop trail. Or continue on and hike a short loop or even further to two spur trails. The short loop has dense mesic flatwoods on the edge of the floodplain swamp, with a large, treeless depression marsh in the center. The Borrow Pit Trail leads north from the small loop through mesic flatwoods and floodplain swamp toward the eastern boundary of the property. The Jones Creek Trail leads south off the small loop and connects three mesic flatwood uplands in a necklace that extends to the southeast corner of the property. The trail then takes a 90-degree turn to the south through mesic flatwoods before ending at CR 514. Hikers can hike straight through from the entrance to the CR 514 access.

# 80. Little Manatee River—Southfork Tract

**GPS:** Lat 27.588467, Long -82.239442

**Address:** 2940 SR 62, Duette, FL 33834

**Trailhead Directions:** From Bradenton, take US 301 north. Head east on SR 62. The property is just past Lake Parrish on the north side of SR 62.

**Size:** 970 acres

**Trail Distance:** 5.5 miles of interior roads

**Hiking Time:** Half-day hike

**Difficulty:** Easy

**Trail Surface:** Sandy soil

**Shade Level:** 0–25%

**Natural Communities:** Mesic flatwoods, bottomland hardwood forest, scrub, scrubby flatwoods

**Wildlife:** Alligator, osprey, Florida black bear, Florida panther

**Maps:** www.swfwmd.state.fl.us/recreation/areas/littlemanatee-southfork.html

**Uses and Restrictions:** Parking, hiking. No motorized vehicles. Family-friendly hiking.

**Trail Highlights:** The trail traverses rare scrub and scrubby flatwoods habitat.

**Additional Hiking:** Lower Manatee Watershed, Little Manatee River State Park, Moody Branch Mitigation Park, Beker State Park, Terra Ceia Preserve State Park, Tampa Bay Estuarine Ecosystem

This property protects the Little Manatee River watershed. It has wetlands crossing the property between which are high and dry scrub and scrubby flatwoods habitat. These areas are rare in Florida because they are sought for development. Hikers will enjoy the uplands and wetlands interspersed throughout this property on five miles of hiking trails.

## Hike Details

From the SR 62 parking area, hike northeast from the trailhead and hike the exterior of scrub and scrubby habitat. This area has white sandy soil and is characterized by oaks of short stature and open sand where scrub jays cache their acorns. Take this triangle-shaped loop back to the entrance for a short 1.75-mile hike. If you would like a longer hike, hike north from the entrance. Cross two creeks before reaching a T intersection. Hike the loop and then a second loop through scrub and scrubby flatwoods before returning back to your vehicle. Backtrack after the loop trail or the out-and-back spur.

## 80. Little Manatee River—Upper Tract

**GPS:** Lat 27.676018, Long -82.269332
**Address:** 3398 CR 579, Wimauma, FL 33598
**Trailhead Directions:** From Bradenton, take US 301 northwest. Take a right heading southeast on Dug Creek Road. Take a 90-degree turn to the northeast (left) on the same road and then a left on CR 579. The entrance will be just north of the intersection of Dug Creek Road and CR 579.
**Size:** 4,364 acres
**Trail Distance:** Network of old trail roads
**Hiking Time:** Day hike
**Difficulty:** Easy
**Trail Surface:** Sandy soils, seasonally flooded trails
**Shade Level:** 0–25%
**Natural Communities:** Floodplain swamp, mesic flatwoods, sand pine scrub, oak hammocks
**Wildlife:** Alligator, osprey, Florida scrub jay
**Maps:** www.swfwmd.state.fl.us/recreation/areas/littlemanatee-upper.html
**Uses and Restrictions:** Fishing, hiking, paddling. No motorized vehicles. Family-friendly hiking.
**Contact:** Hillsborough County Parks, Recreation, and Conservation Department, (813) 672-7876
**Trail Highlights:** Hikers will be amazed at views of the striking Little Manatee River.
**Additional Hiking:** Little Manatee River State Park, Moody Branch Mitigation Bank, Cockroach Bay Preserve State Park, Bullfrog Creek

Mitigation Park Wildlife Environmental Area, Lake Manatee Lower
Watershed

This property is unique because it has high and dry sand pine situated
right next to floodplain swamp along the Little Manatee River. Trails
here afford many miles of hiking in an out-and-back fashion.

## Hike Details

From the Leonard Lee Road entrance, hike east along the sand pine
scrub. This is a high, dry area with tall sand pine and white sandy
soil. Cross the creek and continue hiking on a squiggly path around
the western border of an open area and then on the border of mesic
flatwoods and creek floodplain. The hike will take you south and then
immediately back north across a creek. Hike along the floodplain in a
northeast direction until you reach Grange Hall Loop. You can continue
across the street for more hiking as part of this conservation area or
backtrack to the parking area.

## 81. Myakka River—Deer Prairie Creek

**GPS:** Lat 27.107554, Long -82.318895
**Address:** 7001 Forbes Trail, Venice FL
**Trailhead Directions:**
NORTH ENTRANCE—From Venice, take E. Venice Avenue to the east.
  Turn north onto Jacaranda Boulevard. Turn east onto Border Road.
  Turn south onto S. Moon Drive. Travel under I-75 and turn left onto
  Forbes Trail. Dead-end into the parking area.
SOUTH ENTRANCE—From Venice, take SR 41 South and then east.
  Cross the Myakka River and then turn north into parking area
  opposite Boardwalk Road.
**Size:** 10,128 acres
**Trail Distance:** 75 miles of unpaved trails
**Hiking Time:** Day hike
**Difficulty:** Easy
**Trail Surface:** Dirt paths, seasonally flooded trails

**Shade Level:** 0–25%

**Natural Communities:** Mesic flatwoods, floodplain swamp, wetland strands, depression marshes

**Wildlife:** Alligator, osprey

**Maps:** www.swfwmd.state.fl.us/recreation/areas/myakka-deerprairie.html

**Admission:** None

**Hours:** Daily from sunrise to sunset

**Uses and Restrictions:** Bicycling on 75 miles of unpaved trails, 22 miles of designated equestrian trails, fishing access, hiking, paddling access, picnic facilities, hunting. No motorized vehicles. Property is a wildlife management area. Be sure to visit www.myfwc.com for hunting dates before visiting the property. Family-friendly hiking.

**Contact:** Sarasota County Natural Resources Department, (941) 861-5000

**Trail Highlights:** Enjoy crossing Deer Prairie Creek as well as hiking through thousands of acres of mesic flatwoods and wetlands.

**Additional Hiking:** Myakka River State Park, Myakka River State Forest, Jelks Preserve, T. Mabry Carlton, Jr. Memorial Reserve, Sleeping Turtles Preserve—North

This property protects the floodplains of the Myakka River. The Myakka River flows from west of Bradenton southwest toward Venice and out through the Gasparilla Sound/Charlotte Harbor in Venice. The property is thousands of acres of mesic flatwoods interspersed with wetland swamps and circular depression marshes. There are more than 75 miles of former logging roads turned into trails for ample hiking opportunities.

## Hike Details

Hikers have two access options for 75 miles of hiking opportunities. From the south entrance, many loops pass through mesic flatwoods, wetland strands, and depression marshes. Hike directly north from the south entrance on an old road to cross Deer Prairie Creek and continue hiking on loops throughout to the north side of the property. Or enter from the north end and hike south into the property through pasture before accessing many loops through miles of mesic flatwoods, wetlands, and pasture.

# 82. Myakka River—Flatford Swamp

**GPS:** Lat 27.421817, Long -82.133420

**Address:** 39450 Taylor Road, Myakka City, FL 34251

**Trailhead Directions:** From Bradenton, take SR 64 east and cross the Manatee River. At Wauchula Road, travel south. The parking area will be on your right.

**Size:** 2,357 acres

**Trail Distance:** Around 5 miles in a network of old trail roads

**Hiking Time:** 2 hours

**Difficulty:** Easy

**Trail Surface:** Seasonally flooded trails

**Shade Level:** 0–25%

**Natural Communities:** Bottomland swamp, freshwater marsh, mesic flatwoods, hardwood swamp

**Wildlife:** Alligator, osprey

**Maps:** www.swfwmd.state.fl.us/recreation/areas/myakka-flatford.html

**Uses and Restrictions:** Fishing, hiking. No motorized vehicles. Family-friendly hiking.

**Trail Highlights:** This property provides for a short backcountry hike through mesic flatwoods.

**Additional Hiking:** Manatee County's Duette Park, Lake Manatee State Park, Myakka River State Park

The Flatford Swamp parcel protects more than 2,000 acres of wetlands that are part of the headwaters of the Myakka River. This land protects water quality and water flow to the Upper Myakka Lake, water within the river, and water within Myakka River State Park. Sand Slough, Long Creek, Myakka River, Ogleby Creek, and Maple Creek flow through the property. Hiking is within the uplands on the east side. Mesic flatwoods are the dominant natural community in hiking views.

## Hike Details

From the parking area, hike the loop around the mesic flatwoods. In the middle of the northern loop, hike across the wetland swamp to a second loop. This loop also passes through mesic flatwoods. Additional hiking can be found at a walk-in area off Grainger Farms Road and Wauchula Road south of the main entrance.

## 83. Panasoffkee Outlet

**GPS:** Lat 28.80073, Long -82.153378
**Address:** 3100 CR 413, Lake Panasoffkee, FL 33538
**Trailhead Directions:** From Weeki Wachee, take SR 50 east to SR 98 east to I-75 and head north. Exit on SR 44 and head east. Turn south on CR 470. Veer south on CR 413; the entrance will be on your right with parking available at Marsh Bend County Park.
**Size:** 1,118 acres
**Trail Distance:** Around 3 miles of old woods roads, seasonally flooded, so hiking in dry winter months is advisable
**Hiking Time:** 2 hours
**Difficulty:** Easy
**Trail Surface:** Seasonally flooded trails
**Shade Level:** 50–75%
**Natural Communities:** Mesic flatwoods, freshwater marshes, scrub habitat
**Wildlife:** Avian species and other wildlife
**Maps:** www.swfwmd.state.fl.us/recreation/areas/panasoffkee.html
**Uses and Restrictions:** Bird-watching, fishing, hiking, boating, paddling, picnic facilities. Developed recreation can be found in adjacent county park. No motorized vehicles. Family-friendly hiking.
**Trail Highlights:** Hikers will pass through backcountry wilderness on the fringe of floodplain forest and mesic flatwoods, with direct access to the Withlacoochee River.
**Additional Hiking:** Flying Eagle Preserve, Half Moon-Gum Slough, Jumper Creek Wildlife Management Area, Lake Panasoffkee, Citrus Wildlife Management Area, Chassahowitzka National Wildlife Management Area, Richloam Wildlife Management Area, Chassahowitzka National Wildlife Refuge, Waccasassa Bay Preserve State Park

Just north of Weeki Wachee Springs lie Chassahowitzka and Lake Panasoffkee along the Withlacoochee River. These Native American–

named conservation areas are a natural majesty of the Old Florida kind. Panasoffkee Outlet protects the border of Princess Lake, Panasoffkee Outlet River, and pristine river corridor along the Withlacoochee River. Hiking is along the ecotone, the space where two different natural communities meet and host unique plants and wildlife, between the floodplain swamp and the mesic flatwoods. This hike has access to the Withlacoochee River.

## Hike Details

From the county park entrance, hike due west, crossing over the abandoned railroad. You'll hike with floodplain swamp to your left with old oaks, cypress trees, and wetlands, and on your right, mesic flatwoods with pines and palmetto. Hike west until you reach a three-way intersection and take a left, hiking to the Withlacoochee River and the northernmost point of Princess Lake. Take in views of the river and then backtrack. Hike north at the three-way intersection and continue north, taking a left. At the next intersection, decide whether to continue hiking north to the walk-through at CR 315 or veer to the east and hike through mesic flatwoods to North County Road 470. Hikers must backtrack at this point.

## 84. Potts Preserve

**GPS:** Lat 27.907071, Long -82.278857

**Address:** 2988 North Hooty Point, Inverness, FL 34453

**Trailhead Directions:** From Inverness, take SR 44 west to SR 41 north. Turn north onto CR 581 and follow this until you reach a 90 degree curve to the right. Continue on CR 581 until it turns to the north and changes to E. Turner Camp Road/CR 581. The road then changes into N. Hooty Point Road. Before dead-ending into the Withlacoochee River, take a left and you will drive into the parking area.

**Size:** 8,500 acres

**Trail Distance:** 30 miles open for hiking with a 4-mile marked river trail and a 16-mile loop trail. Orange blaze trails are primary trail, blue blazes indicate side trails, white blazes indicate overnight loop, double blazes indicate a sharp turn in the trail.

Potts Preserve. Photo courtesy Southwest Florida Water Management District.

**Hiking Time:** Day hike
**Difficulty:** Easy
**Trail Surface:** Seasonally flooded trails and old roads
**Shade Level:** 0–25%
**Natural Communities:** Wetlands, depression marshes, mesic flatwoods, scrub habitat
**Wildlife:** Gopher tortoise, avian species, Florida scrub jays, and other wildlife
**Maps:** http://www.swfwmd.state.fl.us/recreation/areas/potts.html
**Uses and Restrictions:** Bicycling, bird-watching, boating and paddling, camping, nonpotable water, equestrian trails, hiking, hunting, picnic facilities available at campsite, portable toilets located at equestrian/ group and primitive campgrounds. No motorized vehicles. Property

is a wildlife management area. Visit www.myfwc.com for hunting dates before you hike. Family-friendly hiking.

**Contact:** Southwest Florida Water Management District, (352) 796-7211 ext. 4470

**Trail Highlights:** Miles and miles of trails guide hikers through wild wetlands and around rough scrub where the Florida scrub jay takes haven.

**Additional Hiking:** Halpata Tastanaki Preserve, Ross Prairie State Forest, Citrus Wildlife Management Area, Panasoffkee Outlet, Lake Panasoffkee

Potts Preserve is a massive expanse of wetlands and high sandy scrub uplands between the Withlacoochee River and the Tsala Apopka Chain of Lakes. This is an important area for groundwater recharge and discharge as well as for the protection of surface water wetlands and wetland habitat. It is also home to rare scrub habitat with the endangered Florida scrub jay. Hikers will enjoy miles upon miles of hiking trails on old roads that traverse through wetlands, scrub habitat, and Florida backcountry.

## Hike Details

Hike north towards River Camp through mesic flatwoods. At River Camp, decide to hike west through depression marshes and mesic flatwoods to an old road trail or hike north to the scrub habitat. If you hike north, you will take River Road and reach the Holly Tree Camp campsite on the edge of the scrub. If you hike west, you will reach the main road and you can then hike north or hike south and then west to the equestrian camp. From here you will hike the north Loop Road through wetlands on an old road. When you reach the intersection of North Loop Road and Otter Side Road, you can take the loop back east and then south, heading back to Hooty Point road. Or you can take the Otter Side Road loop and reach the Tsala Apopka Outfall Canal before looping back to Cow Pen Cutoff and the western side of the scrub habitat, heading south towards the parking area. Be aware that this property provides for miles and miles of hiking with no exit points except for the equestrian and North Hooty Point Road entrances so be prepared with plenty of water and food for your hike.

## 85. Two Mile Prairie

**GPS:** Lat 28.91271, Long -82.402200
**Address:** 7160 N. Lecanto Highway, Hernando, FL 34442
**Trailhead Directions:**

> SOUTH TRAILHEAD—From Inverness, take SR 41 north and head east on CR 491. After passing North Paradise Point, take a left and head into the property to park.

> NORTH TRAILHEAD—From Inverness, take SR 41 north and head east on East Citrus Springs Boulevard. Take a right on East Withlacoochee Trail. The parking area will be on your right at the Oxbow Recreation Trailhead.

**Size:** 2,900 acres
**Trail Distance:** 2.8 miles to 8.3 miles on equestrian hiking trail
**Hiking Time:** 2 hours to day hike
**Difficulty:** Easy
**Trail Surface:** Dirt trails, seasonally flooded
**Shade Level**: 0–25%
**Natural Communities:** Sandhill, scrub, cypress swamp, upland sandhill lake
**Wildlife:** Avian species, other wildlife
**Maps:** http://www.swfwmd.state.fl.us/recreation/areas/twomile.html
**Uses and Restrictions:** Bird-watching, camping, equestrian trails, fishing, hiking, restrooms and nonpotable water at Bear Head Hammock Trailhead (south entrance). No motorized vehicles. Family-friendly hiking.
**Contact:** Florida Forest Service, Withlacoochee State Forest, (352) 754-6898
**Trail Highlights:** Climb to the top of the lookout tower and view the upland sandhill lake of Johnson Pond.
**Additional Hiking:** Halpata Tastanaki Preserve, Marjorie Harris Carr Cross Florida Greenway, Ross Prairie State Forest, Goethe State Forest, Crystal River, Waccasassa Bay Preserve State Park

Two Mile Prairie preserves land on the southern boundary of the Withlacoochee River at the northern end of Tsala Apopka Chain of

Lakes. In this rural area on the western side of Florida, you'll find mesic flatwoods, wetlands, cypress swamps, and scrub. The sandhill upland lake at Johnson Pond provides for clear water and a glimpse into Florida's underground aquifer as sandhill lakes are groundwater-fed, circular sinkholes that reach the groundwater column during times of high water. Experience hiking through rare sandhill and scrub and climbing the lookout tower with views of the Johnson Pond upland sandhill lake!

## Hike Details

From the Johnson Pond Trailhead, hike in and immediately turn east to hike the loop through sandhill to the Johnson Pond Lookout Tower. Enjoy this quiet view! Hike the loop back for a shorter hike. Or continue heading south past the lookout tower to hike through scrub habitat with white sandy soils and low-growing oaks. Hiking south through the scrub takes you on a long loop to the west and back north through sandhill habitat. From the south entrance's Bear Head Hammock Trailhead, hike into the property past the camp sites and restrooms and head north. This route will take hikers on a long loop through sandhill, planted pine, and a wetland pond at the very northern point of the loop.

# 5

## South Florida District

At the northern boundary, the South Florida Water Management District begins with a narrow swath of land sandwiched between the Southwest Florida Water Management District and the St. Johns River Water Management District just west of Orlando. It runs south in this narrow band as a way to manage and protect the Kissimmee River watershed. The eastern boundary widens to the ocean where the Florida Turnpike turns east, just south of Fort Drum Marsh Conservation Area (the beginning of the north-flowing headwaters of the St. Johns River). On the western boundary, the narrow swath runs south from the west side of Orlando to Lake Istokpoga, excluding the placid lakes, and extends a small distance north on the west side of the placid lakes to include Fisheating Creek, which flows southwest into Lake Okeechobee. It then runs west to the Gulf of Mexico to include the Caloosahatchee River and land just north of Ft. Myers. From Ft. Myers to Vero Beach the district covers all the rest of Florida to the south. This boundary was created to manage the Kissimmee River and everything south, including the Everglades system.

The land within the South Florida boundary is flat and historically wet and wild. Ever since Napoleon Bonaparte Broward promoted draining of the Everglades in 1905, the theme of this area has been to dredge and drain and make way for development. The Everglades were altered, drained, and diked as the areas south of Lake Okeechobee were cleared and drained for ranching, and the water was prevented from flowing naturally to the Everglades. Such steps facilitated development on the South Florida coasts, where the large cities of Miami and Ft. Lauderdale on the Atlantic Ocean grew into a massive metroplex, with development and concrete now reaching from Miami west to the Everglades, making up the area known as South Florida.

In 1949, with flooding, wildlife decline, and water quality issues, the State of Florida designated the Central and South Florida Flood Control District to manage flooding issues in the region. This division merged into the South Florida Water Management District, which today manages 2,200 water control structures, 2,300 canals, and the associated pump stations. The South Florida Water Management District must balance water supply, water quality, environmental quality, and water treatment to fulfill its charge of providing a service to 7.5 million residents and farms, as well as manage water concerns in swamps from Orlando to the Florida Keys.

Hiking trails in South Florida offer a mixture of natural and human-engineered environments. Features include large sections of mesic flatwoods and depression marsh ecosystems surrounded by farms, stormwater treatment areas hosting beautiful wetlands with a plethora of avian birds and other wildlife, and levees along canals that overlook glades marshes and tree islands of the Everglades. Hikers will be rewarded with glimpses of beautiful South Florida habitat, the restored Kissimmee River, and swamps and marshes, all preserved by the district and partnering organizations.

## Basics for the South Florida District

Be sure to note whether trails are seasonally flooded (typically in the summer rainy season) and whether there is hunting. Check www.myfwc .com for hunting dates prior to hiking.

Unless otherwise noted, all properties in this region are open from sunrise to sunset, free of charge. For any additional questions, contact the South Florida Water Management District office at (800) 250-4250.

## 86. Shingle Creek

### GPS:
THE VISTAS IN HUNTER'S CREEK—Lat 28.366516, Long 81.452703
HUNTER'S CREEK MIDDLE SCHOOL—Lat 28.367439, Long 81.433959
MARRIOTT ENTRANCE—Lat 28.397247, Long -81.459977

**Address:**

THE VISTAS IN HUNTER'S CREEK—12930 Hunter's Vista Boulevard, Orlando, FL 32837

HUNTER'S CREEK MIDDLE SCHOOL—13400 Town Loop Boulevard, Orlando, FL 32837

MARRIOTT ENTRANCE—5901 Avenida Vista, Orlando, FL

**Trailhead Directions:**

From Orlando, take I-4 to Highway 91 south. Take a left on Highway 417 and travel west. Take a right into Town Loop Boulevard and enter the middle school at the bus entrance. Parking is behind the school along the chain-link fence, only on weekends and during nonschool hours.

THE VISTAS IN HUNTER'S CREEK—Continue west on Highway 417 (Central Florida Greenway, toll road) and take a left into Hunter's Vista Boulevard. Travel approximately 1 mile north to the parking area on the left at Vista Park, just after Flora Vista Drive. Hike north along the power line easement 0.3 miles to the conservation area.

MARRIOTT ENTRANCE—Take I-4 southwest to the Central Florida Parkway exit and head west. From Central Florida Parkway take International Drive and head south. Turn left into the Marriott Grande Vista Resort. Park at the tennis courts.

**Trail Distance:** 5 miles

**Hiking Time:** Half-day hike

**Difficulty:** Easy

**Trail Surface:** Dirt roads, seasonally flooded trails

**Shade Level:** 25–50%

**Natural Communities:** Mixed hardwood swamp, mesic flatwoods, cypress swamp, oak hammock, wet prairies, depression marsh

**Wildlife:** White-tailed deer, alligator, wild turkey, resident and migratory bird species

**Maps:** www.sfwmd.com

**Hours:** Hunter's Point Subdivision access, 10 am to sunset; Hunter's Creek Middle School, sunrise to sunset, weekends and nonschool hours

**Uses and Restrictions:** Bicycling, primitive canoe ramp, kayaking/canoeing, hiking, fishing. No motorized vehicles. Family-friendly hiking.

**Trail Highlights:** Hikers have a choice of loops through islands of higher-elevation mesic flatwoods.

**Additional Hiking:** Lake Louisa State Park, Hal Scott Regional Preserve and Park

Shingle Creek marks the northern boundary of land protected by South Florida Water Management District. It is the first stop on the Everglades Trail, a series of driving destinations planned for seeing and understanding the Everglades ecosystem. The creek joins Reedy Creek and then flows into Lake Tohopekaliga; Shingle Creek is the major water source for the lake. The creek connects to the Kissimmee Chain of Lakes via a series of lakes, creeks, and canals. The Chain of Lakes connects to Lake Okeechobee, which eventually flows to the Everglades through a series of canals and water treatment areas. This property protects the Kissimmee watershed, which is surrounded by development, and even this far north, in Orlando, it protects water flowing into the Everglades. Hikers will experience a 5-mile hike through hardwood hammock and floodplain as well as a loop around an island of mesic flatwoods in pine.

## Hike Details

Hunter's Creek Middle School Shingle Creek Trailhead: Hike northwest into the property and then hike east, crossing a boardwalk bridge across the Shingle Creek canal. Hike north through mesic flatwoods and the fringe of forested wetlands until reaching the power lines. Hike west along the power lines until reaching a wetter area with a north (right) turn. Hike north and travel to the Pine Island East Loop. After completing the loop, hike south and then east, back to the parking area, or continue hiking west and then south to The Vistas in Hunter's Creek trailhead. Or hike north to the second loop at Pine Island West Loop and continue north to the Marriott entrance along an old logging grade.

## 87. Lake Marion Creek Wildlife Management Area

**GPS:**

SNELL CREEK—Lat 28.132396, Long -81.541432

HUCKLEBERRY ISLANDS—Lat 28.140003, Long -81.522979

**Address:**

> SNELL CREEK—County Road 580, Haines City, FL 33844
>
> HUCKLEBERRY ISLANDS—Poinciana, FL 34758

**Trailhead Directions:**

FROM US 27—Take the exit for 17/92 North/East, turn right onto Johnson Avenue, which becomes CR 580, and travel approximately 5 miles.

FROM KISSIMMEE—Take US 17/92, Orange Blossom Trail/John Young Parkway south, and turn left onto Pleasant Hill Road. Travel approximately 15 miles. Pleasant Hill Road becomes Cypress Parkway and then CR 580.

**Size:** 8,000 acres

**Trail Distance:**

> HUCKLEBERRY ISLANDS—6 miles round-trip
>
> SNELL CREEK—2.37 miles round-trip

**Hiking Time:** Day hike

**Difficulty:** Easy

**Trail Surface:** Sandy roads at Snell Creek and dirt trail at Huckleberry Islands. Beware of seasonally flooded trails.

**Shade Level:** 25–50%

**Natural Communities:** Wet flatwoods, floodplain swamp

**Wildlife:** White-tailed deer, feral hog, wading birds such as white ibis, little blue heron, great blue heron, and great egret, the endangered Florida scrub jay, gopher tortoise, and the rare sand skink

**Maps:** www.myfwc.com/media/2791703/Lake-Marion-Creek-Map.pdf

**Uses and Restrictions:** Snell Creek: Hiking trail; Huckleberry Island: Camping, hiking, kayaking, picnicking. No motorized vehicles. The property is a wildlife management area. Be sure to visit www.myfwc.com for hunting dates prior to hiking. Family-friendly hiking.

**Contact:** (850) 488-4676

**Trail Highlights:** At Snell Creek hikers will experience a rare scrubby flatwoods hike near the creek. At Huckleberry Islands, hikers will pass through wetlands as they visit three islands that reach greater elevations as they travel north.

**Additional Hiking:** Lake Marion Creek Horse Creek, Lake Marion

Creek Baltic Road, Allen David Broussard Catfish Creek Preserve, Lake Kissimmee State Park

This area is split into five access points that all boast hikes through different types of natural communities. Two access points are in Snell Creek, a high and dry hike through a scrub ridge. The Huckleberry Islands host trails through wetlands to reach three islands with different natural communities as they rise higher in elevation from island to island. This area is part of the Upper Lakes Basin Watershed, an area that protects Lake Marion, Snell Creek, and the Kissimmee Chain of Lakes, which connect the Kissimmee River to Lake Okeechobee and the Everglades.

## Hike Details

Snell Creek: From the trail entrance, hike west. Meander along a strand of wetlands and continue west. Hike north toward Snell Creek and continue around a loop through scrubby flatwoods and return to the entrance. Huckleberry Islands: Hike north along swampy wetlands and reach an island of mesic flatwoods; continue north and reach a circular island that has a four-way intersection. Continue north and reach the final island with white scrubby soils and oak scrub, the highest of the three in elevation.

## 88. Kissimmee River Public Use Area: Hickory Hammock Wildlife Management Area: Hickory Hammock Trailhead (Bluff Hammock Management Area hiking, Boney Marsh Management Area hiking)

**GPS:** Lat 27.402585, Long -81.168626
**Address:** Hickory Hammock WMA, Lorida, FL 33857
**Trailhead Directions:** From Ft. Pierce, take SR 70 west to Okeechobee. Take Highway 98 northwest to Basinger. Continue west until you cross the Istokpoga Canal. The entrance is 0.5 miles past the canal on your left.
**Size:** 4,000 acres

The Florida National Scenic Trail. Photo courtesy South Florida Water Management District.

**Trail Distance:** 11 miles

**Hiking Time:** Day hike or overnight

**Difficulty:** Easy

**Trail Surface:** Dirt path

**Shade Level:** 25–50%

**Natural Communities:** Marsh, scrub, hickory and cabbage palm hammocks

**Wildlife:** White-tailed deer, feral hog, wild turkey, gopher tortoise, swallow-tailed kite

**Maps:** www.myfwc.com/media/2791324/Hickory-Hammock-Map.pdf

**Uses and Restrictions:** Hiking, air boating, bicycling, boating, primitive camping, canoeing, equestrian trails and camping, fishing, hunting, kayaking, shelters. No motorized vehicles. Family-friendly hiking.

**Trail Highlights:** Hikers will find a 25-foot-high bridge over the Kissimmee River 3 miles north of Hickory Hammock.

**Additional Hiking:** Kissimmee Prairie State Park, Lake Wales Ridge National Wildlife Refuge, Taylor Creek/Nubbins Slough

This property provides protection for the Kissimmee River, which meanders south on its path toward Lake Okeechobee. The hiking trails on the property include about 6 miles of hiking-only paths on the west side of the Kissimmee River if entering from the Hickory Hammock Equestrian Center Campground, or a 10-mile hike if starting from SR 98 Istokpoga Creek Boat Ramp. The trail wanders along hardwood hammock interspersed with depression marshes as the hiker moves north through the property.

Hike Details

From Istokpoga Creek Boat Ramp at the Hickory Hammock hiking trailhead, hike northeast and then north. After around 4 miles you will reach the Hickory Hammock Equestrian Center Campground. Hike in a north-northwest direction along the western boundary through hardwood hammock. The trail continues north and on through the water management district's Boney Marsh property. Turn back at any time to return to your vehicle.

## 89. Kissimmee River Public Use Area: Chandler Slough Management Unit

**GPS:** Lat 27.356070, Long -81.013015
**Address:** 12190 Lofton Road, Okeechobee, FL 34972
**Trailhead Directions:** From Okeechobee, take Highway 98 northwest for 15 miles. Take a left on Lofton Road and dead-end into the designated parking area.
**Size:** 3,722 acres
**Trail Distance:** 8 miles on the eastern trailhead of the Florida Trail
**Hiking Time:** Day hike or overnight
**Difficulty:** Easy
**Trail Surface:** Dirt path
**Shade Level:** 25–50%

**Natural Communities:** Cypress swamp, oak and cabbage palm hammock, marsh

**Wildlife:** Bobcat, opossum, river otter, rabbit, gopher tortoise, wading birds, alligator

**Maps:** www.sfwmd.com

**Uses and Restrictions:** Bicycling, bird-watching, camping, canoeing, fishing, hiking, horseback riding, hunting, kayaking, wildlife viewing. Be sure to visit www.myfwc.com for hunting dates prior to hiking. No motorized vehicles. Family-friendly hiking.

**Trail Highlights:** Hikers will enjoy skirting the edge of the large Chandler Slough wetland.

**Additional Hiking:** Hickory Hammock Wildlife Management Area, Kissimmee Prairie State Park, Lake Wales Ridge National Wildlife Refuge, Taylor Creek/Nubbins Slough

This property provides protection for the Kissimmee River. It boasts oak and cabbage palm hammocks, cypress swamps, and marsh habitat for hikers on the Florida Trail. Wildlife can be viewed on the property as well as evidence of prescribed burns. Hikers must cross through pasture to enter wilderness bordering Chandler Slough, the characteristic wetland feature and resident water contributor to the Kissimmee River.

## Hike Details

From the entrance, hike west and then north through pasture on the Florida Trail. Hike between the Chandler Slough and the eastern border of the property along a hammock. Hike northeast along the border of the property to Highway 98 and then take a left and travel northwest. Continue west along Chandler Slough and then hike south, heading to the Kissimmee River. Cross the river to leave the property and continue on the Florida Trail.

## 90. Sumica

**GPS:** Lat 27.858443, Long -81.374556

**Address:** 12993 SR 60/Hesperides Road, Lake Wales, FL 33898

**Trailhead Directions:** From Lake Wales, take SR 60 east for 10 miles. The entrance will be on your right on SR 60/Hesperides Road, just north of Sam Keen Road.

**Size:** 4,301 acres

**Trail Distance:** 9 miles of trails, including 5-mile multiuse equestrian trail

**Hiking Time:** Day hike or overnight

**Difficulty:** Easy

**Trail Surface:** Sandy soil or dirt path

**Shade Level:** 0–25%

**Natural Communities:** Basin marsh, baygall, depression marsh, floodplain swamp, floodplain marsh, mesic flatwoods, upland mixed forest, wet flatwoods, wet prairie

**Wildlife:** Bald eagle, sandhill crane, wild turkey, hawk, wading birds, white-tailed deer, bobcat, fox, gopher tortoise

**Maps:** www.sfwmd.gov

**Uses and Restrictions:** Parking, hiking, equestrian trail, primitive camping. No motorized vehicles. Not friendly for family hiking.

**Trail Highlights:** Hikers can walk to the top of a former railroad bed to enjoy views of the surrounding area.

**Additional Hiking:** Lake Wales Ridge State Forest, Lake Kissimmee State Park, Allen David Broussard Catfish Creek Preserve, Kissimmee River Public Use Area

This property is found on the east side of the Lake Wales Ridge and back into the wetlands characteristic of Florida. On the east side of Lake Weohyakapka, or Lake Walk-in-Water, it plays host to mesic flatwoods, depression marshes, and an oak hammock. Hikers will gain views of marsh and cypress as well as go over the top of a former railroad bed that provides a view of the countryside.

## Hike Details

From the parking area, hike southwest through mesic flatwoods. Hike south on the old railroad bed. This bed traverses mesic flatwoods and skirts depression marshes on the way to an observation tower. Climb the tower to take in views of a large basin marsh as well as the surrounding countryside. This is an out-and-back trail. Also from the parking area, consider taking the equestrian trail to the north and west and then crossing the railroad bed to head south through mesic flatwoods. This path leads to a loop that skirts hardwood hammock and depression marsh with a large cypress dome in the middle before heading back to the main parking area.

## 91. Kicco Wildlife Management Area

**GPS:** Lat 27.768418, Long -81.197561

**Address:** Kicco Grade Road, River Ranch, FL 33867

**Trailhead Directions:** From Vero Beach, take SR 60 west through Yeehaw Junction. Continue west until you cross the Kissimmee River. Take a left on River Ranch Road just west of the river.

**Size:** 12,164 acres

**Trail Distance:** 11 miles

**Hiking Time:** Day hike or overnight

**Difficulty:** Easy

**Trail Surface:** Dirt path

**Shade Level:** 25–50%

**Natural Communities:** Depression marsh, scrub, mesic flatwoods

**Wildlife:** More than 150 species of birds, including the listed Florida scrub jay, burrowing owl, grasshopper sparrow, peregrine falcon, southeast American kestrel, wood stork

**Maps:** www.sfwmd.com

**Uses and Restrictions:** Air boating, bicycling, bird-watching, boating, boat ramp, primitive camping, canoeing, equestrian trails, fishing, hiking, hunting, kayaking, picnicking. No motorized vehicles. Visit www.myfwc.com prior to hiking to review hunting dates. Not friendly for family hiking.

**Contact:** SFWMD at (561) 686-8800 to arrange for lock operator to allow passage across the Kissimmee River on an optional side trip

**Trail Highlights:** Hikers will enjoy hiking a former Old Florida cattle ranch along with stellar birding opportunities along the Kissimmee River.

**Additional Hiking:** Kissimmee Prairie Preserve State Park, Allen David Broussard Catfish Creek Preserve, Lake Wales Ridge State Forest, Blue Cypress Conservation Area, Fort Drum Marsh Conservation Area

This property is on the west side of the Kissimmee River on the site of an old cattle ranch, Kissimmee Island Cattle Company, that operated from 1915 until the late 1920s. Pronounced kiss-oh, the Kicco company helped develop the cattle towns of Kissimmee and Sebring. The property once had its own schoolhouse and steamboat landing that helped with beef production and river trading. Today the area hosts campsites and 11 miles of the Florida National Scenic Trail. Preserving these old cattle ranches and protecting them from development is a huge component of water management district work, as many of these Old Florida ranches have natural areas bordering rivers and contribute to protecting watersheds. This is a unique hike across a former cattle ranch on the Florida Trail!

## Hike Details

From the trailhead near SR 60, hike east and then south. You'll be hiking through scrub habitat with sandy soils and densely growing oaks. The hike then meanders south through mesic flatwoods before heading east toward the Kissimmee River, with hiking on a dirt path. Here hikers fringe an expansive marsh heading south on Kicco Grade, paralleling the river.

After about 2 miles of hiking south, take a right before heading south again through scrub and mesic flatwoods. After about 2 miles, take a left at Tick Island Slough and go east through hardwood hammock. The Florida Trail continues east across the Kissimmee River (hikers must contact SFWMD before crossing the Kissimmee to arrange with the lock operator to allow hikers across). Once hikers cross the river, they can either go south through Kissimmee River Prairie Preserve State Park to continue hiking, or cross back over the Kissimmee River and return north to their vehicles. When returning west across the river, hikers have the option to enjoy a loop hike at Tick Island Slough before heading north to their vehicles.

## 92. Allapattah Flats Wildlife Management Area

**GPS:** Lat 27.163004, Long -80.440413

**Address:** 13653-14337 SW Martin Highway, Palm City, FL 34990

**Trailhead Directions:** From Stuart, take CR 714 west about 15 miles. The gated entrance to a shell-rock road will be on your right.

**Size:** 20,945 acres

**Trail Distance:** 1.5 miles

**Hiking Time:** 1 hour

**Difficulty:** Easy

**Trail Surface:** Shell-rock. Beware of seasonally flooded trails.

**Shade Level:** 0–25%

**Natural Communities:** Wet flatwoods, depression marsh

**Wildlife:** Alligator, wading birds

**Maps:** www.myfwc.com/media/2530744/Allapattah-Flats-Map.pdf

**Uses and Restrictions:** Hiking trail, biking, hunting, and camping. No motorized vehicles. The property is a wildlife management area. Hikers should check www.myfwc.com prior to hiking for hunting dates. Not friendly for family hiking.

**Contact:** Florida Fish and Wildlife Conservation Commission, (561) 625-5122

**Trail Highlights:** Hikers will traverse wet flatwoods to an open expanse of marsh with wading birds.

**Additional Hiking:** Atlantic Ridge Preserve State Park, Jonathan Dickinson State Park, DuPuis Management Area, J. W. Corbett Wildlife Management Area

Allapattah Flats is just that: wet flatwoods intermixed with large, circular depression marshes and a large marsh at the culmination of the hike, all flat. Allapattah means alligator in the Seminole language, so watch out for them here. This property is part of the Everglades restoration project, an area the Seminole Native American tribe once inhabited in larger numbers. Typical of these flat areas, large areas of pasture have been cleared for ranching and drained to allow cattle to roam in dry areas; the trail, however, moves through natural flatwoods and around a large marsh.

## Hike Details

Hikers will travel west across pasture and skirt the north side of a large, circular depression marsh. Hike the first north trail intersection to head through wet prairie, with pasture on your right. Continue north until reaching a T-intersection and take a right along a canal edge. Take a left, crossing the canal, and make a loop around the large marsh. You'll notice a campground on the western edge of the marsh. Complete the loop and hike back along the canal past two left turns. At the third turn, hike left (east) through the wet flatwoods and back to the entrance.

## 93. DuPuis Management Area

**GPS:** Lat 27.011157, Long -80.550774
**Address:** 22500 SW Kanner Highway, Indiantown, FL 34956
**Trailhead Directions:** From Okeechobee, take Highway 98 south and then head east on Highway 76. The property entrance will be on the south side of Highway 76.
**Size:** 21,875 acres
**Trail Distance:** 22 miles
**Hiking Time:** Day hike or overnight
**Difficulty:** Easy
**Trail Surface:** Dirt path
**Shade Level:** 25–50%
**Natural Communities:** Depression marsh, wet prairie, cypress dome, mesic flatwoods, Everglades marsh
**Wildlife:** Red-cockaded woodpecker, white-tailed deer, wild turkey, quail, fox, bobcat, alligator, hawk, wading birds, bald eagle, sandhill crane, wood stork, eastern indigo snake
**Maps:** www.myfwc.com/media/2530759/Dupuis-Map.pdf
**Uses and Restrictions:** Auto tour from Gate 1, fishing, hiking, bicycling, camping, hunting, picnicking, horseback riding. Motorized vehicles limited to auto tour. No dogs. Public access to archaeological sites restricted to designated trails. The property is a wildlife management area. Hikers should check hunting dates at www.myfwc.com prior to hiking. Family-friendly hiking.

**Contact:** DuPuis Management Area, (561) 924-5310

**Trail Highlights:** Hikers will enjoy the wide expanse of Old Florida mesic flatwoods and wetlands as well as get a glimpse of the endangered red-cockaded woodpecker.

**Additional Hiking:** J. W. Corbett Wildlife Management Area, Loxahatchee Slough Natural Area, Jonathan Dickinson State Park, Atlantic Ridge Preserve State Park, Ocean to Lake Hiking Trail of the Florida National Scenic Trail

This property is just west of Lake Okeechobee. Surrounded by squares and lines of farmlands, this area is an oasis affording a glimpse of what the region once looked like. It is an expanse of mesic flatwoods interspersed with a mosaic of depression marshes, wet prairies, cypress domes, and remnant Everglades marsh wetlands. There are 22 miles of hiking trails divided into loops for long or short hikes. Hiking includes the Ocean to Lake Trail, which is part of the Florida National Scenic Trail. This was once a ranch with cattle, sheep, and goats; restoration has included repairing a levee on the southern boundary to restore Everglades marsh, and reconnecting partial flow to the adjacent J. W. Corbett Wildlife Management Area to the east. Hikers will love this Old Florida hike.

## Hike Details

From the Gate 2 entrance, hike south into the property through mesic flatwoods. Continue south across the Jim Lake Grade. Take a left to travel east to the family campground or continue south to the Governor's House Picnic Area. From this point you can travel south on a short 3.9-mile loop, continue to Loop 2 to hike 6.3 more miles, continue to Loop 3 to hike 11.1 miles, or continue to Loop 4 to hike 15.2 miles. At the southern tip of Loop 4 you can continue southeast on the Ocean to Lake Trail/Corridor (Corbett Connector) to J. W. Corbett Wildlife Management Area. All hiking passes through mesic flatwoods with a mosaic of wetlands throughout.

## 94. John C. and Mariana Jones/Hungryland Wildlife and Environmental Area, Pal-Mar East/Nine Gems

**GPS:** Lat 27.000178, Long -80.270125

**Address:** Pratt Whitney Road, Jupiter, FL 33478

**Trailhead Directions:** From Jupiter, take SR 706 west. From I-95, travel west 9 miles past Jupiter to CR 711. Take CR 711 north for about 2 miles. The Pal-Mar hiking entrance will be on your right on CR 711/Pratt-Whitney Road.

**Size:** 3,320 acres

**Trail Distance:** 7 miles of marked trails

**Hiking Time:** Day hike

**Difficulty:** Easy

**Trail Surface:** Dirt path, seasonally flooded. Hiking is drier in winter.

**Shade Level:** 0–25%

**Natural Communities:** Mesic flatwoods, depression marsh

**Wildlife:** Sandhill crane, Florida panther, white-tailed deer, birds

**Maps:** www.sfwmd.com

**Uses and Restrictions:** Bicycling, bird-watching, hiking, equestrian use, primitive camping, hunting. No motorized vehicles. Visit www.myfwc.com prior to hiking to review hunting dates. Not friendly for family hiking.

**Trail Highlights:** Hikers will experience Old Florida mesic flatwoods around depression marsh expanses in a peaceful area surrounded by farmland and development.

**Additional Hiking:** Hungryland Slough Natural Area, Sweetbay Natural Area, Grassy Waters Preserve

The Pal-Mar East/Nine Gems property is part of an oasis of natural area that remains amidst improved farmland to the west and coastal South Florida development to the east. It is part of a conservation corridor connecting DuPuis Management Area, J. W. Corbett Wildlife Management Area, and Loxahatchee Slough Natural Area between Jupiter and Lake Okeechobee. Historically it provided a haven for the Seminole Native Americans during the Seminole Indian War of 1835, but living off the land here was difficult. Hundreds of hungry Native Americans were gathered and moved to Oklahoma, and the area became known as "The Hungryland." Today it boasts the South Florida beauty of mesic flatwoods intermixed with depression marshes. With seven miles of trails, the hiker will enjoy a peaceful respite and Florida backcountry experience, in contrast to the coastal beaches just west of the property.

## Hike Details

If you have two cars, you can park one at the east entrance so you can hike straight through and return to your first car at the SW Pratt-Whitney Road parking area. From the parking area, hike south into the property through mesic flatwoods, past two depression marshes. At the intersection, take a right or left to complete a wide loop through the flatwoods. Take an additional small loop around a large depression marsh and stop to quietly observe any wildlife that might come to drink freshwater. Decide whether to continue across the canal and hike a third loop through flatwoods with many circular depression marshes in the middle.

## 95. Cypress Creek Management Area and Loxahatchee River Management Area

**GPS:** Lat 26.956799, Long -80.190670
**Address:** Jupiter, FL 33478
**Trailhead Directions:** From Jupiter, take Highway 706/Indiantown Road west. Past I-95 and the Florida Turnpike, continue for 2.5 miles. Immediately after a left (south) turn for Jupiter Farms Road, take a right. The Palm Beach County Cypress Creek Natural Area parking area will be on your right. From there you can travel without vehicle 1 mile north to access the SFWMD Cypress Creek Management Area.
**Size:** 10 miles of the Upper Suwannee River Basin
**Trail Distance:** 7 miles of marked trails at Cypress Creek, 2.21 miles at Loxahatchee Management Area from Highway 706 to Florida Turnpike. More trails south of Highway 706.
**Hiking Time:** Day hike
**Difficulty:** Easy
**Trail Surface:** Dirt path, seasonally flooded; drier hiking in winter
**Shade Level:** 0–25%
**Natural Communities:** Mesic flatwoods, depression marsh, forested wetlands along creeks

**Wildlife:** Sandhill crane, Florida panther, white-tailed deer, birds

**Map:** www.sfwmd.com

**Uses and Restrictions:** Bicycling, bird-watching, hiking, hunting. No motorized vehicles. Visit www.myfwc.com prior to hiking to review hunting dates. Not friendly for family hiking.

**Trail Highlights:** Hikers will experience Old Florida mesic flatwoods around depression marsh expanses in a peaceful area surrounded by farmland and development.

**Additional Hiking:** Jonathan Dickinson State Park, Juniper Ridge Natural Area, DuPuis Management Area, J. W. Corbett Wildlife Management Area, Atlantic Ridge Preserve State Park, Hungryland Wildlife Environmental Area, Loxahatchee Slough Natural Area

This area preserves land surrounding tributaries of the Loxahatchee River, Florida's only federally designated Wild and Scenic River. These properties make up a corridor of protected land from Highway 706 north and east to Jonathan Dickinson State Park protecting the headwaters of the Loxahatchee River. Cypress Creek Management Area hosts Cypress Creek, which travels east to the Loxahatchee River. Hikers can cross this creek multiple times on their hike. The property has a 2-mile segment of the Ocean to Lake Hiking Trail, a spur of the Florida National Scenic Trail, heading north and south, as well as three loops within the property. The Loxahatchee River Management Area and Natural Area protects the Loxahatchee River where it begins as a small creek as it heads north. South of Highway 706 there are many marked trails, including the Ocean to Lake Hiking Trail, which goes under Highway 706 heading north and continues on a multiuse trail that dead-ends into a loop at the Florida Turnpike. Hikers will be rewarded with mesic flatwoods and depression marsh views as well as crossing Cypress Creek and skirting the Loxahatchee River.

## Hike Details

From the Cypress Creek trailhead, hike north through mesic flatwoods and cross Cypress Creek to get on the Ocean to Lake Hiking Trail. Or, to stay within the property, hike northwest for the white trail loop. This trail meanders through mesic flatwoods before crossing Cypress

Creek. It continues on through areas of thinner pine and then an area that has been well maintained by prescribed burning. Head south at the western point of the white trail and skirt a large depression marsh before coming to an intersection. Here you can hike west or south for a long loop on the green trail or head back east. If you hike east through more mesic flatwoods you can utilize a loop on the red trail and cross the creek again or continue east to the parking area.

Loxahatchee Management Area: From the Highway 706 walk-in entrance, hike west along a canal and then north through forested wetlands. The trail crosses a small creek and then continues north through mesic flatwoods until reaching a loop at a white sandy area. Here you can loop along the southern border of the Florida Turnpike before backtracking south to the entrance.

## 96. Harold A. Campbell Public Use Area (Stormwater Treatment Area 3/4)

**GPS:** Lat 26.335248, Long -80.547294

**Trailhead Directions:** From Ft. Lauderdale, take I-75 west and travel north on US Highway 27. Look for the Palm Beach/Broward County line and large overhead power lines that cross the road and go west along the paved L-5 levee road. Look for brown recreation road signs.

**Size:** 17,000 acres

**Trail Distance:** 4 miles of marked trails

**Hiking Time:** Day hike

**Difficulty:** Easy

**Trail Surface:** Sidewalk

**Shade Level:** 0–25%

**Natural Communities:** Constructed marsh

**Wildlife:** Wading birds, duck, turtle, fish, alligator

**Maps:** www.sfwmd.com

**Hours:** Friday through Monday, sunrise to sunset

**Uses and Restrictions:** Bicycling, bird-watching, boat ramp, boating, canoeing, fishing, hiking, hunting, kayaking. No motorized vehicles. Visit www.myfwc.com prior to hiking to review dates for hunting in public small-game hunting area. Family-friendly hiking.

**Trail Highlights:** Hikers will enjoy stellar birding opportunities.

**Additional Hiking:** Holey Land Wildlife Management Area, Everglades Wildlife Management Area, Okaloacoochee Slough State Forest, Florida Panther National Wildlife Refuge

Don't let the name sway you! It may be a man-made stormwater treatment area (endearingly titled STA by local waterfowl hunters), but it is a beautiful hike with waterfront views and wading birds galore, the largest constructed wetland in the world! The stormwater treatment areas handle water running from development in the east as well as agricultural runoff from the north, just south of Lake Okeechobee. This area used to be part of the Everglades, but it was drained, ditched, and diked to allow for agriculture. The runoff previously ran directly into the Everglades, causing high levels of mercury and affecting wildlife in food webs that connect fish to birds to alligators to larger wildlife. Today these treatment wetlands allow pesticides and fertilizers and phosphorus to be soaked up by wetland plants and then settle to the bottom before the water flows south into the Everglades. It was genius for land managers to open these wetlands to public access to share the beauty of improved water and the wildlife that flock here. Hikers can utilize the sidewalk path.

## Hike Details

From the parking area, hike north to the main levee and then east or west to hike a large diamond loop and return to the parking area. Or continue on for longer hiking.

## 97. Corkscrew Regional Ecosystem Watershed (CREW)

**GPS:**
CREW MARSH TRAILS (GATE 1)—Lat 26.492224, Long -81.534081
CYPRESS DOME TRAILS (GATE 5)—Lat 26.456266, Long -81.562224
BIRD ROOKERY SWAMP TRAILS—Lat 26.311946, Long -81.633470
**Address:**
CREW MARSH TRAILS (GATE 1)—4600 Corkscrew Road (CR 850), Immokalee, FL 34142

CYPRESS DOME TRAILS (GATE 5)—3980 Corkscrew Road (CR 850), Immokalee, FL 34142

BIRD ROOKERY SWAMP TRAILS—1295 Shady Hollow Boulevard West, Immokalee, FL

**Trailhead Directions:**

CREW MARSH TRAILS (GATE 1)—From Bonita Springs, take I-75 north to CR 850. Travel east on CR 850 for 18 miles, past the Cypress Dome Trails, and you will see CREW Marsh Trails on your right. Brown trailhead signs provide direction.

CYPRESS DOME TRAILS—From Bonita Springs, take I-75 north to CR 850. Travel east on CR 850 for 14 miles. Cypress Dome Trails will be on your right, just after a large curve to the north. Brown trailhead signs provide direction.

BIRD ROOKERY SWAMP TRAILS (GATE 5)—From Bonita Springs, take I-75 south to Highway 846. Take 846 east until it curves north and changes to Immokalee Boulevard. Take a left on Shady Hollow Boulevard West. The parking entrance to the hiking trails will be on your right past the lake.

**Size:** 28,910 acres

**Trail Distance:** 24 miles of trails

**Hiking Time:** Day hike or overnight

**Difficulty:** Easy

**Trail Surface:** Graded levee, seasonally flooded trails, boardwalk

**Shade Level:** 0–50%

**Natural Communities:** CREW Marsh Trails—mesic flatwoods, ephemeral ponds, glades marsh, oak hammock; Cypress Dome Trails—scrubby flatwoods, mixed oak/pine forest, cypress dome, popash slough; Bird Rookery Swamp Trails—maple-cypress swamp

**Wildlife:** Alligator, river otter, Florida panther, bobcat, white-tailed deer, short-tailed hawk, swallow-tailed kite, songbirds, wading birds

**Maps:** www.sfwmd.com

**Uses and Restrictions:** Bicycling, hiking, bird-watching, equestrian trails, camping, geocaching, hunting. No motorized vehicles. Visit www.myfwc.com prior to hiking to review hunting dates. Not friendly for family hiking.

**Trail Highlights:** Hikers will be rewarded with spring wildflower blooms and an observation tower overlooking the glades marsh and tree islands at CREW Marsh Trails.

**Additional Hiking:** Okaloacoochee Slough State Forest, Picayune Strand State Forest, Fakahatchee Strand State Preserve, Florida Panther National Wildlife Refuge

CREW is a 60,000-acre wetland acquisition project. It consists of marshes, flatwoods, oak hammocks, and cypress swamps just north of Naples. The CREW Wildlife and Environmental Area consists of three units: Corkscrew Marsh, Flint Pen Strand, and Bird Rookery Swamp, totaling more than 28,000 acres currently. Three hiking opportunities are found here. The CREW Marsh Trails (Gate 1 to the northwest) offer 5 miles of trails through mesic flatwoods, ephemeral ponds, glades marshes, and oak hammocks. It has an observation tower overlooking the Corkscrew Marsh. The Cypress Dome Trails (Gate 5) offer 6.5 miles of trails and host scrubby flatwoods, mixed oak/pine forest between two cypress domes, and popash slough. This trail leads to Caracara Prairie Preserve, another 3 miles of hiking adjacent to CREW. Bird Rookery Swamp off Shady Hollow Boulevard in the south-central offers 12 miles of multiuse trails with maple-cypress swamp, boardwalk, and trails that are seasonally flooded, with drier hiking in winter. Hikers can spend time here exploring all the habitats.

## Hike Details

CREW Marsh Trails (Gate 1): From the trailhead, hike southeast into the property through mesic flatwoods with pine and palmetto. When you hit an intersection, continue straight to dead-end on a hiking deck overlooking a large depression marsh. Then take a right and hike south on the Pine Flatwoods Trail to point number 3. Hike southeast to point 4, continuing on the Pine Flatwoods Trail until you reach the Marsh Loop Trail. At the Marsh Loop Trail, stay to the right and hike south until you reach the observation tower overlooking the glades marshes and tree islands. Enjoy a view of a marsh that has been preserved among miles and miles of farmland. Notice the slight elevational differences that create tree islands among the wetlands, creating a completely different natural community from the community inches lower in the marsh. After your respite on the tower, hike west along the Pop Ash Slough Trail across two boardwalks. At point 12 on the map, you can take the 1.5-mile hike to a primitive campsite or decide to head back to the parking area. If you are completing your hike at this point, hike north at point 12 and then northeast. Take the Hammock Trail back to the Pine Flatwoods Trail and then head north, back to the trailhead.

Cypress Dome Trails (Gate 5): From the parking area, hike east and then south on the Green Loop Trail. On your hike south you will pass through scrubby flatwoods and oak hammock as well as skirt the western edge of pasture where you might see wildlife passing through. Follow the trail east and after heading north and then east again, look to the north for an opening in the tree line and you'll notice a large depression marsh. Continue east and hike between two large cypress domes. The Green Loop Trail takes a sharp curve back to the northwest and heads up to the Yellow Loop Trail. When you come to the intersection of the Yellow Loop Trail, veer to the right and hike north through more hammock. When you hit the next intersection, hike west, taking the Blue Trail (shortcut). Here you will hike past another large depression marsh called Alligator Flag Pond. You'll dead-end at the Yellow Loop Trail and can take a left and hike south, or take a right and head west to the parking area.

Bird Rookery Swamp Trails (Shady Hollow Boulevard): From the entrance, hike north and then follow the trail east until dead-ending at a water body. Hike north and continue hiking through Bird Rookery Swamp. When you reach the two-way intersection, you can decide to hike north or veer to the left to hike west as you take the square loop around the swamp. Enjoy the peace of the swamp and listen for sounds of birds and wildlife.

## 98. Water Conservation Areas 2 and 3: Everglades and Francis S. Taylor Wildlife Management Area

**GPS:** Lat 26.144744, Long -80.441685
**Address:** Weston, FL
**Trailhead Directions:** From Deerfield Beach, take the Hillsboro

Hiking the levee at Everglades and Francis S. Taylor Wildlife Management Area

Boulevard exit from I-95, Highway 810, and head west. Take a right and head north on US 441. Take a left on Highway 827/Loxahatchee Road and head west until the road ends at the parking area and boat ramp.

**Size:** 671,831 acres
**Trail Distance:** 40 miles of levee trails
**Hiking Time:** Day hike
**Difficulty:** Easy
**Trail Surface:** Graded levee
**Shade Level:** 0–25%
**Natural Communities:** Glades marsh, wet prairies/sloughs, tree islands
**Wildlife:** Everglades kite, river otter, Florida black bear, Florida panther, marsh rabbit, alligator, cottonmouth, dusky pygmy rattlesnake, green anole, green tree frog, many wading birds

**Maps:** www.myfwc.com

**Uses and Restrictions:** WCA 2—Bicycling, bird-watching, hiking, hunting, boating, airboating. WCA 3—Frogging, stargazing. No motorized vehicles, visit www.myfwc.com prior to hiking to review hunting dates. Family-friendly hiking for short distances.

**Trail Highlights:** Hikers will gain views of glades marsh and tree islands characteristic of the Everglades ecosystem.

**Additional Hiking:** Jonathan Dickinson State Park, Juniper Ridge Natural Area, DuPuis Management Area, J. W. Corbett Wildlife Management Area, Atlantic Ridge Preserve State Park, Hungryland Wildlife Environmental Area, Loxahatchee Slough Natural Area

Construction of water control structures, canals, and levees in this area began in 1949 and ended in 1962. Water sheet flow has been disrupted by these alterations and major highway systems, and water is impounded and maintained according to regulation schedules. The area now serves as fish and wildlife habitat and offers recreation opportunities like hiking, hunting, bicycling, and stargazing at night. It is used as flood retention during high rainfall years along with serving as a reservoir for urban and agriculture water use during dry years. Researchers study the Everglades marsh systems here. It is hoped that one day the area will be reconnected to the Everglades system through the lowering of levees, helping in the overall restoration of the region.

## Hike Details

L-35 Levees: From Sawgrass Recreation Area (shown on FWC hunting map), walk along L-35B to the northeast and out to Sawgrass Expressway and back, about 12 miles. Or travel the whole levee loop for slightly more than 30 miles of hiking. An easy out-and-back of your choice of distance will provide views of tree islands, glades marsh, and wildlife. Another popular hike is the L-67 canal system from Holiday Park. From the park area, hike southwest, south, and then back to the northeast. Or hike as long as you'd like out and back for views of the glades marsh and tree islands.

## 99. Southern Glades Wildlife and Environmental Area and Frog Pond Wildlife Management Area

**GPS:** Lat 25.403152, Long -80.559077

**Address:** CR 9336/Ingram Highway, Miami-Dade County, FL

**Trailhead Directions:** From Homestead/Florida City, take Highway 9336 west toward the Everglades. The Southern Glades Trail is just west of SW 202nd Avenue, west of US 1, along Canal C-111. The next trail is about 2 miles farther west, just west of SW 224th Avenue. Just west of this trail is Aerojet Road/SW 232 Avenue with additional hiking on canal levees C-111, C-111E, and C-110.

**Size:** 30,000 acres

**Trail Distance:** 16 miles of levee trails, plus additional hiking on levees off Aerojet Road

**Hiking Time:** Day hike

**Difficulty:** Easy

**Trail Surface:** Graded levee

**Shade Level:** 0–25%

**Natural Communities:** Glades marsh, marl prairie, tree islands

**Wildlife:** Cape Sable seaside sparrow, wood stork, roseate spoonbill, other wading birds

**Maps:** www.myfwc.com

**Uses and Restrictions:** Air boating, bicycling, bird-watching, hiking, boating, canoeing, horseback riding, hunting, kayaking, picnicking. No motorized vehicles. Visit www.myfwc.com prior to hiking to review hunting dates. Family-friendly hiking for short distances.

**Trail Highlights:** Hikers will see glades marsh and tree islands characteristic of the Everglades ecosystem.

**Additional Hiking:** Everglades National Park, Big Cypress National Preserve, Biscayne National Park

Southern Glades is located at the very southwestern tip of farmland and development of Homestead/South Florida and on the fringe of the Everglades system. Even though it is bound by canals and levees, it plays host to a large expanse of Everglades marsh and tree islands. Hikers can explore 16 miles of trails on levees with views of glades marsh, migratory birds in the winter months, and endangered birds such as Cape Sable seaside sparrow and wood stork as well as many wading birds.

## Hike Details

From US 1, follow Highway 9336 west to Canal-111E southeast, then go south on the levee on the Southern Glades Trail. Hikers can view Holiday Hammock Preserve on the west side of the canal and other mesic flatwoods on the east side. The views gradually turn to glades marsh and tree islands divided by levees and canals. From Highway 9336, hike Canal-111 south on the Southern Glades Trail on the west side of the canal. The hike has farmland on the east, but wetlands on the west. Just before a large curve to the east, there are views of hammock before the scenery merges into glades marsh and tree islands. Additional hiking within the preserve is found on Aerojet Road and Canal-110.

## 100. Water Conservation Area 1/STA 1E and STA 1West: Loxahatchee National Wildlife Refuge

**GPS:**
20 MILE BEND ENTRANCE—Lat 26.683654, Long -80.379712
HEADQUARTERS ENTRANCE—Lat 26.498976, Long -80.212115
**Address:**
20 MILE BEND ENTRANCE—Palm Beach County, FL
HEADQUARTERS ENTRANCE—10216 Lee Road, Boynton Beach, FL
    33473
**Trailhead Directions:**
20 MILE BEND ENTRANCE—From West Palm Beach, take I-98 west. Take
    a left on CR 880. Take an immediate left just after the green bridge
    onto 20 Mile Bend Road. Take a right into 20 Mile Bend Boat Ramp
    Road to automatic gate.
HEADQUARTERS ENTRANCE—From West Palm Beach, take I-98 west
    and then head south on US 442. Take a right on Lee Road and the
    headquarters building will be on the north side of the road.
**Size:** 145,800 acres
**Trail Distance:** 16 miles of levee trails, plus additional hiking on levees
    off Aerojet Road

**Hiking Time:** Day hike
**Difficulty:** Easy
**Trail Surface:** Graded levee
**Shade Level:** 0–25%
**Natural Communities:** Sloughs, wet prairies, glades marsh, tree islands
**Wildlife:** More than 250 species of birds, 23 mammal species, alligator, 40 species of butterflies, 11 species of frogs and toads, 10 species of turtles, 46 species of fish
**Maps:** www.fws.gov/refuge/arm_loxahatchee
**Uses and Restrictions:** Air boating, bicycling, bird-watching, hiking, boating, canoeing, kayaking, picnicking. No motorized vehicles. Family-friendly hiking.
**Contact:** Arthur R. Marshall Loxahatchee National Wildlife Refuge, (561) 732-3684
**Trail Highlights:** Hikers will find views of glades marsh and tree islands characteristic of the Everglades ecosystem.
**Additional Hiking:** Everglades Wildlife Management Area, Holeyland Wildlife Management Area, DuPuis Management Area, J. W. Corbett Wildlife Management Area, Everglades National Park

Water Conservation Areas 1, 2, and 3 were constructed by the U.S. Army Corps of Engineers in the 1940s and placed under management of the district. The areas, formerly part of the Everglades system, are bound by levees and connected by a series of canals to provide for water needs of agriculture and population expansion and serve as water storage areas. Through a license agreement with U.S. Fish and Wildlife Service in 1951, the 143,954-acre Loxahatchee National Wildlife Refuge was created at Water Conservation Area 1. This area is the only remnant of the northern Everglades in Palm Beach County. The surrounding land comprises farms planted in sugar cane, winter vegetables, and sod, and cattle ranches. To the east is urban development. To the south are Water Conservation Areas 2 and 3 and Everglades National Park. Hikers have options to hike on a series of square levees overlooking marsh and two observation towers at the main headquarters entrance or hiking longer mileage along the L-40 Levee overlooking marsh. Beautiful views of the Everglades system await.

## Hike Details

From the headquarters building, hike a series of rectangular levees around treatment marshes to two observation towers. From 20 Mile Bend, hike east and then south along the levee to enjoy views of glades marsh and tree islands, wading birds and ducks, and sloughs of the Everglades ecosystem.

# Acknowledgments

Thank you to all the land management staff and recreation managers of Florida's water management districts who take care of Florida's backcountry. Thank you to the many partners that assist in maintaining recreation on these lands, including federal agencies, the Florida Forest Service, Florida Park Service, local counties, and volunteer groups like the Florida Trail Association. These heroes of Florida conservation work with few staff, few resources, and little acknowledgment, yet they thrive with the charge of preserving Florida's wonders for future generations.

Also, thank you to J. B. Miller, Steven R. Miller, Robert Christiansen, and Jack Eckdahl, who brought me in for the interview and took a chance on hiring me. Especially to Steve, who asked if I'd be interested in learning about prescribed burning, a question that would change my life.

Thank you to the land management field staff who took me in as one of their own, taught me everything they knew, were always kind and hardworking, yet made everything fun. Especially Danny Mills, my favorite cowboy, Pete Henn, Doug Voltolina, R. H. Davis, Crystal Morris, Jo Anna Emanuel, Brian Emanuel, and Maria Zondervan. And I also can't forget the horse, Fat Joe. Also, thank you to the many "Old Florida" cattle ranchers who welcomed me into their homes and shared their lives and histories.

Thank you to my husband, Hugh; without his edits to my book proposal, the contract would not have been possible. And thank you to Nels Parson, who reviewed the book, to the other district recreation managers who were kind in phone interviews, to Sian Hunter and Marthe Walters at the University Press of Florida for guiding the manuscript through the process, and to Lucinda Treadwell for copy editing.

# Bibliography

Florida Natural Areas Inventory (FNAI). 2010. Guide to the natural communities of Florida: 2010 edition. Florida Natural Areas Inventory, Tallahassee.

St. Johns River Water Management District. "Recreation." Accessed August 26, 2016. http://sjrwmd.com/recreation.

Suwannee River Water Management District. "Recreation." Accessed August 26, 2016. http://www.mysuwanneeriver.com.

South Florida Water Management District. "Come Out and Play." Accessed August 26, 2016. http://www.sfwmd.gov/portal/page/portal/ xweb%20protecting%2 0and%20restoring/recreation.

Northwest Florida Water Management District. "Recreation." Accessed August 26, 2016. http://www.nwfwater.com/Lands/Recreation.

Southwest Florida Water Management District. "Recreation Areas." Accessed August 26, 2016. https://www.swfwmd.state.fl.us/recreation/.

Florida Fish and Wildlife Conservation Commission. "Wildlife Management Area Brochures." Accessed August 26, 2016. http://www.myfwc. com.

# Index

TERRI MASHOUR is a second-generation Florida native from Jacksonville. She has contributed articles to *Footprint* magazine of the Florida Trail Association, the *Ponte Vedra Recorder*, and *Forest Policy and Economics* journal.

With her sister, she cofounded www.fun4firstcoastkids.com, and she reviews the top places to hike, camp, and get out into nature in and around Jacksonville for the website's blog.

She has received two master's degrees from the University of Florida, one in forest resources and conservation and a second in ecological restoration. Before taking a brief career break to care for her young children, she worked almost a decade in Florida's forests, swamps, sandhills, and prairies as a land management planner and land management specialist with the St. Johns River Water Management District. She proudly earned her Florida Certified Burner certification while seven months pregnant and has participated in almost 100 burns or wildfires.

# Wild Florida

EDITED BY M. TIMOTHY O'KEEFE

Books in this series are written for the many people who visit and/or move to Florida to participate in our remarkable outdoors, an environment rich in birds, animals, and activities, many exclusive to this state. Books in the series will offer readers a variety of formats: natural history guides, historical outdoor guides, guides to some of Florida's most popular pastimes and activities, and memoirs of outdoors folk and their unique lifestyles.

*30 Eco-Trips in Florida: The Best Nature Excursions (and How to Leave Only Your Footprints)*, by Holly Ambrose (2005)

*Hiker's Guide to the Sunshine State*, by Sandra Friend (2005)

*Fishing Florida's Flats: A Guide to Bonefish, Tarpon, Permit, and Much More*, by Jan S. Maizler (2007)

*50 Great Walks in Florida*, by Lucy Beebe Tobias (2008)

*Hiking the Florida Trail: 1,100 Miles, 78 Days, Two Pairs of Boots, and One Heck of an Adventure*, by Johnny Molloy (2008)

*The Complete Florida Beach Guide*, by Mary and Bill Burnham (2008)

*The Saltwater Angler's Guide to Florida's Big Bend and Emerald Coast*, by Tommy L. Thompson (2009)

*Secrets from Florida's Master Anglers*, by Ron Presley (2009)

*Exploring Florida's Botanical Wonders: A Guide to Ancient Trees, Unique Flora, and Wildflower Walks*, by Sandra Friend (2010)

*Florida's Fishing Legends and Pioneers*, by Doug Kelly (2011)

*Fishing Secrets from Florida's East Coast*, by Ron Presley (2012)

*The Saltwater Angler's Guide to Tampa Bay and Florida's West Coast*, by Tommy L. Thompson (2012)

*High Seas Wranglers: The Lives of Atlantic Fishing Captains*, by Terry Howard (2013)

*Backcountry Trails of Florida: A Guide to Hiking Florida's Water Management Districts*, by Terri Mashour (2017)